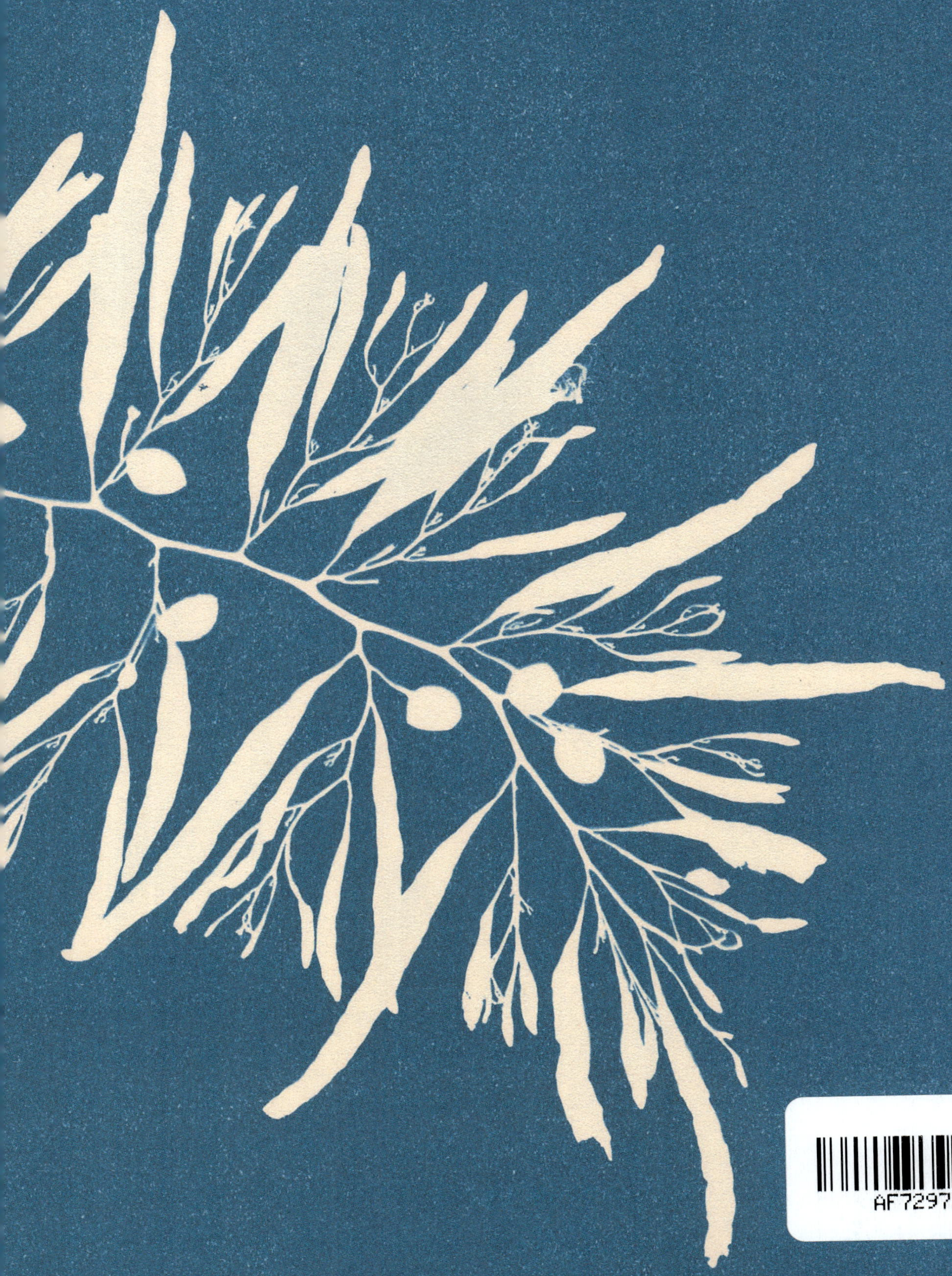

Women Photographers Are Dangerous

Front endpapers: Anna Atkins, 'Sargassum plumosum', 1850, cyanotype on paper, New York, The New York Public Library
Back endpapers: Anna Atkins, 'Cystoseira granulata', 1843, cyanotype on paper, New York, The New York Public Library

978 1 78884 371 3

First published in French under the title *Les femmes photographes sont dangereuses* in 2024 by Flammarion

This translation published by ACC Art Books Ltd in 2026 by agreement with Flammarion

www.accartbooks.com

A CIP catalogue record for this book is available from the British Library

French Edition
Editorial Director: Julie Rouart
Editorial Administration Manager: Delphine Montagne
Editors: Marion Doublet, Adèle Ehlinger
Proofreader: Colette Malandain
Graphic Design: Marie Pellaton
Picture Research: Lucía Pasalodos
Production: Chloé Brossard
Reprographics: Hyphen

English Edition
Publisher: James Smith
Translator: David Watson
Editor: Stewart Norvill
Production: Steven Farrow

EU GPSR Authorised Representative:
Easy Access System Europe Oü, 16879218
Address: Mustamäe tee 50, 10621 Tallinn, Estonia
Email: gpsr@easproject.com
Tel: +358 40 500 3575

MIXTE
Papier | Pour une gestion forestière responsable
FSC® C118234

Printed in Bosnia and Herzegovina by GPS
for ACC Art Books Ltd, Woodbridge, Suffolk, UK
www.accartbooks.com

ACC ART BOOKS

Laure Adler & Clara Bouveresse

Women Photographers Are Dangerous

ACC ART BOOKS

Laure Adler is a journalist, writer and historian, who specialises in women studies and feminism in the 19th and 20th centuries. She contributed to *Dangerous Women: The Perils of Muses* and *Femmes Fatales* (Flammarion, 2010) and has authored numerous essays and books, including *Marguerite Duras: A Life* (Phoenix, 2001), whose French edition was awarded the Prix Femina.

Clara Bouveresse is a photography historian, a member of the Institut Universitaire de France and a lecturer in English studies at the University of Évry Paris-Saclay. Her books include *A History of the Magnum Agency* (2017) and *Photographs Straight Out of Bed* (2020). She curated the exhibitions Unretouched Women: Eve Arnold, Abigail Heyman, Susan Meiselas (2019) and Erica Lennard: Women, Sisters (2025) at the Rencontres de la Photographie d'Arles, as well as co-curating An Imperfect World, with Isabella Seniuta and Guillaume Blanc in 2020–21 and exhibitions dedicated to Didier Lefèvre and to Stanley Greene's work.

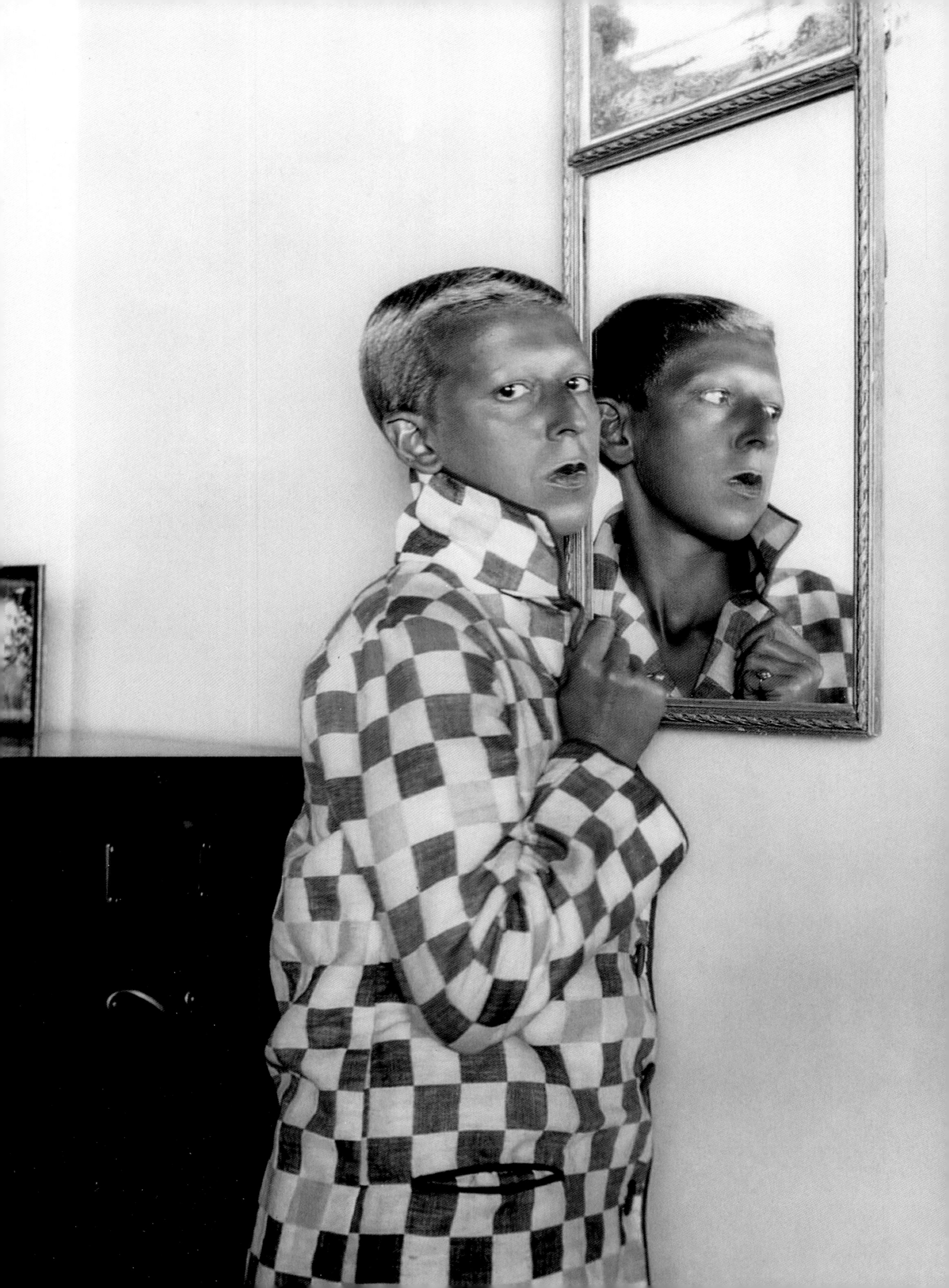

OPENING UP THE INFINITY OF THE WORLD

By Laure Adler

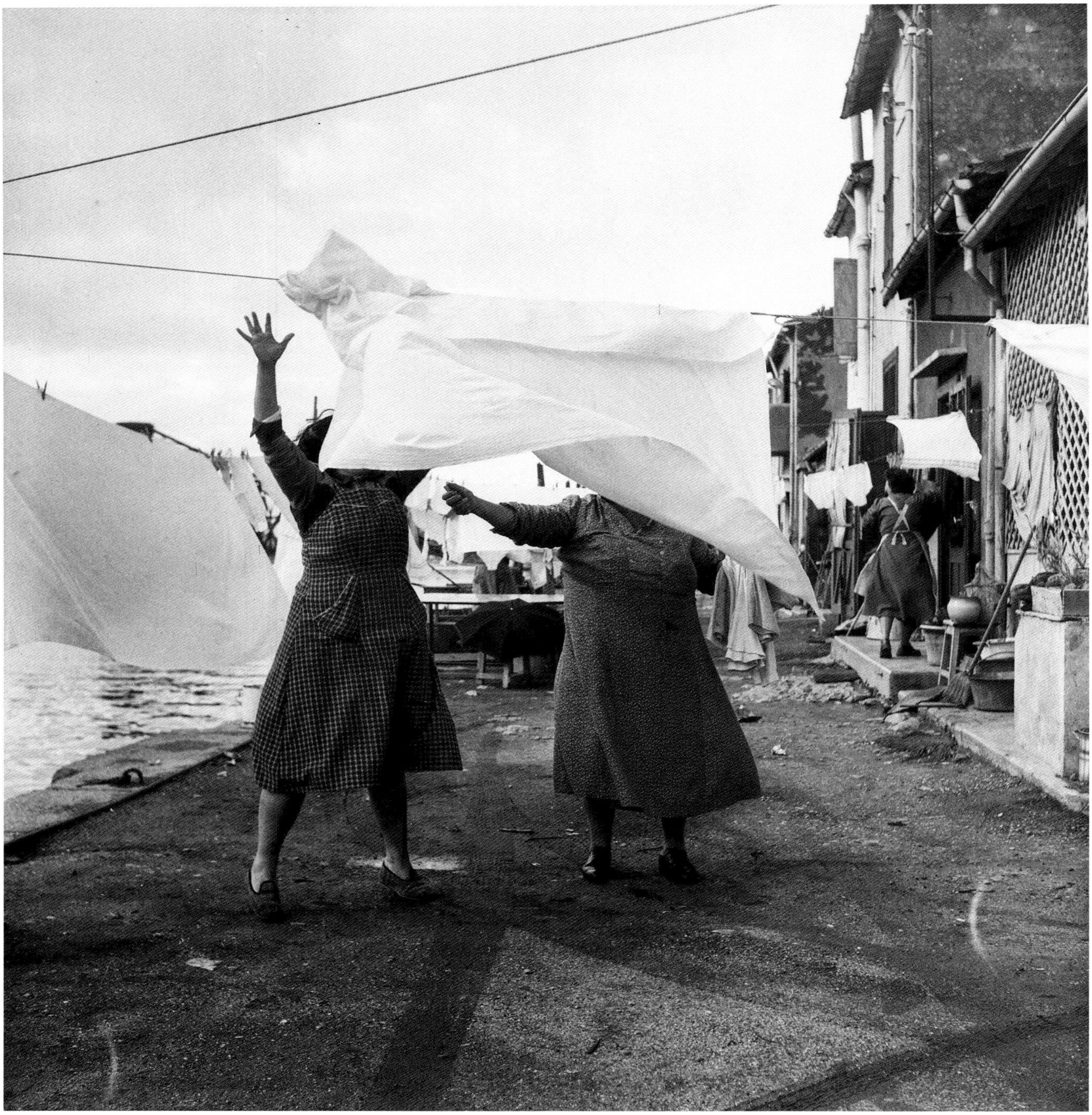

AGNÈS VARDA
'Washing on the Quai du Mistral', from her film, *La Pointe Courte,* March 1954, Agnès Varda Estate – Agnès Varda Archive, held at the Institut pour la photographie

p. 6
CLAUDE CAHUN
'Self-Portrait', *c.* 1928, private collection

Move along, nothing to see here. Just some women in aprons in their husbands' or brothers' studios; ever compliant and obedient women doing the preparation for a work that will eventually be signed… by the man.

Multitasking women, minor-tasking women, women reduced to silence for decades, even those who were artists themselves; we are now very familiar with the implacable mechanism that renders women in the art world and the world in general invisible. Yet what is so distinctive about the major art of photography is that, from its very beginnings, it was regarded, not least by its inventor, as an activity so simple that it lay within the competence of women and children.

In 1838, Louis Daguerre announced his invention to the public by saying: 'Even though the result is achieved by chemical means, this little task might well be found pleasing by ladies.' The more photography was practised, the more accessible it became for persons of the feminine sex, who, as we all know, are not greatly endowed with technical or creative skills. Thus, the invention of the portable camera, the Kodak – a device so easy to use that its publicity made a point of saying that it was designed for women to play around with. Of course, it's well-known that all women are ditzy. Likewise, the Leica made out-of-focus pictures a thing of the past. Likewise, the Polaroid: just press a button and it's done. Click.

The problem is, to the chagrin of certain gentlemen who police the art world, women have never simply played around with photography. On the contrary, from the very beginning, they have taken it very seriously indeed and wielded it as a tool of emancipation, research, resistance, the documentation of real life, the exploration of self and other, and a way of finding beauty.

In many cases, they have appropriated the medium and turned it into an art, following its various technical developments, testing its boundaries and constantly redefining it.[1] For if you know how to see, you can capture reality, and this representation of the real that photography offers us is capable of changing our perception, our vision. This is probably what is so particular about the act of looking at photographs. Unlike paintings or drawings, they create an effect of truth (even if it is constructed) that goes straight to the heart and moves us immediately. We project ourselves. We are there. The art of photography opens up the infinity of the world, whether imaginary or real, introspective or

1. There are many books on the subject of photography. See Peter E. Palmquist, *A Bibliography of Writings by and about Women in Photography, 1850–2000*, Arcata, published by the author, 1994; or Liz Heron and Val Williams, *Illuminations: Women Writing on Photography 1850s to the Present*, London, I. B. Tauris, 1996.

objective, dreamlike or scientific. By means of a simple device, it captures that fragment of the unexpected that only one person sees and then offers it to others; it crosses a frontier.

This is exactly what women did: they used the camera from the very start to open doors in every sense of the term; no longer confining themselves to the home, trapped in their role as mother and wife, but discovering the outside world, which had been forbidden to them for centuries.

They would expand their vision and break down their prohibitions while opening their eyes and developing their skills. At first, they would do it bravely, modestly, patiently in the shadow of their men, assisting them in their studios; but then they acquired the technical skills to be artists themselves. Do you know, for example, that a woman, Constance Talbot, was one of the first people to make photographic images? That it was another woman, Anna Atkins, a botanical artist, who would make the first photographic album using dried algae? She used the cyanotype procedure, where an impression is made through direct contact with the paper, creating a photo without any need of a camera. These 'photogenic' drawings move us today by their sheer beauty and poetry.

In the middle of the 20th century, photography was seen as a means of reproducing what was all around us and the women who engaged in it were seen as skilful transmitters of these images. However, they very quickly moved beyond such ladylike pursuits to more risqué undertakings, bending genres and social codes. The family portrait garlanded with flowers was one area exploited by many women, as sisters and wives, whose names we now know only because of the efforts of art historians, as their very existence had been lost from sight. I am thinking in particular of Julie Vogel, or Amélie Guillot-Saguez, or Constance Talbot, mentioned above, who assisted her husband William in his experiments in the negative/positive process, but who was also the first woman to produce photographic images. Who remembers her? And there are hundreds of others hidden in the shadows, waiting to be discovered. With the boom in photography, many women were recruited by photographic portrait studios, where they were employed to retouch negatives or make prints, which could be used as visitor's cards and so on. Retouchers, splicers, assistants, all soldiers of silence, demanding nothing, content just to be there. They were creators, innovating without asking for recognition, even if it meant being lost to history. Did you know that Harriet C. Tytler, in 1857, photographed the revolt of the Sepoys against the British East India Company, yet her images are still attributed to her husband Robert?

Often, women have made a virtue out of necessity, showing their empathy, kindness, gentleness and attention to detail to make portraits

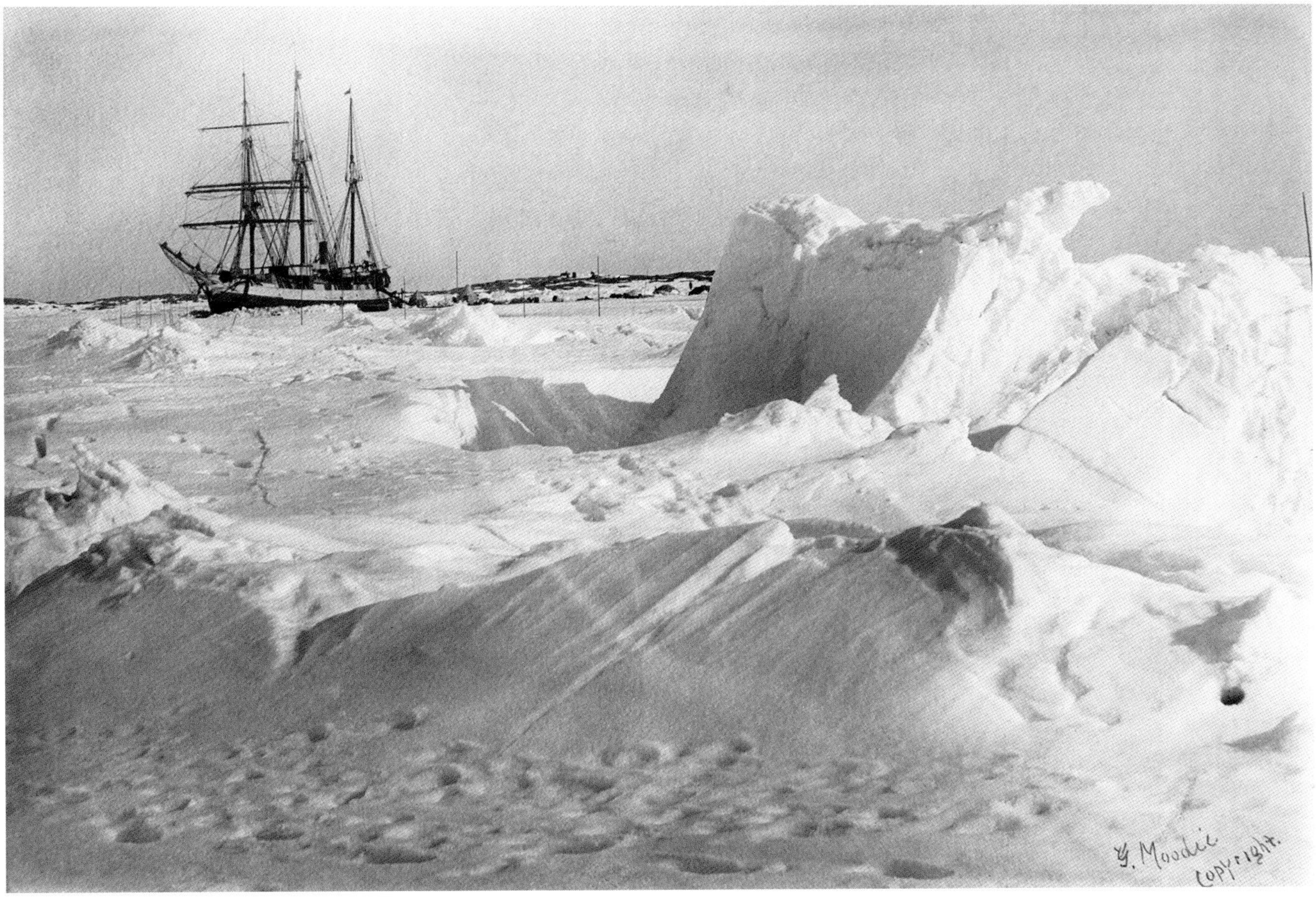

GERALDINE MOODIE
'DGS *Arctic* Frozen in Ice, Fullerton Harbour, Nunavut', April 1905, Calgary, Glenbow Museum

of women – a specialism that their husbands or their brothers couldn't dispute. In addition, some of them abandoned the domestic world and decided, at no little risk to themselves, to travel far from their familiar milieu to bring back images of worlds they wanted to discover, such as Isabella Bird, who made a solo trip across Asia in 1894; Geraldine Moody, who explored the Arctic in 1897; and Helen Messenger Murdoch, who went round the world in 1913. Their remarkable work was more like anthropological research than mere pandering to a taste for exoticism. For some, the escape from the studio was an expression of their desire to represent what was happening in the public sphere. Thus, throughout Europe, a new breed of female photographers documented demonstrations, particularly demonstrations by women, bequeathing us inspiring historical records of the suffragette movements in Britain and France. Just as many made images of feminist demonstrations before the First World War, such as Julie Laurberg in Denmark and Christina Broom in Britain. Without their work, would we have known about the pulse and scale of these feminist pacifist movements?

After the First World War, women began to behave differently, and photography became for them a tool of social and political engagement. Further, they were able to benefit from teaching by schools such as the Bauhaus or New Objectivity, who welcomed them, and some among them would take this instrument and turn it into an art, no longer merely a reproduction of reality. In Germany in the 1920s, women were cropping up more and more, not just in front of, but also behind, the lens. Reductions in the cost of photography and the proliferation of publications, notably popular and women's magazines, created a whole new market. The press needed images and women were lining up to provide beautiful ones. They were also seeking to create art.[2] They found art in the street. I am thinking of Margaret Bourke-White, who captured the architectural beauty of the city and was featured in *Life* in 1936.[3] I am also thinking of Tina Modotti, with her now iconic photo of a woman walking down the street with a flag. And of course I am thinking of Dora Maar, belatedly celebrated in a retrospective at the Pompidou Centre – because she was a painter but also a 'partner of…' – who was an incomparable experimenter in photography and who, for example in *The Pisser*, gave us an unsettling body of work in

2. See Christian Bouqueret (ed.), *Les Femmes photographes de la Nouvelle Vision en France* [Women Photographers of the New Vision in France], Paris, Marval, 1998.

3. See Melissa A. McEuen, *Seeing America: Women Photographers Between the Wars. Doris Ulmann, Dorothea Lange, Marion Post Wolcott, Margaret Bourke-White, Berenice Abbott*, Lexington, The University Press of Kentucky, 2000.

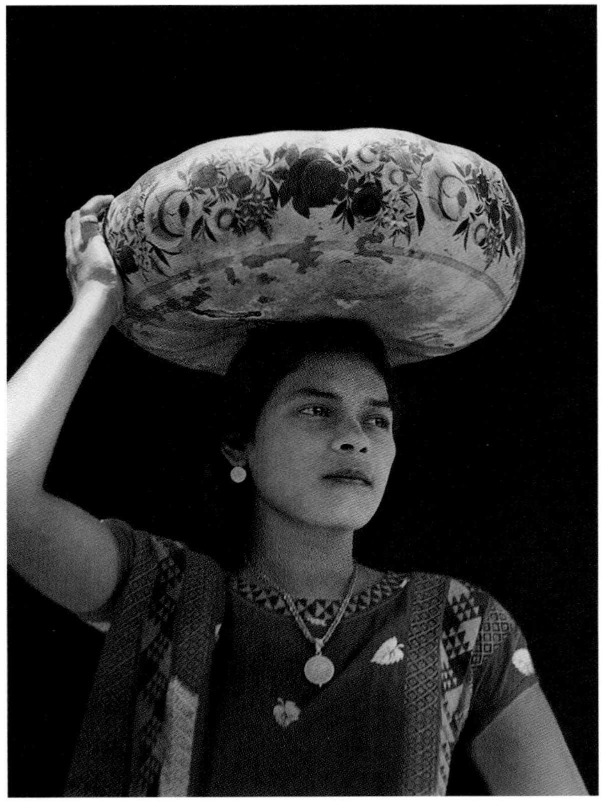

TINA MODOTTI
'Mujer en Tehuantepec (con un Jicalpextle)' [Tehuantepec Woman Carrying a *Jicalpextle* (painted calabash)], 1929, platinotype signed in pencil by Ava Vargas, New York, Throckmorton Fine Art Gallery

which desire is expressed through the light employed, the framing, the grain of the skin, the poses. For women, such as for example Harriet Thorn or Ergy Landau, did not shy away from nudes, including male nudes. No subject was out of bounds and for them nudity was not titillation for men in search of erotic excitement but a celebration of the strength of the new woman, who assumed multiple identities and wore various masks. Female artists began to explore and interrogate sexuality, the attractions of androgyny, the anxiety provoked by disconnecting from their own personality and used self-portraiture to play self-reflexively with appearances more deeply. I am thinking of the series of masquerades by Gertrud Arndt, who represented herself multiplied through her forty-three variations. Who am I? I can portray myself as I would like to be without ever being the actual person you see.

In the game of introspection, women took many risks as they interrogated the border between private space and the deliberate construction of their persons or their personae. The still-young science of psychoanalysis is evident throughout the work of many women across the world: it feeds through the artistic endeavour, as in the work of Marianne Breslauer, whose images represent the split self; or Claude Cahun, one of the major photographers of the 20th century, relatively unknown in their lifetime but a huge inspiration to younger generations. A gay Jewish socialist, Claude Cahun defied social convention their whole life long; they overturned codes of representation, placing themself in some danger. Throughout, they dedicated themself to exploring the divided *I*. One side in light, the other in darkness. They constantly fought against all social conventions and left behind a journal, *Cancelled Confessions*, in which they created two androgynous personae: their artistic self, Claude Cahun, and their official identity, Lucy Schwob. Rather than trying to reconcile the two, they set them in dialogue, maintaining the split between them.

All across Europe and in the United States, photography became increasingly democratic and accessible to women. Of course, no one stopped them from travelling to the ends of the Earth if that was what they wanted, but when they came back with thousands of remarkable photos,

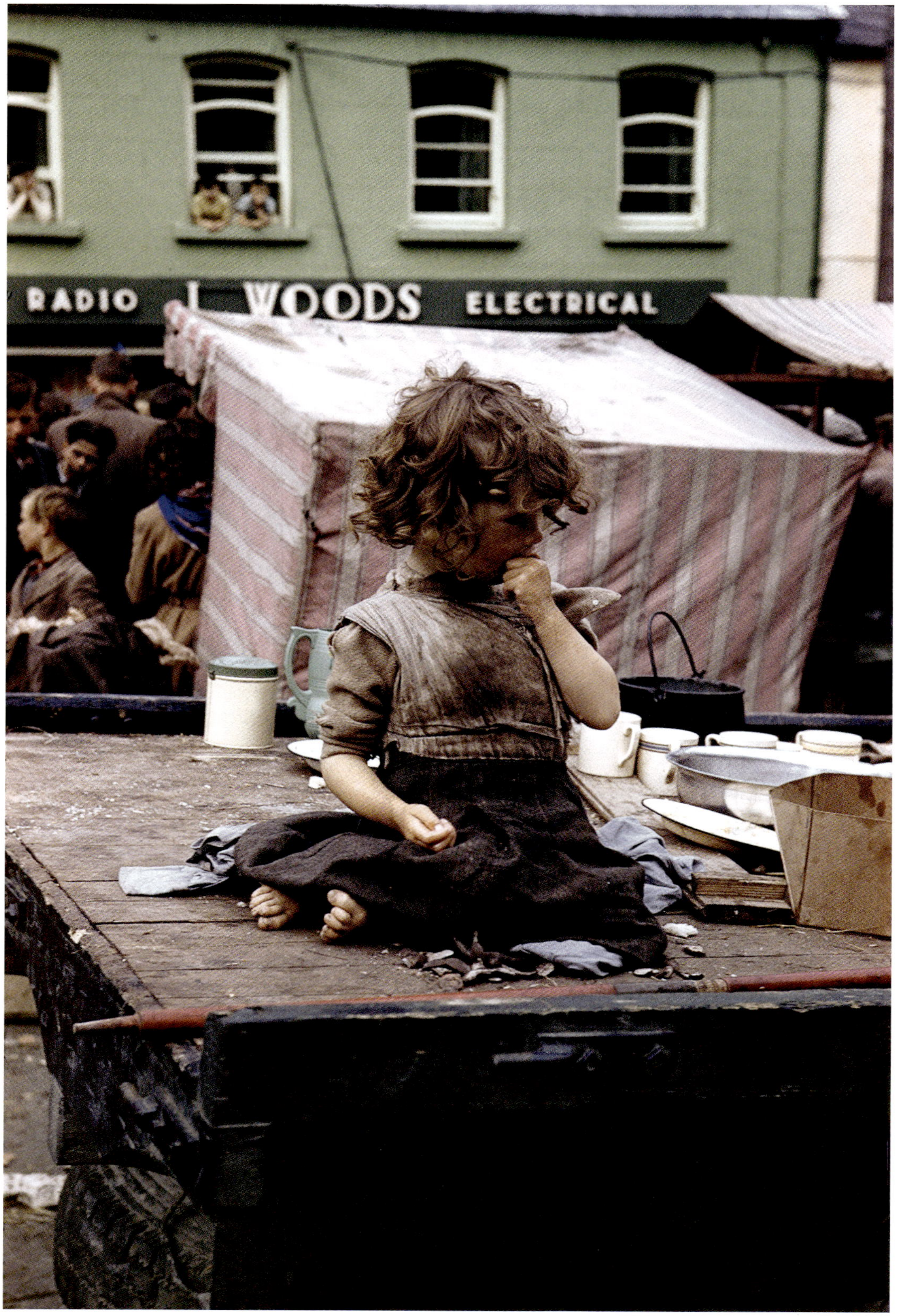

INGE MORATH
'Ireland, Killorglin, County Kerry. Park Fair',
1954,
Magnum Photos Archive

they didn't always find willing buyers in the press, as there was stiff male competition. This is what happened to Agnès Varda on her return from China in 1957, and to Martine Franck, partner of Henri Cartier-Bresson, when she obtained visas for the Far East. Sometimes women remained in the shadows of their own accord – indeed, Martine Franck said that she lived 'in the shade of a mighty tree' and Cartier-Bresson encouraged her to believe in herself, to pursue her work. In doing so, Martine joined the Magnum agency, a sanctum to which only a few women – Eve Arnold, Susan Meiselas, Inge Morath, Marilyn Silverstone – gained access.

The legacy of these humanistic camerawomen is considerable: as journalists opposing exclusion – whether based on class, skin colour or age – they redefined so-called 'travel' photography, transforming it into a road movie, a search for faces, intimate situations, subjective approaches. Not everything was suitable to be photographed. These female photographers all adopted a different ethical code from the journalistic sensationalism that was then at its peak. They were concerned about what was happening in the world and involved in what was all around them. Their ambition was not only to 'document' reality but also to understand it and communicate what they had perceived. From the middle of the 19th century to the present day, not a single conflict in the world has passed them by, nor any social change. Attentive to different ways of living, to the history of ideas, they were the first to produce long reportages on the hardship of work, child labour, poverty and the precariousness of the dispossessed, with nothing to guide them but their own feelings. No one had taught them how to take photos, and when asked, they would respond: it's life.

That doesn't mean, however, that male and female photographers should be treated separately, let alone set in opposition. It would be a clever person who could distinguish their work in the absence of a signature. Many of them didn't wish to be regarded as female photographers but simply as photographers, not defined by their gender. That is totally understandable. It wasn't because they were women that they took photos… of women. Conversely, the fact that they had a common experience of the many difficulties in being able to practise their art and the often complete erasure of their work which went on for decades, their ways of seeing and understanding reality and their interest in things that did not seem worthy of being photographed might all be seen as characteristics of their work and define a homogeneous way of looking. Put male and female photographers in the same public space and they will not see the same things and take the same photos. Does this mean women perceive or interpret reality differently? Some said so, loud and clear, like Běla Kolářová, who declared in 1963: 'Little by little I began to perceive a world which was disdained, ignored by photographers, a negligible everyday world, as if it took exception to being photographed.' Agnès Varda also embraced the vision of the world by photographing whatever she saw when she left her home: a shop, walls, children playing in the street, customers at the bar of a café. There was adventure at the corner of the street. You didn't have to travel far to be captivated, it was all in the way you looked at things. Beauty was to be found in the everyday, the overlooked, the insignificant stuff. This redefinition of the real was a major inspiration of their creativity wherever they worked in the world.

Photography doesn't take up a lot of space. You can carry a camera in a bag, it doesn't cost very much; you can set up a darkroom in a bathroom and a timer allows you to turn the lens on yourself. The body and identity would become favourite themes for women to express themselves in narrative or performance, such as the cross-dressing and multiple identities of Cindy Sherman; or Alexis Hunter with her *Approach to Fear* series of hands; Valie Export, with her *Identity Transfer* cycle; and Orlan, who has been metamorphosing for decades and uses her body as a medium for our feminist grievances. These artists used provocatively inventive means to raise consciousness of the violence that women often experience, anticipating what later became the gender question. They disguised themselves, upended conventions, sowed romantic confusion and offered new visions of sexuality far removed from sexist codes.

The emancipation of women that came about through feminist struggles in Europe and the USA was accompanied by an unwavering engagement on the part of female photographers who documented it in quality photojournalism.[4] Feminists would also use the camera as an instrument of revolution, of subversion[5] – for example, the 71 artists who, especially in Austria at the beginning of the 1970s, constructed a new image of woman in opposition to sexism, social inequalities and the structures of patriarchal power. Their self-portraits were especially powerful: Annagret Soltau covered her face with masks stitched with pins. These radical works of art were showcased just a couple of years ago in the exhibition The Feminist Avant-Garde at the Rencontres d'Arles following legitimate protests by the La Part des Femmes collective, a group of

4. See Carol McCusker, *Breaking the Frame. Pioneering Women in Photojournalism*, San Diego, Museum of Photographic Arts, 2006; and Martin W. Sandler, *Against the Odds: Women Pioneers in the First Hundred Years of American Photography*, New York, Rizzoli, 2002.

5. See Diane Neumaier (ed.), *Reframings: New American Feminist Photograpàhies*, Philadelphia, Temple University Press, 1995; and Abigail Solomon-Godeau, *Chair à canons, Photographies, discours, féminisme* [Cannon Fodder, Photographies, Discourses, Feminism], Paris, Textuel, 2016.

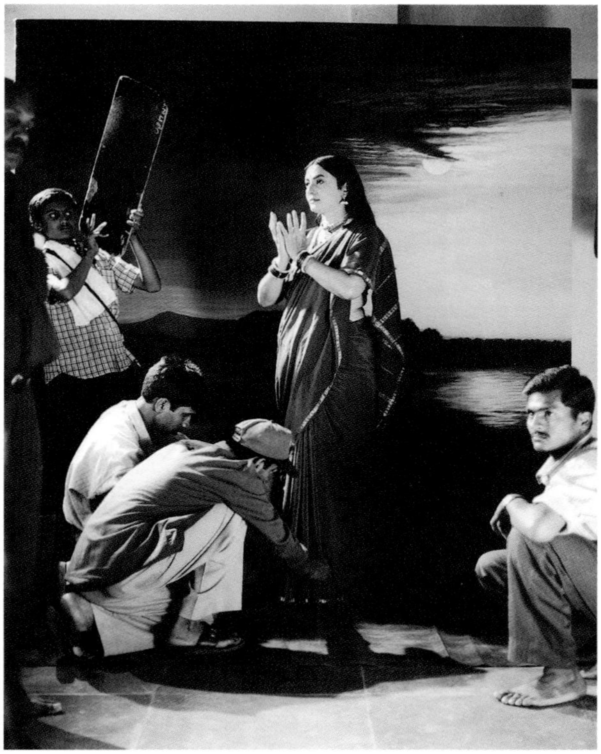

PUSHPAMALA N. IN COLLABORATION WITH CLARE ARNI
'Lady in Moonlight E-9',
The Process series,
black-and-white photograph

activists opposed to the occlusion of women.[6]

This is just the beginning. The fight must go on! For the demotion of female artists persists, in terms of exposure, of money – the gaps between men and women are huge, with the exception of artists such as Cindy Sherman – and of recognition too. Of course, there are always exceptions, such as Agnès Varda, who was exhibited in international biennials and prestigious institutions, but she had to struggle to achieve that and not everyone is endowed with her energy… Just like in painting, you have to wait until you are old or dead to merit a retrospective. I am thinking of Louise Bourgeois in terms of painting, and of Sabine Weiss, among others, in terms of photography – the latter displayed her work in group exhibitions her whole life but had to wait 50 years to be exhibited at the Maison Européene de la Photographie and was 90 years old before she had a solo exhibition at the Rencontres d'Arles, rather than being displayed collectively in badly lit basements of museums. I was lucky enough to visit her in her studio on several occasions towards the end of her life, and when I sang her praises to directors of cultural institutions to encourage them to exhibit her works, I was told rather sniffily that she had already been amply acknowledged but she was no longer much sought after. That phrase stuck with me. It seemed overused in relation to women photographers, who in fact ask so little, given that so many are content simply to be *shortlisted*. As ever, it is a battle for acceptance, even if attitudes are changing, very slowly.

Views about women photographers are changing and they are beginning to be taken seriously by galleries and museums, albeit without being fully included in the art world. They are seen more as skilled practitioners of what was once called 'ladies' work' than artists imagining and expressing a vision of the world. Some of them poke malicious fun at this, subverting patriarchal codes, the better to denounce them, as Annette Messager did over several decades, digging underneath the stereotypes

6. See Gabriele Schor, *Une avant-garde féministe. Photographies et performances des années 1970 de la collection Verbund* [A Feminist Avant-garde. Photographies and Performances of the 1970s in the Verbund Collection], Vienna/Paris, Delpire, 2022.

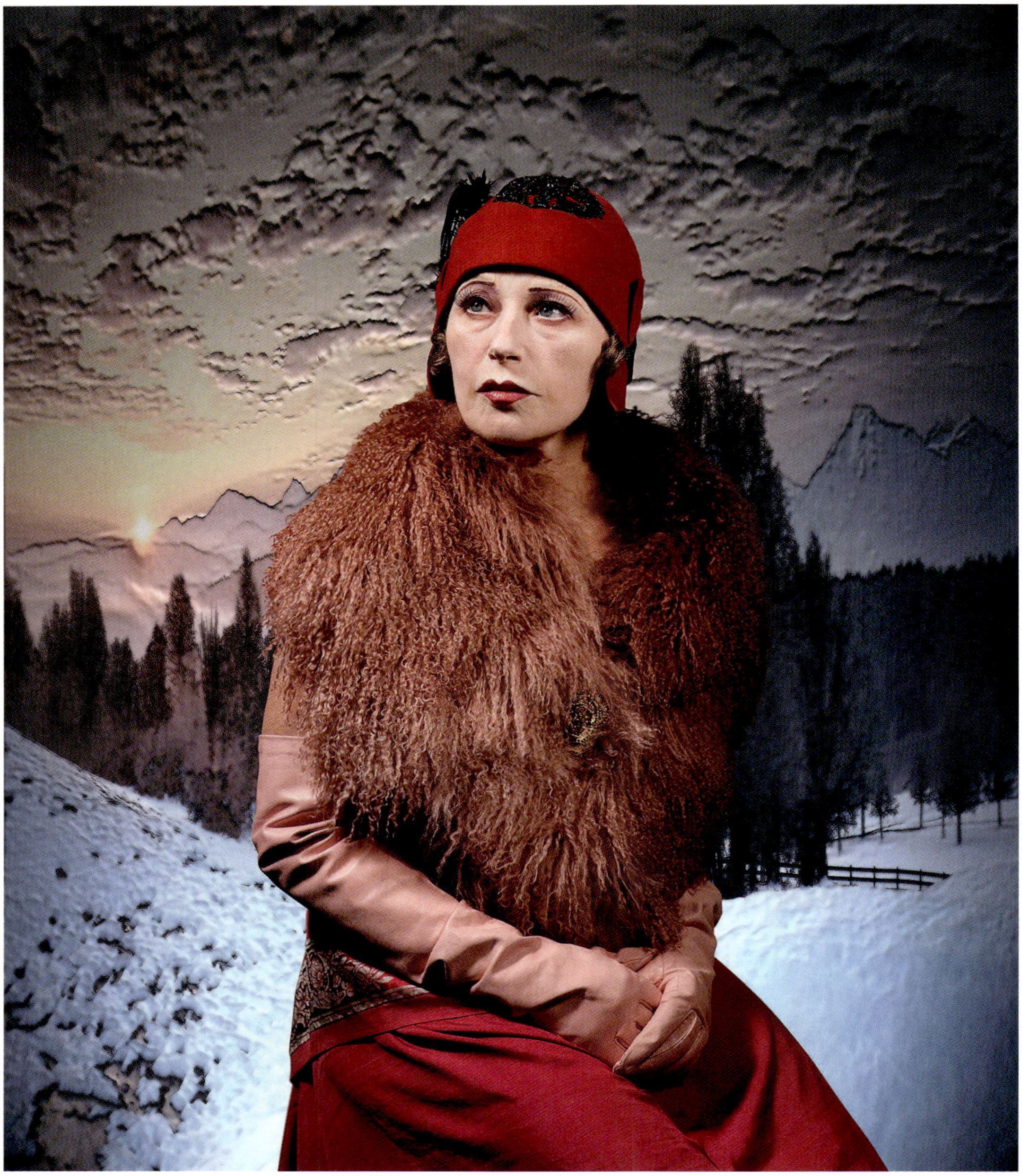

CINDY SHERMAN
'Untitled #576',
2016,
thermal
sublimation print
on metal

attached to one idea of femininity. Irreverent, funny, audacious, like Cindy Sherman and Eleanor Antin, they increasingly refute the very idea of assignment by deliberately upsetting our whole mythology of representations of self and others. Disguise as a form of reinvention in role plays that call into question representations of femininity is also a way of making us reflect on the violence that has been inflicted on women's bodies, their psyches and on their status as object – sexual object more often than not – in which they have been imprisoned and indeed still are.

Unfortunately, social media are churning out representations of females which confirm and amplify the worst caricatures of toxic masculinity. Once readily overlooked by scholars of photography, they are now included (somewhat, still too little) in the shared story of photography.[7] Female curators now hold positions of cultural influence and, while not yet achieving parity, are at least beginning to redress the balance.

And then there is the public, increasingly interested in discovering works by women. In 2013, a government report criticised the under-representation of women in photography, which still wallowed in the male mythology of the creative genius and his muses. In 2016, under the direction of Marie Robert, an inspiring exhibition was mounted under the title of Who's Afraid of Women Photographers?[8] Apparently quite a lot of people, since women continued to be under-represented in the major photographic exhibitions despite the creation of the Women Exhibit festival in Houlgate and the periodical *Femmes photographes*. The #MeToo movement has kick-started this new awareness and the necessity of staking a claim. There have been noticeable changes at the Rencontres d'Arles, where this is now the predominant view and some minor efforts at Paris Photo, where one artist in three is female – but their works made up only 31% of new public acquisitions in 2020.[9] Proactive policies at state level have been accompanied by a significant increase in female teachers

7. See, for example, Anne Tucker, *The Woman's Eye*, New York, Knopf, 1973; Margery Mann and Anne Noggle, *Women of Photography. An Historical Survey*, San Francisco, Museum of Modern Art, 1975; Jenne Moutoussamy-Ashe, *Viewfinders: Black Women Photographers*, New York, Dodd Mead, 1986; Lothar Schirmer and Naomi Rosenblum, *Women Seeing Women: A Pictorial History of Women's Photography from Julia Margaret Cameron to Annie Liebovitz*, New York, Norton, 2003; Constance Sullivan, *Women Photographers*, New York, Abrams, 1990; Naomi Rosenblum, *A History of Women Photographers*, Abbeville Press, 1994, reissued 2010; or Luce Lebart and Marie Robert (eds.), *Une histoire Mondiale des femmes photographes* [A Global History of Women Photographers], Paris, Textuel, 2020.

8. Thomas Galifot, Ulrich Pohlmann and Marie Robert (eds.), *Qui a peur des femmes photographes?* [Who's Afraid of Women Photographers?], Paris, Hazan, 2015.

9. https://ellesfontla.culture.gouv.fr/infographie.

in the subject, who will pass on their knowledge to younger generations. You will never convince those of an inveterate macho disposition, but you can at least point out that the two market leaders are both women: Cindy Sherman and Rosalind Fox Solomon. It's not all about the market, of course, but nevertheless… And then you have Diane Arbus, Lee Miller, Claude Cahun, Nan Goldin. There are many others, dead or alive, who haunt our imaginations and have left their mark on our memories.

RENATE EISENEGGER
'Hochhaus (Nr.1)' [Apartment Block No. 1], 1974, black-and-white photograph laminated on wood, Vienna, Verbund Collection

It has been an immense pleasure to work with Clara Bouveresse, author of a remarkable book on women photographers as well as a historian of the Magnum agency and… a particular fan of love in the early hours, with her poetic essays *Photographies au saut du lit* [Photographs Straight Out of Bed]. We wanted to pay special attention to the younger generation of women photographers for several reasons: because they are finding new forms of expression and new techniques, but also because #MeToo is embedded deep in their way of seeing the world, in how they bear witness to it and revolt against it. As evidence, the Iranian Gohar Dashti, the American Tarrah Krajnac and the Belgian Bieke Depoorter, who holds a silent dialogue with those whose photos she 'takes'. In France too, there are many who see their artistic practice as a form of feminist activism, unwittingly reconnecting with the aims of the first women photographers: to bear witness and advocate for freedom.

We have both attempted the impossible: to synthesise, to choose. Please forgive us for our omissions… some must wait to be included in some future book that will pay them their due, as the struggle for recognition for women photographers continues: so says the collective La Part des Femmes, who in 2018 wrote a manifesto for Paris Photo, which I found so strong and of-the-moment that it merits reading, rereading and meditating upon… It starts off:

'We are all photographers!
Look at us. Take your time.
Really, we are many.
Self-taught, some of us. Others educated in the finest art schools, where we make up more than 60% of graduates. And yet we account for barely 20% of the artists exhibited in France and in other Western countries […]
Look at us. Take your time.'

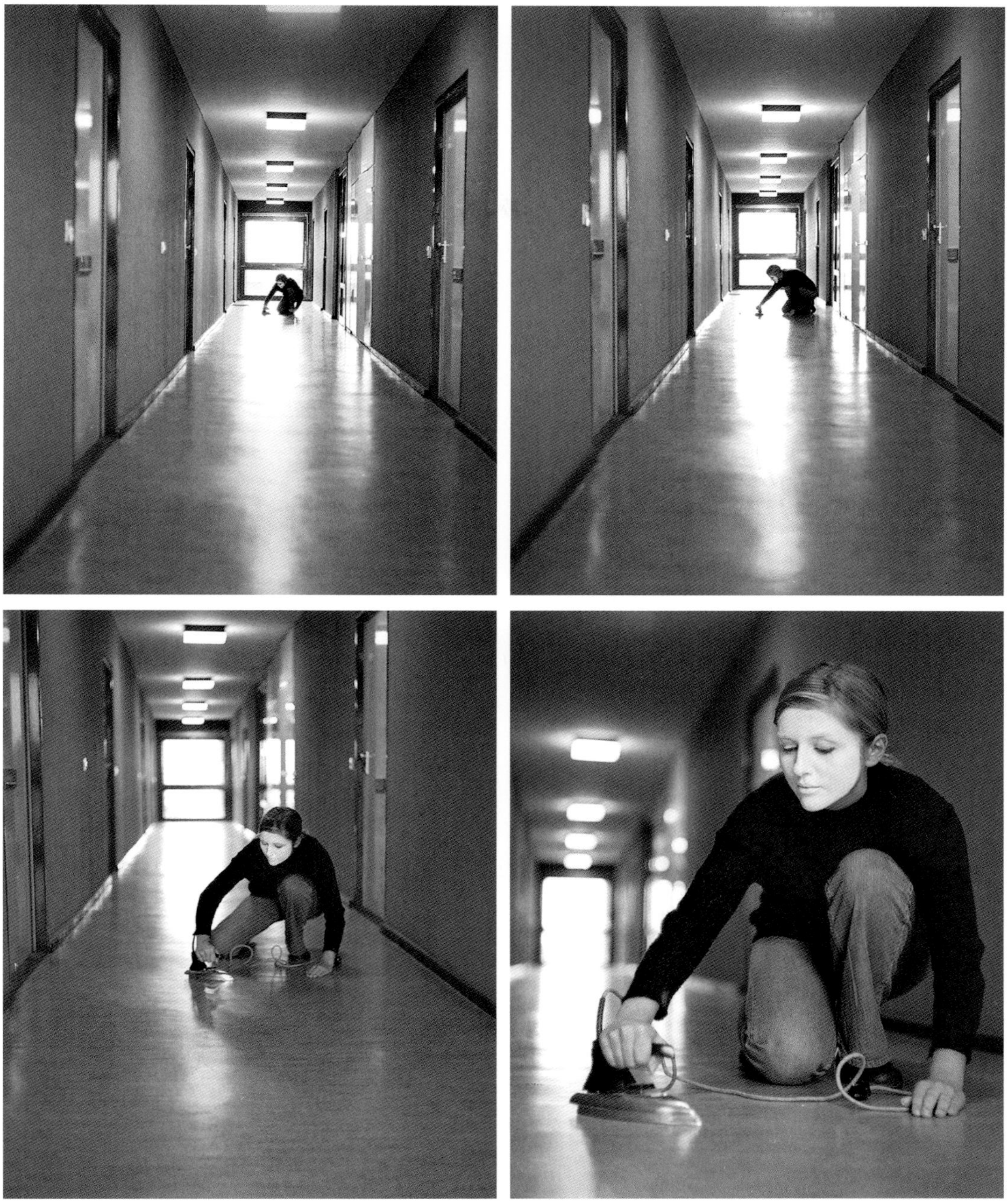

p. 23
DOROTHEA LANGE
'Migrant Mother, Nipomo, California', March 1936, digital print from the original negative, retouched in the 1930s, Washington, Library of Congress

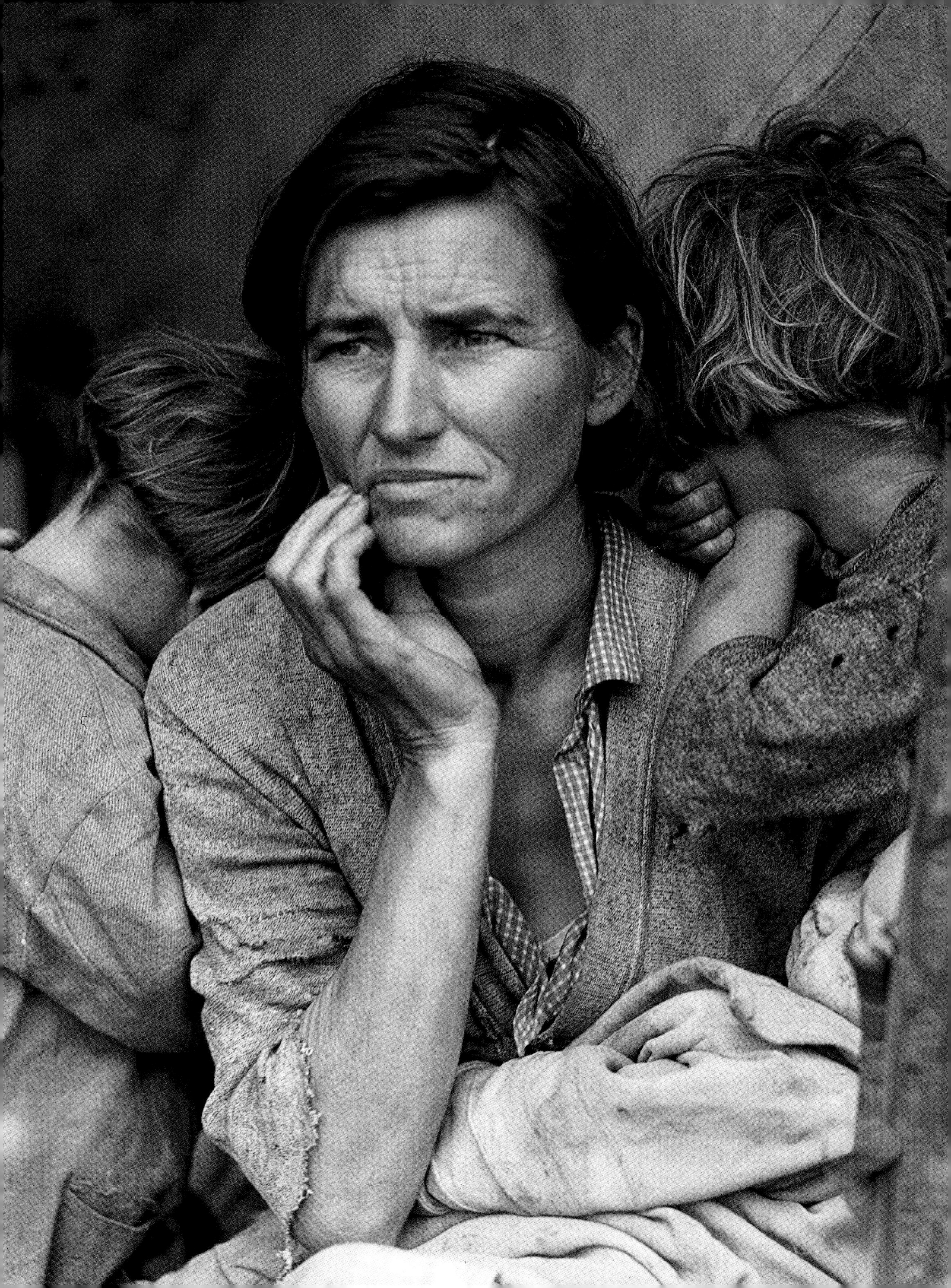

ANNA ATKINS

1799–1891, UK

The daughter of naturalist John George Children, in 1823 Anna Atkins provided the illustrations for his translation of Jean-Baptise Lamarck's book on molluscs. A watercolourist and lithographer who had an interest in the natural sciences, in 1838 she became a member of the London Botanical Society, one of the very few scientific institutions that accepted women. She transformed scientific publishing and illustration through her use of a new photographic technique, namely the cyanotype method, developed by the astronomer John Herschel. This involved making an image through contact, without the use of a camera, by exposing an object on a surface coated in iron salts that reacted to sunlight. The contours of the plants were picked out in white in extraordinary detail when the print was developed, contrasting with the paper, which was tinted Prussian blue.

Between 1843 and 1853, she used this method to illustrate William Henry Harvey's work on algae. The silhouette of each specimen, accompanied by its Latin name, seemed to unfurl in a translucid liquid. She later published a book of 160 plates of plants and ferns dedicated to her friend Anne Dixon, who helped her produce her collections and prints. On the opening page, the plants formed an elegant crown around the title, illustrating the combination of erudition and formal harmony that she brought to each fascicle.

These books were reference works for the scientific community and established the new medium of photography as a tool of scientific discovery, exploration and record, prized for its rigour and precision. Their pared-down aesthetic, bringing to mind stencils and herbariums, also attracted art collectors. Anna Atkins invented the genre of the photographic book in all its diverse forms, opening the way to its use in education and science, but also art.

'Dictyota dichotoma',
1849–50,
cyanotype on paper,
New York, The New York Public Library

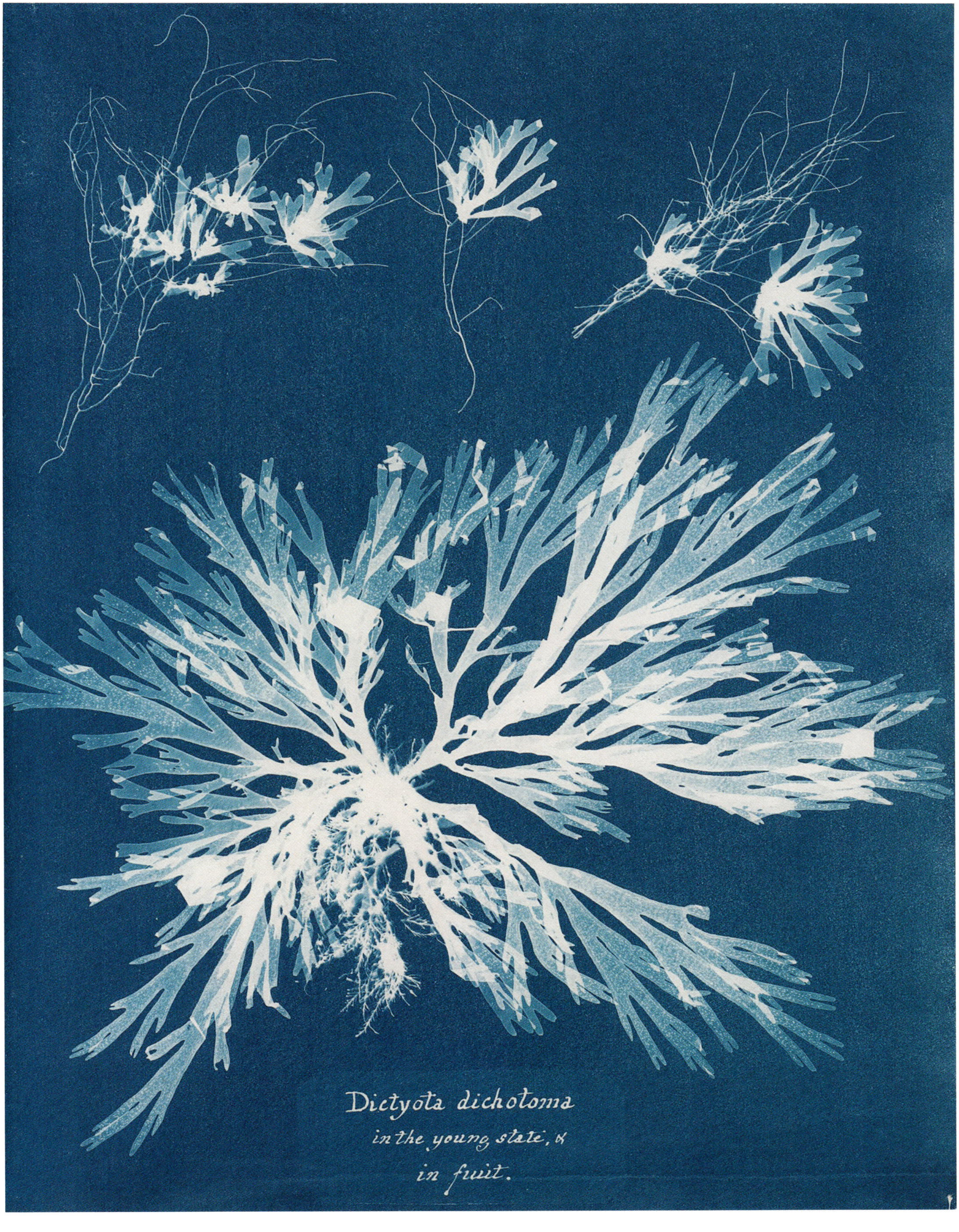
Dictyota dichotoma
in the young state, &
in fruit.

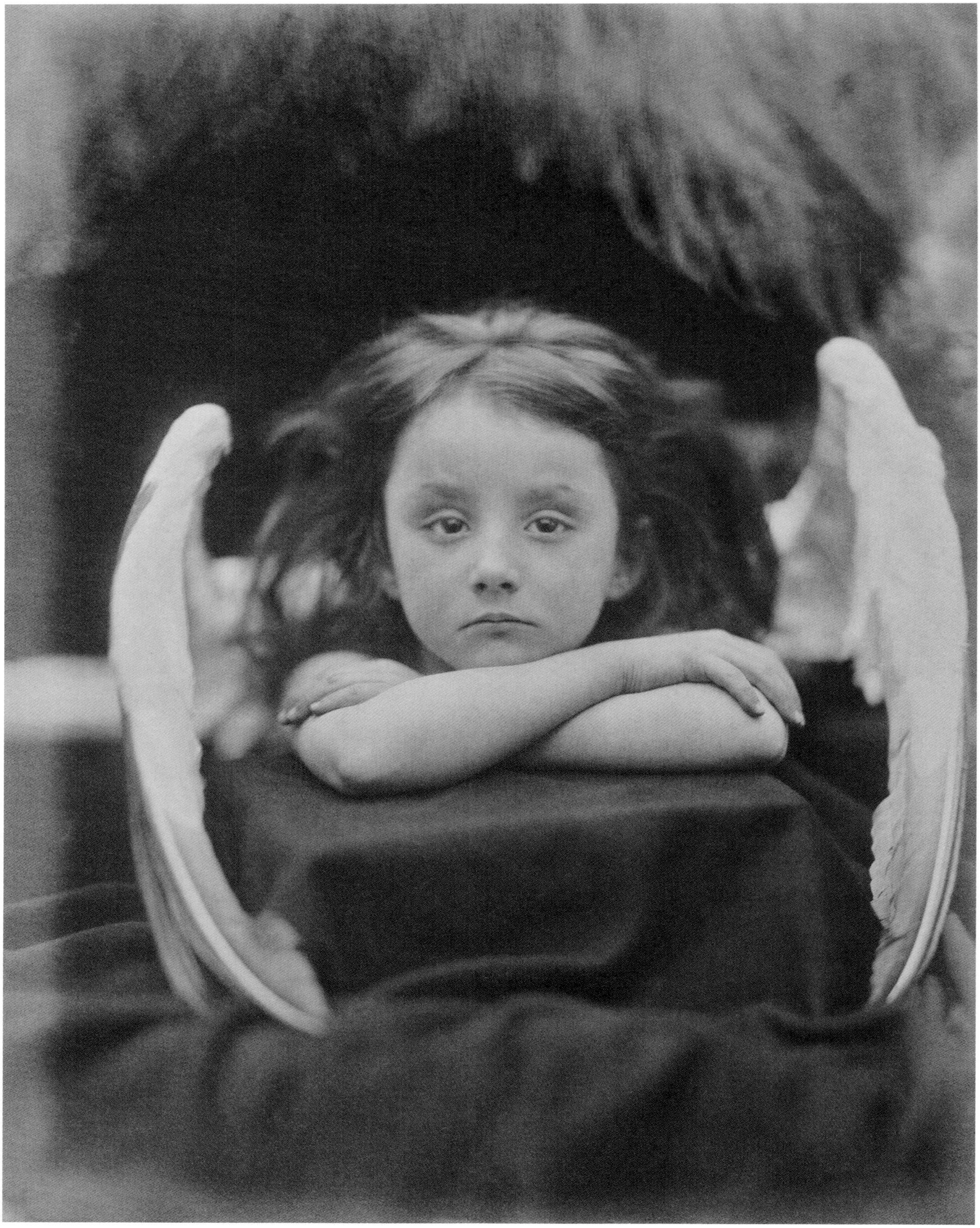

JULIA MARGARET CAMERON

1815, India–1879, Sri Lanka

Julia Margaret Cameron was given her first camera in 1864, at the age of 48, and she soon had everyone posing for her – friends, family and servants. Sometimes *au naturel*, sometimes dressed as angels, madonnas or allegories, her subjects incarnated various religious or literary characters for her camera. She provided sets and costumes with elaborate drapery based on pre-Raphaelite paintings. She was a friend of Alfred Lord Tennyson, a neighbour of hers on the Isle of Wight, where she lived, and illustrated one of his poetry collections on the legend of King Arthur, depicting Merlin, Lancelot and Guinevere. She also became well known for her portraits of children and celebrities of the Victorian era such as the astronomer John Herschel, the naturalist Charles Darwin and the playwright and poet Henry Taylor. She sold prints through the Colnaghi Gallery, sometimes signed by their illustrious models to make them more valuable and to top up the family coffers. From 1865 she exhibited at the Victoria & Albert Museum and from 1868 had the use of two rooms where she installed her studio.

Her work is characterised by an innovative use of close-ups and soft focus, sometimes creating a luminous halo around the faces. Some critics saw this as a lack of expertise, even though this new technique was distinguished by its sharpness and transparency. Contrary to the norms of clarity, she was quite willing to make prints from damaged negatives, showing traces of fingerprints or scratches, accentuating the materiality and physical thickness of the displayed object. She therefore opened the way to modernism and the experimentation of pictorialist avant-gardes, who saw her as a pioneer who raised this infant medium to the level of artistic expression.

'I Wait (Rachel Gurney)',
1872,
silver albumen print,
Los Angeles, J. Paul Getty Museum

VIRGINIA DE CASTIGLIONE

1837, Italy–1899, France

A leading light in Parisian high society, the Countess de Castiglione used photography as an instrument of self-publicity. In the studio of Pierre-Louis Pierson, she produced more than 400 self-portraits displaying her lavish fashions and legendary beauty. Sometimes retouched or colourised by her own hand, printed as calling cards or blown up, her images were a record of her triumphant social and political career.

Newly arrived in Turin in 1856, she was commissioned by King Victor-Emmanuel III to lobby for Italian unity with Emperor Napoleon III, whose mistress she became. She turned every one of her public appearances into an event which was reported in all the papers. She played on the fad for fancy dress at the imperial balls, dressed in Etruscan costume or disguised as the queen of hearts or a peasant woman. A handwritten note under one of her portraits was categorically damning of any potential rivals: 'I equal them by my birth. I surpass them in beauty. I judge them with my wit.'[1]

She was a provocateur, never shy of showing her bare legs, then of documenting the signs of ageing on her body, capturing for example her feet as if viewed in her own coffin. After a gap of twenty-six years, she took up her photographic chronicle again, so to speak, and posed in dresses from her regal years, ambivalently fascinated by her own physical decline, yet in denial of the ravages of time.

In 1897, she asked to be given the status of exhibitor when one of her portraits was shown at the Universal Exposition, demanding the role of creator even though she hadn't technically clicked the shutter. As both model and artist of her own image, the Countess de Castiglione redefined the limits of photography and created her own myth. Her work marked the beginnings of photographic performance and autofiction, presaging our modern narcissistic obsession with our own image and with norms of beauty.

1. Cited by Benedeatta Craveri, *La Contessa*, Paris, Flammarion, 2021.

With the collaboration of Pierre-Louis Pierson, 'Scherzo di Follia' [Mad Pleasantry],
c. 1863–66,
albumen print from a glass negative with collodion,
New York, The Metropolitan Museum of Art

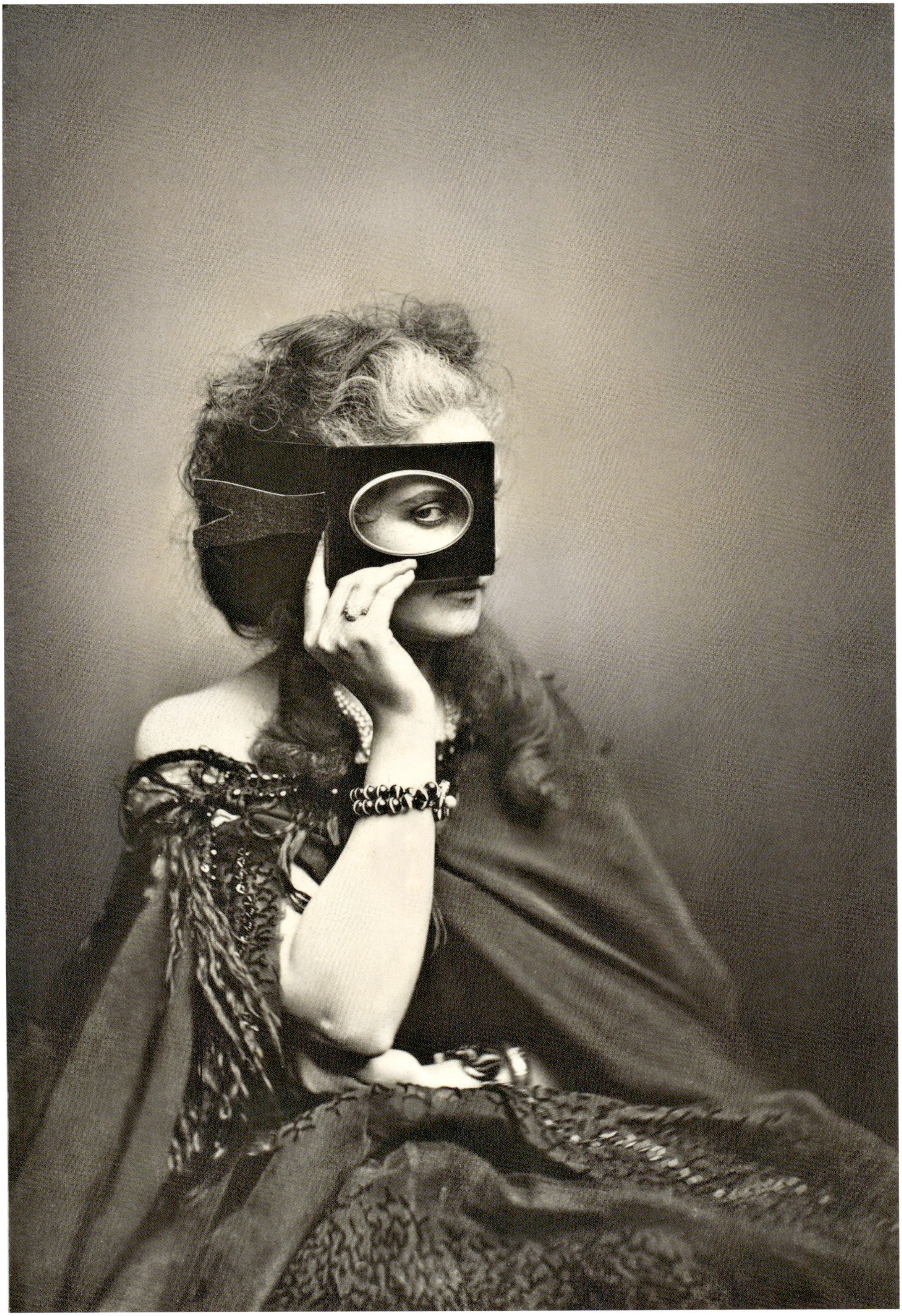

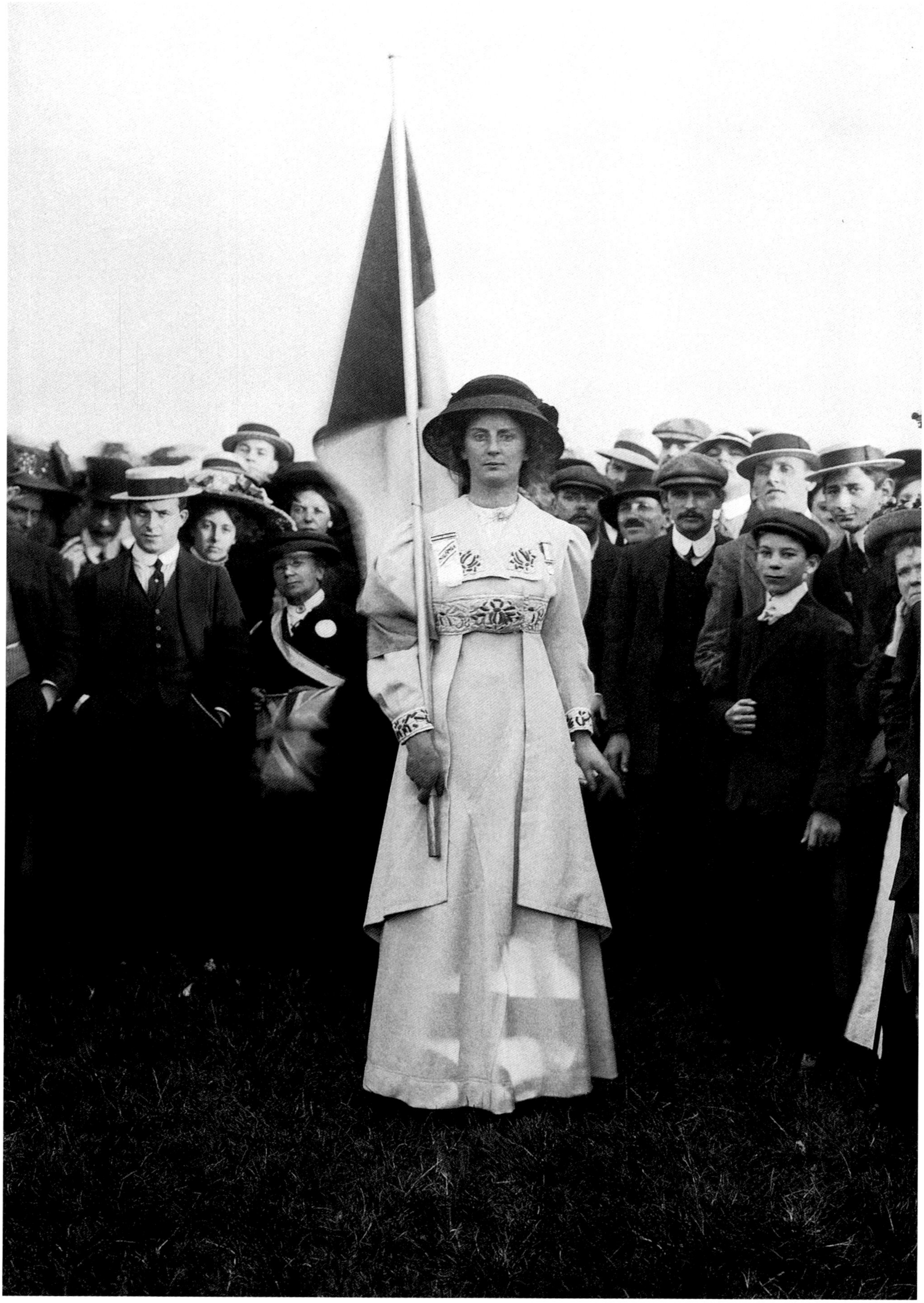

CHRISTINA BROOM

1862–1939, UK

Christina Broom is the creator of magnificent photos of Suffragette marches demanding votes for women prior to the First World War. Her images are a record of the ferment and diverse forms of activism, the banners with elaborate coats of arms carried by the regional and professional delegations, and the posters used for fundraising. She got up close with the militants with her cumbersome equipment and her tripod and took full-length photos of the leaders of the marches, giving a human face to the growing feminist movement. Boldly she went out her studio to capture the political action on the streets and she exploited her photos commercially by producing much sought-after postcards, which gave the movement a great deal of publicity.

Self-taught, Christina took up photography in 1903 in order to provide for her family. She documented university boat races and public appearances by the royal family. Her daughter acted as her assistant, working in the darkroom to produce the postcards that made money for the family business. As the official photographer of the royal guard, she managed to go behind the parades and the pomp to capture moments of rest and camaraderie. Taken on the occasion of the rally on 23 July 1910, one of her best-known images features Charlotte Marsh, standing out in white against a largely male crowd dressed in black. Charlotte had been incarcerated the previous year and had been force-fed during her hunger strike in prison. She proudly carries the flag of the Women's Social and Political Union, whose upright pole gives her an authority that seems to part the crowd, emphasising her stature and her direct gaze.

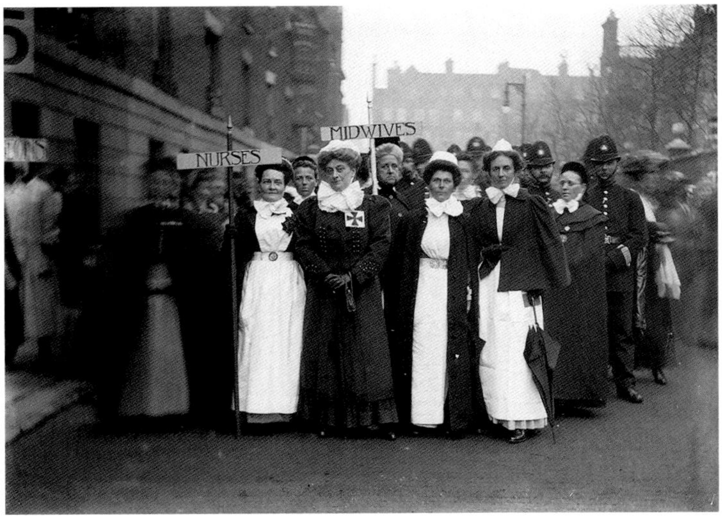

← 'Suffragette Charlotte (Charlie) Marsh at Hyde Park Rally',
1908,
silver emulsion on cellulose acetate

↗ 'Nurses and Midwives Marching to the Albert Hall',
27 April 1909,
silver emulsion on glass plate

FRANCES BENJAMIN JOHNSTON

1864–1952, USA

After studying art in Paris, Frances Benjamin Johnston trained as a photographer in Washington and began to publish her images in the illustrated press in the 1890s. She opened her own studio in 1895, attracting a prestigious clientele from the political class in the federal capital. She took part in pictorialist exhibitions and put together a presentation of the works of her American sisters at the Universal Exposition in Paris in 1900. She was interested in education and documented the activities of various public and professional schools, notably an institute in Virginia open to African Americans and Native Americans. She was also involved in photographing architecture and gardens and opened a specialist studio in New York in 1913. She travelled in Europe and the Middle East and then, towards the end of the 1920s, undertook a huge project documenting the historical legacy of the American South.

Her archive, held today at the Library of Congress, is testament to how, in its early years, photography opened up new possibilities, offering various professional options to women. Posing in her studio or dressed as a man, Frances Benjamin Johnston embodied a bold and enterprising modernity. In 1987, she wrote an article for *Ladies Home Journal*, 'What a Woman Can Do with a Camera', which defended women's access to this new and growing profession. Part practical guide and part aesthetic manifesto, the article described the qualities needed for success – common sense, patience, tact, good taste, a quick eye, a talent for detail – saying that, 'to an energetic, ambitious woman with even ordinary opportunities, success is always possible, and hard, intelligent and conscientious work seldom fails to develop small beginnings into large results.'

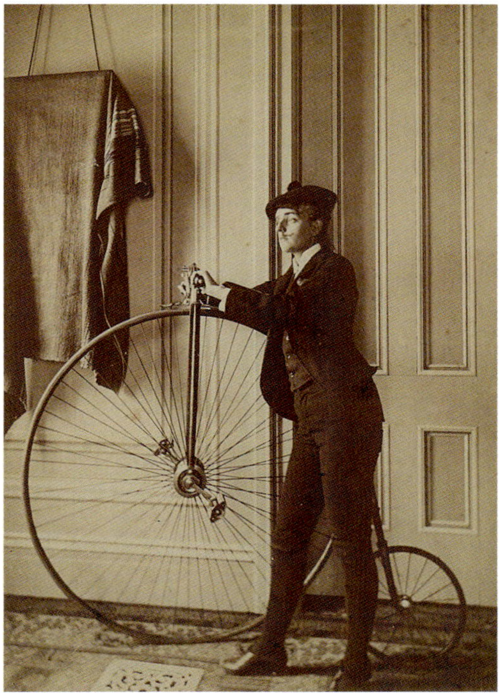

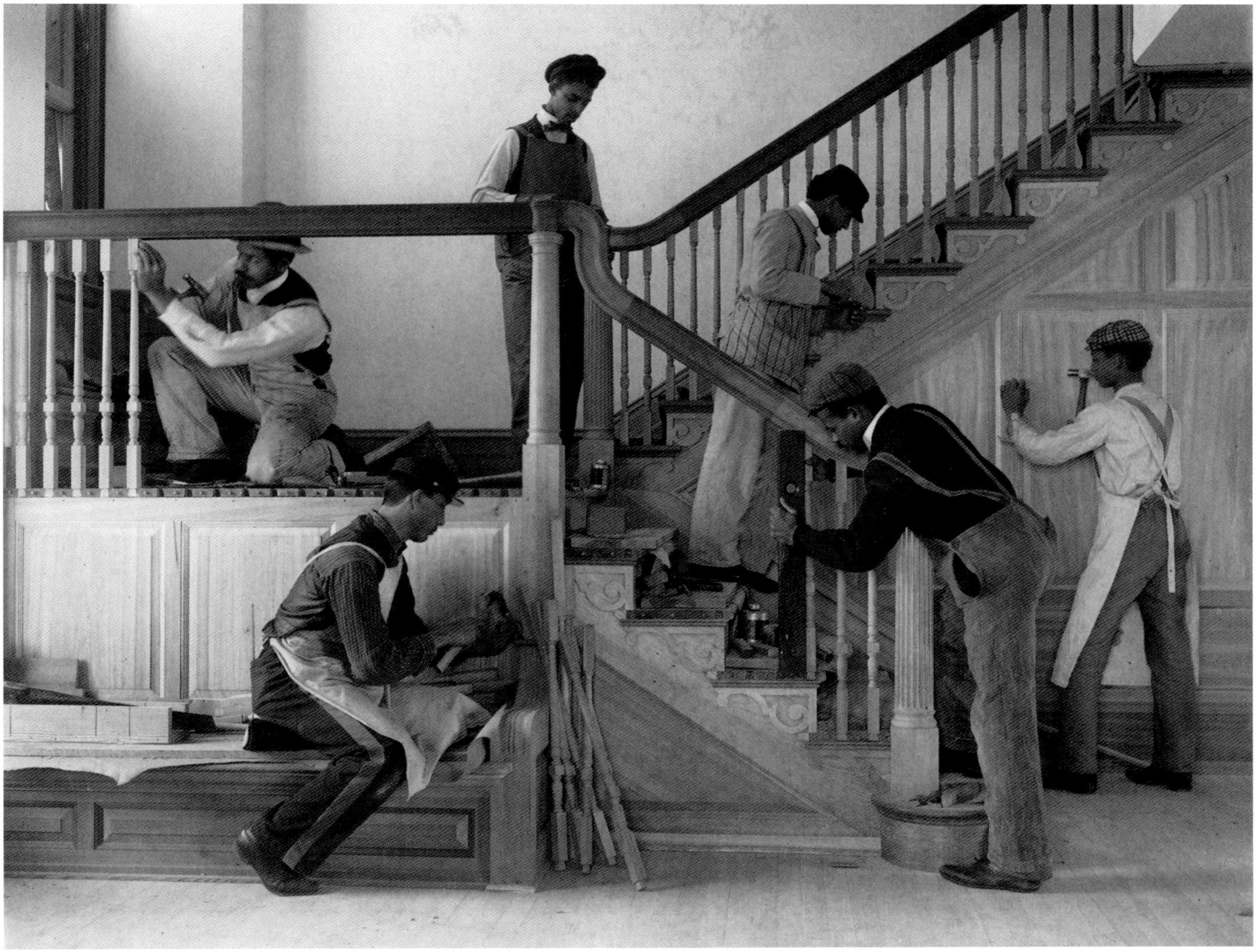

← 'Full-Length Self-Portrait Dressed as a Man with a False Moustache, Posed with a Bicycle',
c. 1890,
albumen print,
Washington, Library of Congress

↑ 'Stairway of the Treasurer's Residence: Students at Work',
1899–1900,
platinum-palladium print,
New York, Museum of Modern Art

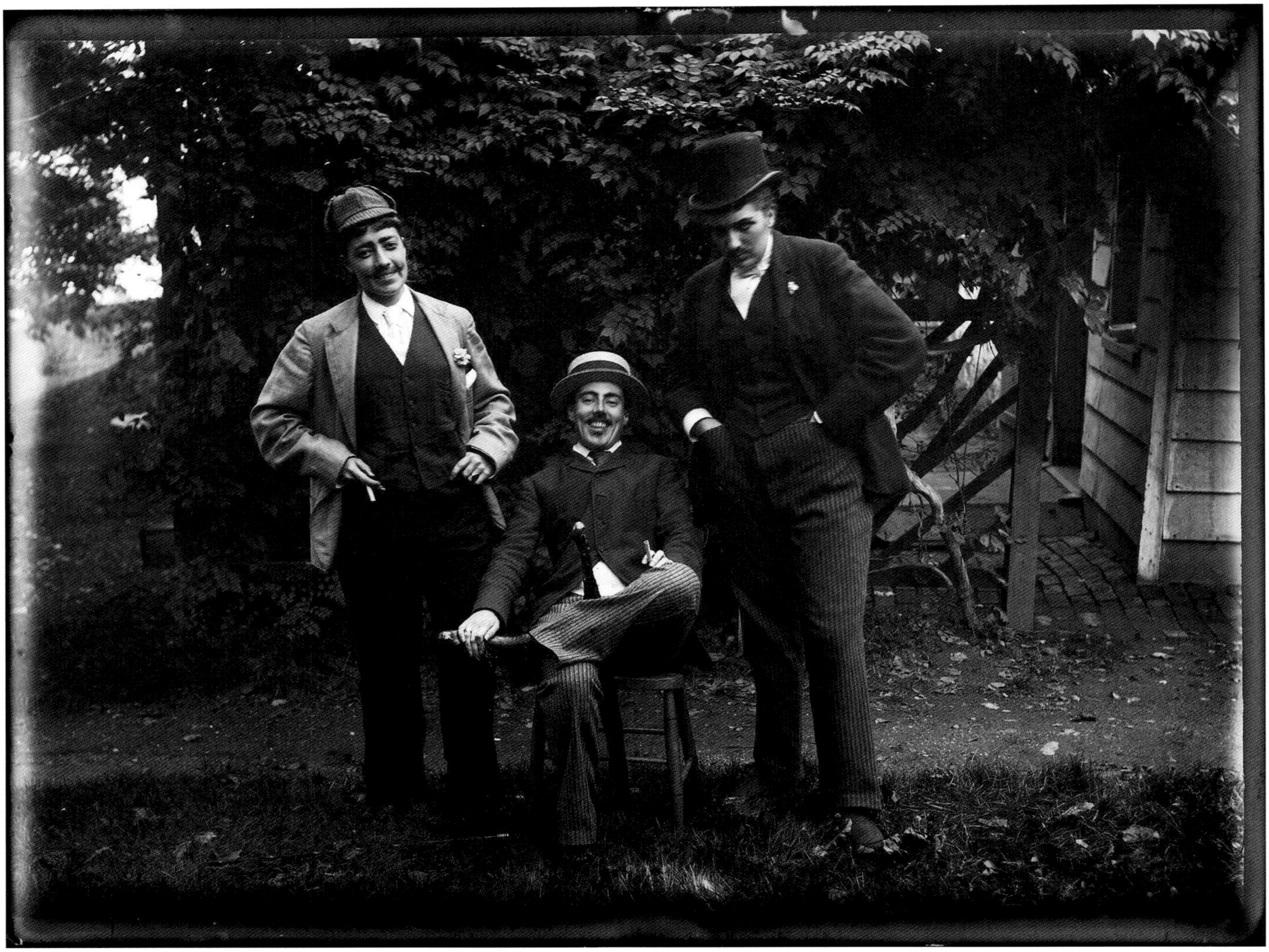

↑ 'Julia Martin, Julia Bredt and Self Dressed Up, Sitting Down',
15 October 1891,
silver emulsion on glass plate,
Staten Island, Alice Austen House Museum

↗ 'The Darned Club',
1891,
silver emulsion on glass plate,
Staten Island, Alice Austen House Museum

ALICE AUSTEN

1866–1952, USA

Bicycling for Ladies, Violet Ward's 1896 book defending women's right to ride bicycles, was replete with illustrations showing how to negotiate bends or do repairs. The images were based on photos taken by Alice Austen, who had a personal interest, as she went about herself on two wheels, carting her heavy photographic equipment with her. Her boldness didn't end there. A non-conformist, she lived more or less openly for nearly 56 years with her partner Gertrude Tate. Indeed, their house on Staten Island, New York, is today a museum dedicated to her work and her role in the history of homosexuality.

Alice Austen started taking photographs at the age of 10 and was entirely self-taught. She developed her own negatives, created albums and used the new invention of the flash to work indoors in poor light. She photographed people she knew as they played sport or went on excursions, recording the lifestyles of the better-off. In 1895, she began a series on the workers and shopkeepers on the streets of New York, from the ragpickers to the errand boys to the organ grinders. She also documented life in the quarantine station on Staten Island, where would-be immigrants were processed.

She lost her fortune in the crash of 1929 and had to leave her house in 1945. Rediscovered in the 1950s, her work includes around 7,000 images. Many of them subverted the conventional ways of taking portraits then in vogue. Austen sometimes posed her female friends dressed as men, embracing or sharing a bed, providing a rare insight into relations between women at the turn of the 20th century.

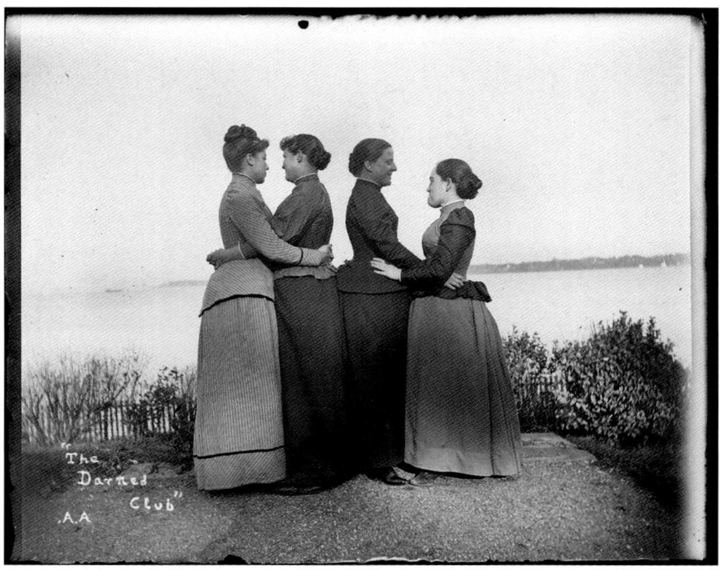

OLIVE EDIS

1876–1955, UK

Olive Edis opened her first studio with one of her sisters in a Norfolk seaside town in 1905. She photographed landscapes, weddings, newborn babies and fishermen and published a few postcards for holidaymakers. She was an innovator in the use of colour, inventing an autochrome viewing device for her clientele, which bore her logo. She opened a second studio in London in 1913 and became a member of the Royal Photographic Society. Her portraits of politicians, of the suffragette Emeline Pankhurst and of the members of her family consolidated her reputation.

In 1918, she was commissioned by the Imperial War Museum to document the work of women on the Western Front in France and Belgium. She received permission to travel only in March 1919, after the cessation of hostilities. Over four weeks, equipped with a heavy and fragile camera, she visited 37 different locations in order to document the involvement of women across different sectors. She photographed an aircraft repair workshop, communication stations, logistics, the ambulance service and medical staff in hospitals. She also took pictures of the devastated landscapes of the battlefields.

The following year, she was invited by a Canadian railway company to travel across their country and photograph its landscapes. She also went to Hong Kong and the USA, where she made a portrait of the British ambassador in Washington.

A renowned portrait photographer, Olive Edis ran a much sought-after studio and contributed to the advancement of colour photography through her technical innovations. She left a detailed record of the involvement of women in the war effort and their crucial role in every link of the chain connecting the front to the rear.

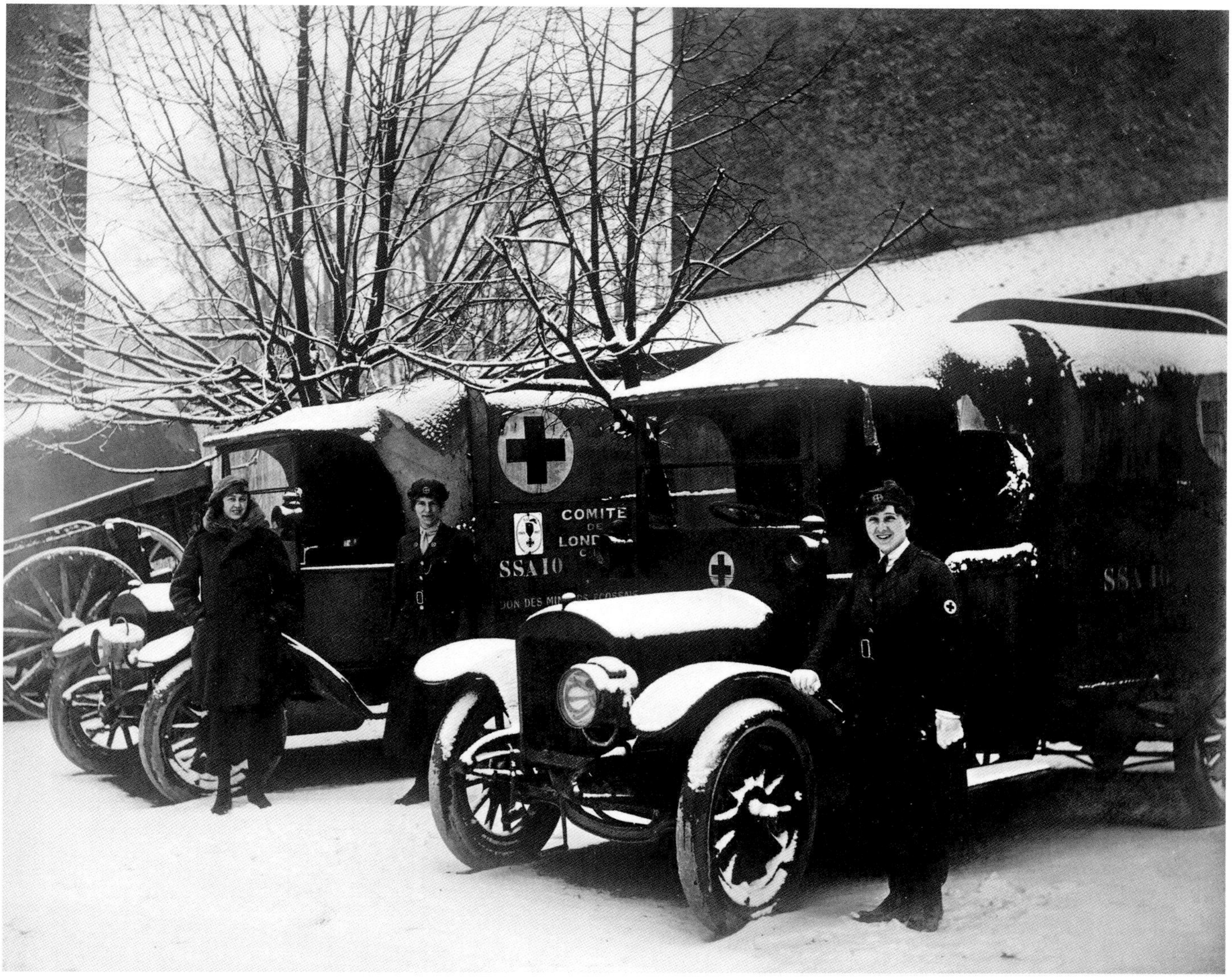

'First Aid Nursing Yeomanry Drivers',
1919,
London, Imperial War Museum

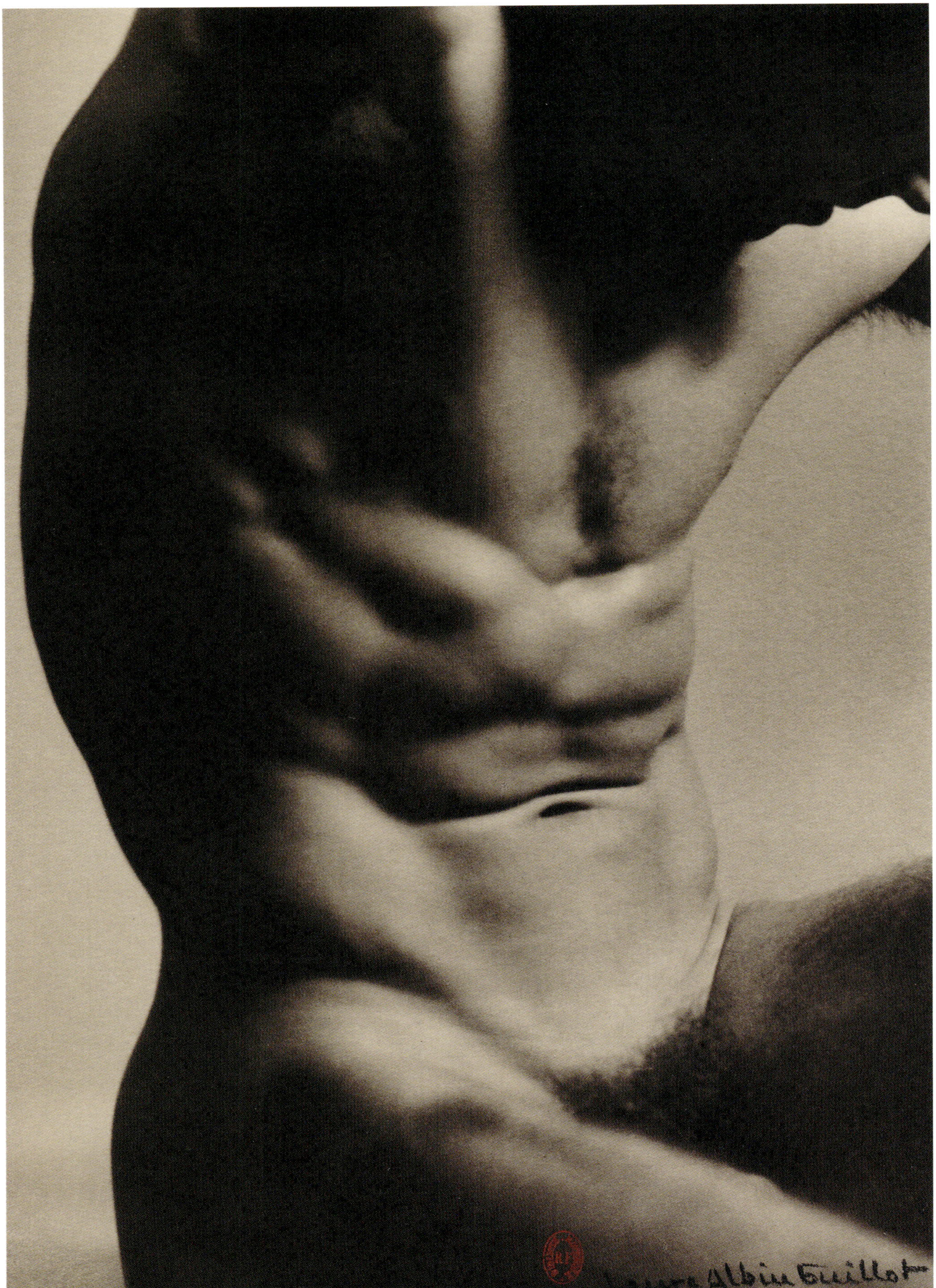
Laure Albin Guillot

LAURE ALBIN GUILLOT

1879–1962, France

Laure Albin Guillot began her career in the 1920s. She became known for the pared-down elegance and refinement of her portraits and her fashion photographs with their halos of soft lighting. Inspired by antique statues, she was one of the rare women to attempt male nudes. On the occasion of the 1925 International Exposition of Modern Industrial and Decorative Arts she presented a series of portraits of designers. Influenced by Japanism, she created fire guards and screens with photos embedded in them. She considered photography as a form of artistic craft based on technical virtuosity.

In 1931, she published *Micrographie decorative* [Decorative Micrography], a series of 20 plates of microscopic views of rocks and plants. The individual graphic shapes combined in an ornamental harmony that was adaptable into patterns of fabrics or objects. *Photographie publicitaire* [Advertising Photography] in 1933 pulled together her research conducted over the course of her commissions for luxury brands and the pharmaceutical and cosmetics industries. She also collaborated with writers such as Paul Valéry and the composer Claude Debussy to create luxury collectors' editions combining words and images, which were sold to subscribers.

She was appointed director of photographic archives at the Direction Générale des Beaux-Arts and became the first female curator at the Cinématheque Nationale the following year. In 1937, she worked on the *Women Artists of Europe Exhibit at the Jeu de Paume Museum* project. She also chaired the Union Féminine des Carrières Libérales et Commerciales [Female Union of Liberal and Commercial Careers], which defended the interests of women practising these professions. In 1939, she documented the evacuation of the Louvre and the protection of monuments and coordinated the transfer of funds that she was responsible for. With her preponderant place in cultural institutions, she embodied the classicism of a certain 'French style'.

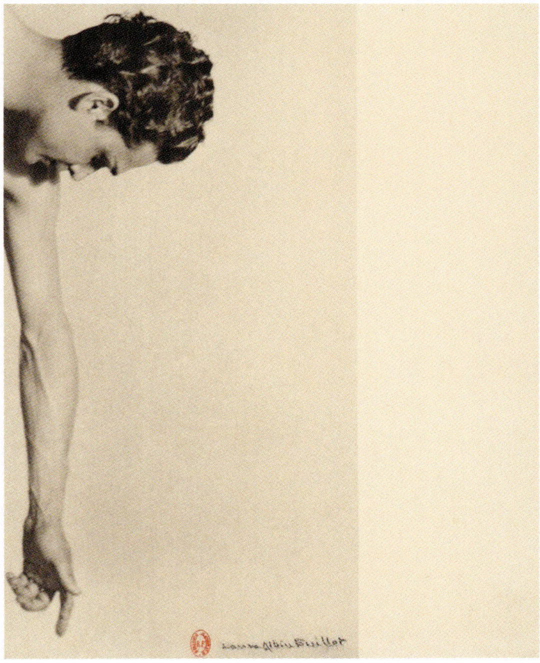

← 'Photograph from an illustrated edition of *La Cantate du Narcisse* by Paul Valéry', 1942,
gelatin silver print, in-4° format,
Paris, Bibliothèque nationale de France

↑ 'Photograph from an illustrated edition of *La Cantate du Narcisse* by Paul Valéry', 1942,
gelatin silver print, in-4° format,
Paris, Bibliothèque nationale de France

IMOGEN CUNNINGHAM

1883–1976, USA

Imogen Cunningham studied painting and drawing before taking up photography at the age of 18. She was totally self-taught. She pursued a course in chemistry in Washington then worked in Seattle in the studio of Edward Curtis, who was known for his portraits of Native Americans. The women's support association at her university gave her a grant in 1909 to finance her studies in Dresden and her thesis on platinum printing and photographic papers. In 1913, in the association's newsletter, she published a plea for women to be given access to the photography profession.

On her return to the USA in 1910, she opened a portrait studio in Seattle and became part of the pictorialist tradition, imitating the compositions and blurred effect of their paintings and watercolours. She dabbled in nude photography – especially male – and made headlines. After getting married in 1915, she closed her studio and moved to San Francisco. She raised three boys and concentrated on subjects near to hand, her family and her garden. She then produced extreme close-ups picking out the shapes of plants with great precision, reviving the genre of botanical illustration. She also created luminous abstract compositions and industrial landscapes and experimented with multiple exposures in collaboration with the dancer Martha Graham.

In 1932, she participated in the work of the f/64 group, breaking with pictorialism and the imitation of painting to find a way that was proper to photography, a 'direct' approach, accentuating its qualities of clarity and sharpness. She worked for magazines such as *Vanity Fair* and *Life* and had her first solo exhibition in 1956 at the pioneering gallery Limelight, opened by Helen Gee in New York. She continued to be active in many different fields, from street photography to technical manipulation (solarisation, superimposition, inversion, etc...). Her last series, *After Ninety*, assembled portraits of people in their 90s and was published posthumously in 1977.

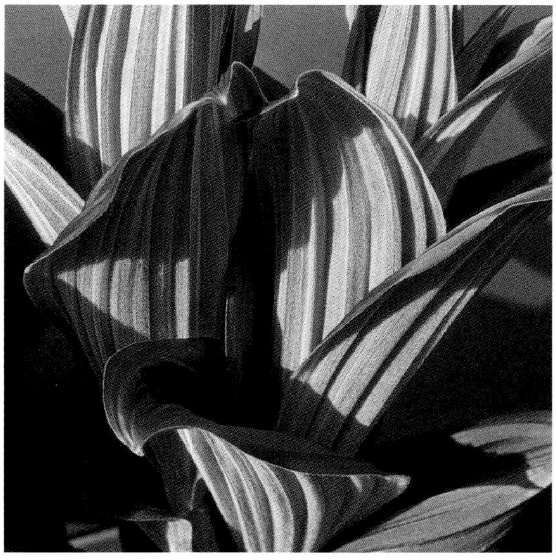

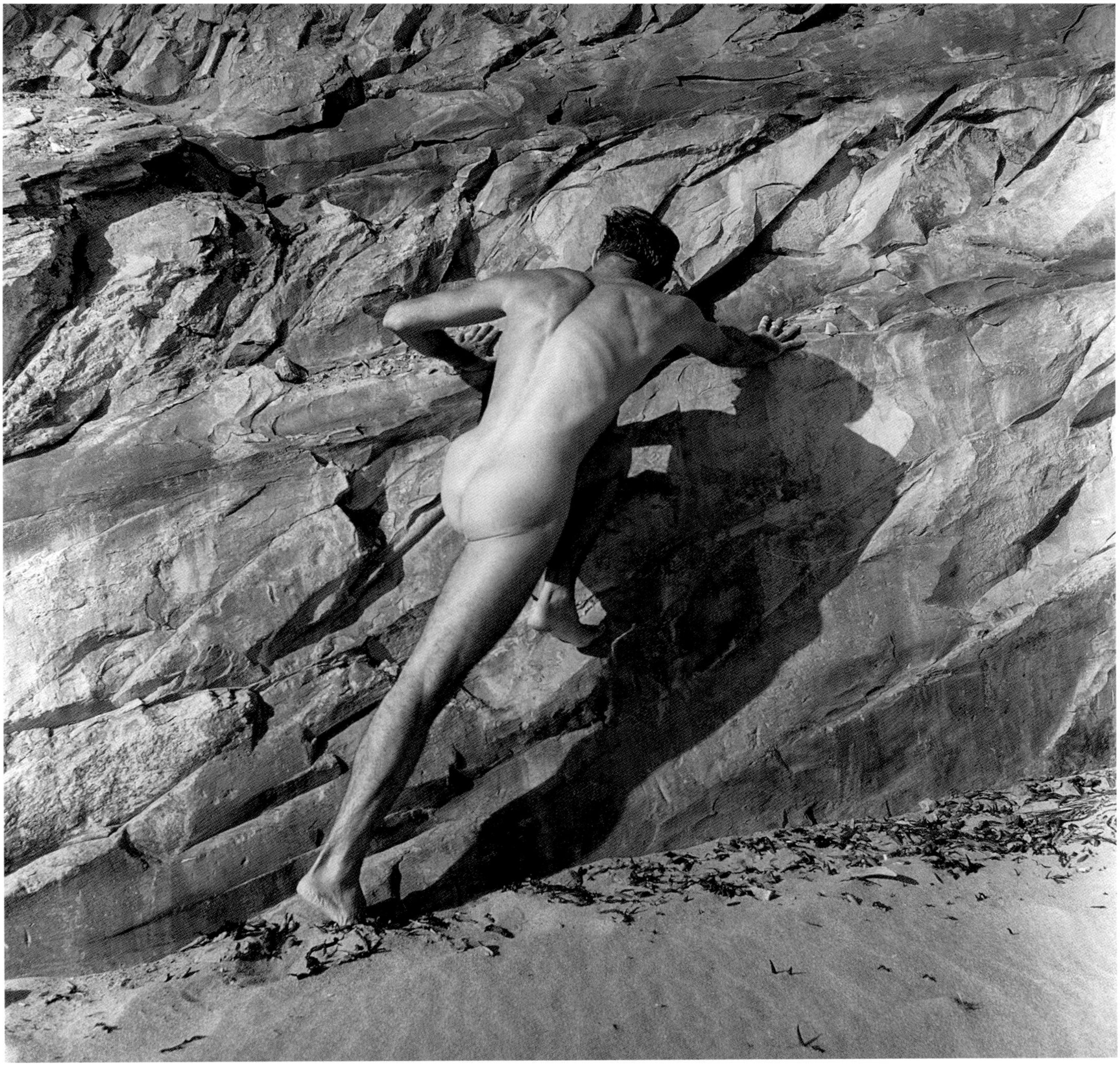

← 'Glacial Lily', now titled 'False Hellebore',
1927,
gelatin silver print,
Imogen Cunningham Trust

↑ 'Rainwater on Oregon Beach 4',
1967,
Imogen Cunningham Trust

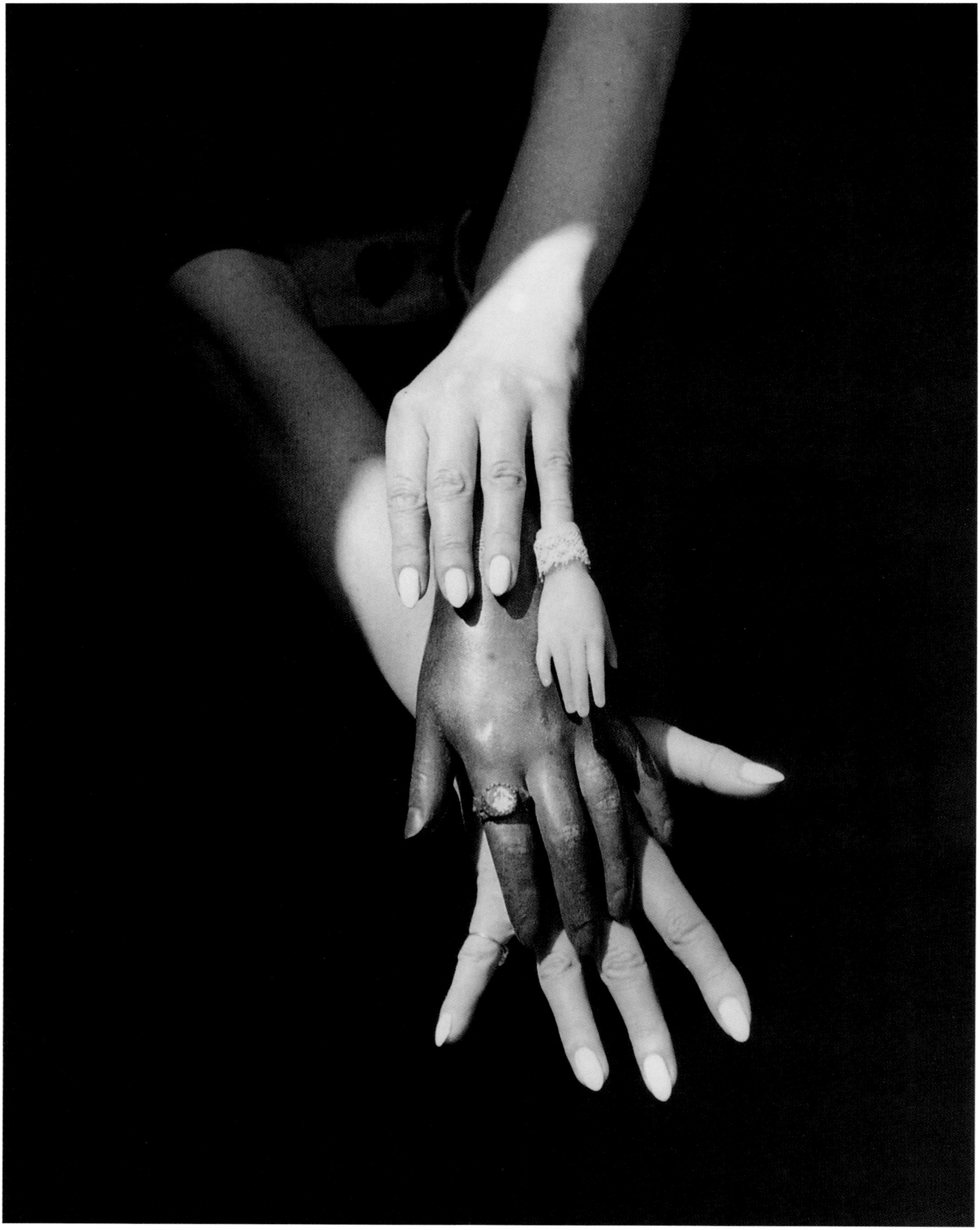

CLAUDE CAHUN

1894, France–1954, Jersey

Born into a middle-class family in Nantes, Lucy Schwob studied philosophy and literature at the Sorbonne. They adopted the pseudonym Claude Cahun in 1917, while their partner Suzanne Malherbe, whom they first met at school, would take the pen name Marcel Moore. The couple lived in Paris between 1918 and 1937, frequented surrealist circles and worked in the theatre, creating costumes, scripts and illustrations, even acting on stage. In 1930, they published *Aveux non avenus* [Cancelled Confessions], which combined poems and photomontages in which Cahun took on a number of different personae. Dressed as either a man or a woman, androgynous, with long hair or a shaved head, they explored sexual ambiguity, codes of femininity and masculinity through dressing up, reflections and doublings (see p. 6). 'Masculine? Feminine? Well, that depends on the situation. Neuter is the only gender that always fits,' they wrote.

In 1934, Claude Cahun signed *Les Paris sont ouverts* [Place Your Bets], a pamphlet against the cultural policy of the Communist Party, criticising the views of Louis Aragon. They participated in the foundation of the revolutionary group Contre-Attaque [Counterattack] with André Breton and Georges Bataille in 1935. In parallel, they created photographic images of objects as various as puppets, dolls, utensils, scraps of fabric, pens, playing cards, sticks, enhanced with gouache, notably their illustrations to Lise Deharme's collection of poems *Le Cœur de pic*.

In 1938, the couple moved to a farm on Jersey, which they called the Farm with No Name. At the start of the Second World War, they joined the Resistance, printing and distributing pamphlets. They were arrested in July 1944 and sentenced to death but saved by the liberation of the island in May 1945. A large part of their work was destroyed at the time of their detention. Claude Cahun's work was rediscovered in the early 1980s and was appreciated for its avant-garde subversion of gender norms.

'Untitled',
c. 1936–39
gelatin silver print,
Paris, Centre Pompidou

DOROTHEA LANGE

1895–1965, USA

Dorothea Lange trained in photography at Columbia University in New York and opened a portrait studio in San Francisco in 1918. In the early 1930s, she began taking photographs of the mass unemployment caused by the Great Depression. She joined the Resettlement Administration – a federal agency set up under the New Deal to support ruined farmers, which became the Farm Security Administration in 1937 – and undertook the huge task of documenting the economic hardship. She photographed seasonal workers employed at harvest time in California and refugees fleeing whirlwinds and drought in the Dust Bowl. Her sober and precise portraits, some of them shot from a low angle, paid homage to the courage of the victims of the economic crisis. Their aim was to raise consciousness and get the public to sign up to government programmes. One of them shows Florence Owens Thompson (see p. 23), a mother of seven children who became an iconic image of that sombre period and the heroism of these 'ordinary people' who form the history of the nation.

In 1938, with her husband, the economist Paul Taylor, she published *An American Exodus*, a collection of writings and photos of the migrations that provided the main corpus of testimonies of the homeless and displaced farmers. During the Second World War, she documented the internment of families of Japanese origin who lived in the USA, the naval shipyards in California and the importation of Mexican labour. She later worked for *Life*, travelled abroad extensively and collaborated with Edward Steichen to put together the major humanist exhibition The Family of Man at the Museum of Modern Art in New York. She also helped the same museum organize a retrospective of her work, which took place in 1966, a few months after her death.

'A sign of the Times – Depression – Mended Stockings',
1934,
photonegative,
Oakland, Oakland Museum of California,
The Dorothea Lange Collection

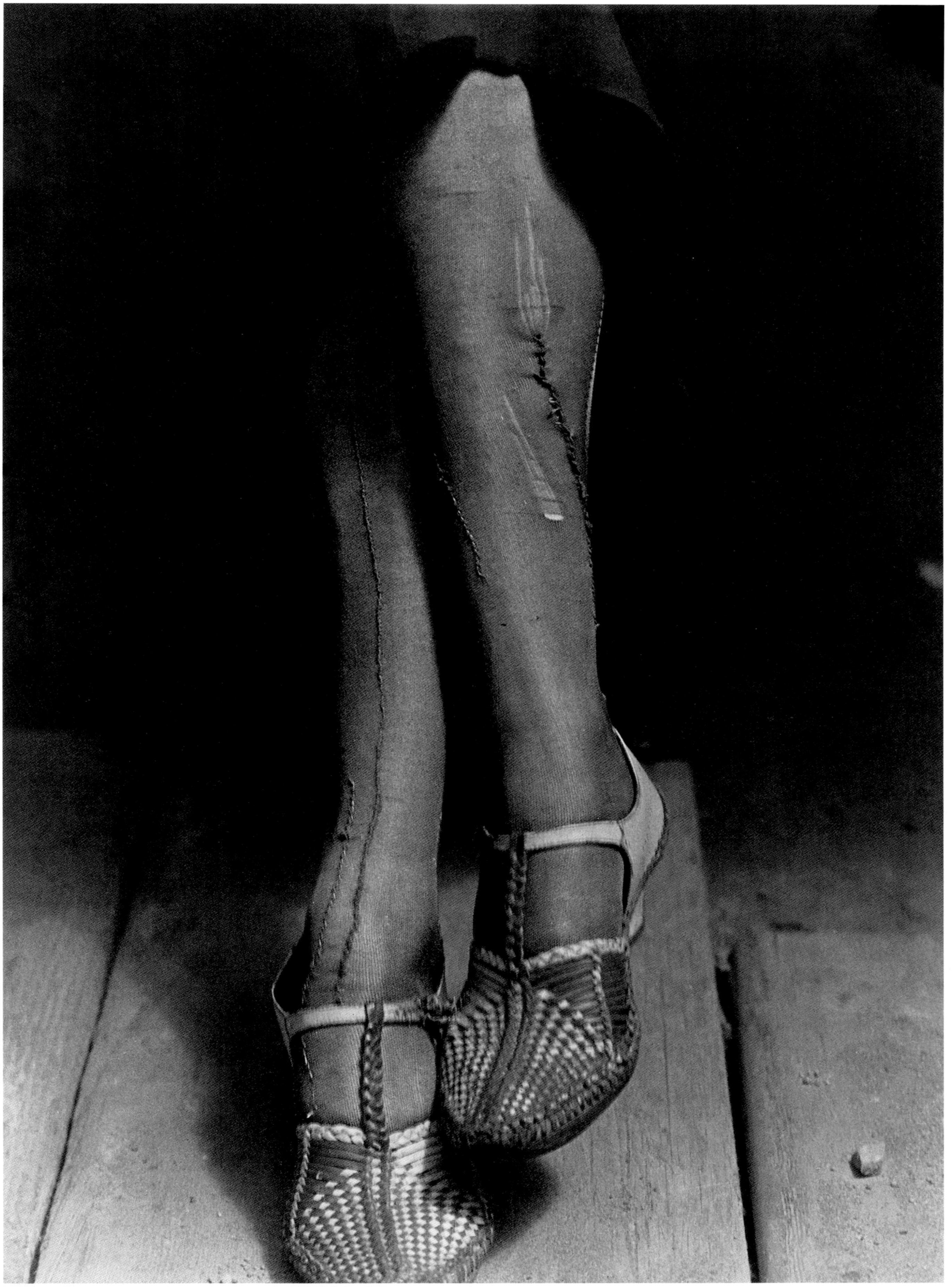

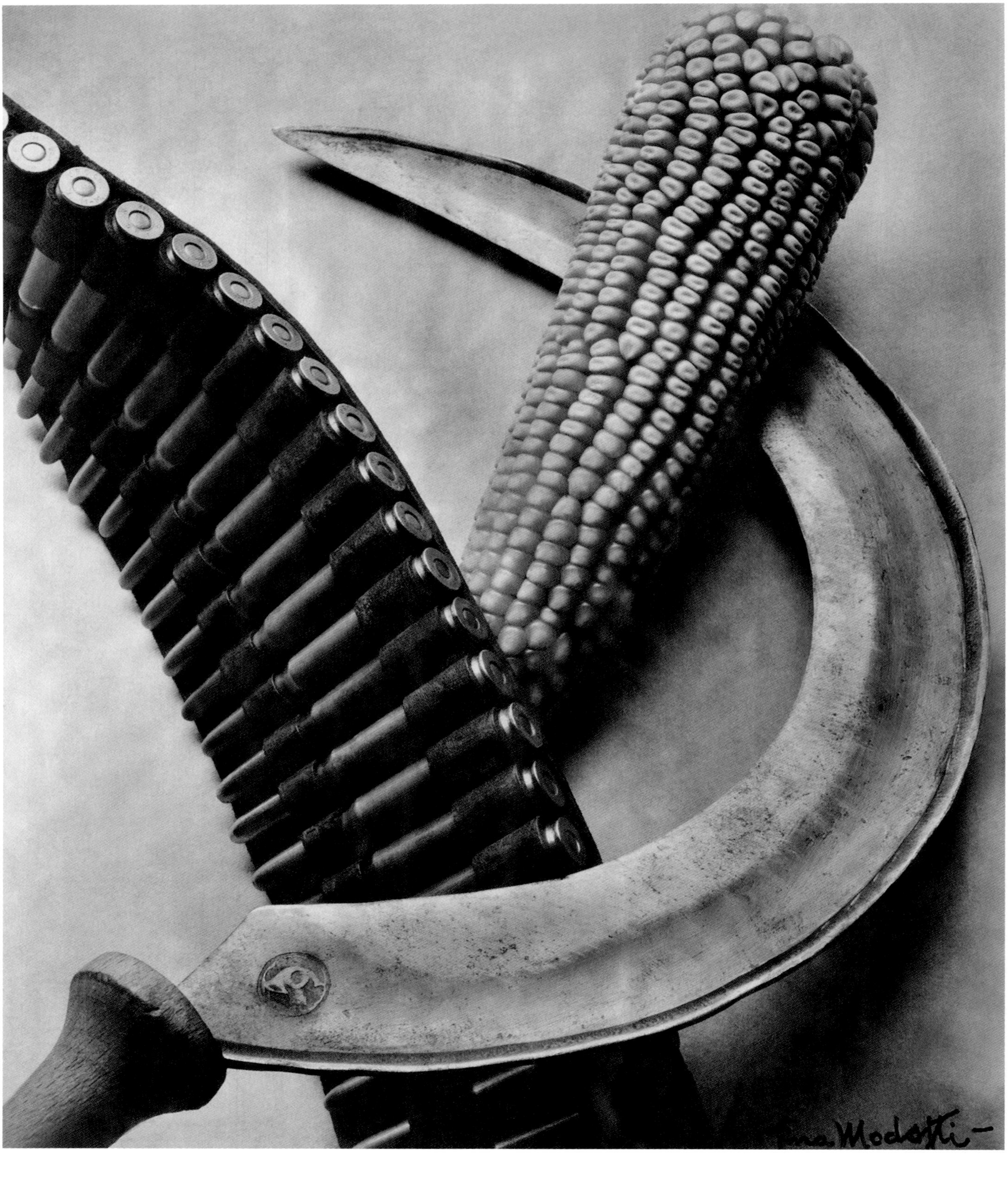
Modotti

TINA MODOTTI

1896, Italy–1942, Mexico

Tina Modotti grew up in a working-class family in Italy before emigrating to the USA in 1913. Originally a fashion designer, she debuted as an actress in the amateur theatre of the Italian community in San Francisco in 1917 before moving to Los Angeles. She appeared in three silent films produced in Hollywood and became the model and mistress of the photographer Edward Weston. They moved to Mexico in 1923, where she managed his studio. Weston went back to California the following year, but Tina Modotti stayed in Mexico, where she hung out with artists and left-wing intellectuals. She photographed the large socialist murals depicting Mexican workers and culture. In 1927, she joined the Mexican Communist Party and put together a series of images symbolising her political stance, juxtaposing a hammer and sickle with a sombrero, an ear of corn and a gun belt. She photographed her adopted country, particularly the working people, the religious art, the folklore and female figures (see p. 13).

In 1929, on the occasion of an exhibition at the National Library of Mexico, she wrote a defence of her aesthetic and political views. Rejecting 'tricks', 'manipulation' and 'artistic effects', she wanted to make 'honest photographs' for use by the 'social revolution which we must all contribute to'.[1]

Suspected of being part of an attempted political coup against the president, she had to leave Mexico in 1930 for Berlin, Moscow and then Paris. Like a number of radical artists and intellectuals on the left she went to Spain during the Civil War to support the republican side as part of Red Aid International. She managed to sneak back into Mexico under a false identity two years before her death. Alternately model, photographer and political activist, Tina Modotti participated in avant-garde experiments between the wars before devoting herself completely to the revolutionary cause.

1. Tina Modotti, 'Sur la photographie' [On Photography], *Mexican Folkways*, vol. 5, no. 4, Mexico, October–December 1929, pp. 196–8.

'Hoz, canana y mazorca' [Sickle, Gunbelt and Ear of Corn],
1927,
gelatin silver print,
Mexico, Fundación Televisa

BERENICE ABBOTT

1898–1991, USA

Berenice Abbott started out as a sculptor and frequented the artistic circles of New York before leaving for Paris in 1921. She served an apprenticeship in the flourishing studio of her compatriot Man Ray before opening her own portrait studio in 1926. The intellectual elite all posed in front of her lens. As the editor Sylvia Beach put it, 'having your portrait "done" by Man Ray or Berenice Abbott was a sign that you were somebody'.[1] Known for her ability to capture the personality of her models with refinement and precision, she made portraits of several prominent lesbians, contributing to the creation of new visual codes.

In parallel, she made the acquaintance of Eugène Atget, the remarkable chronicler of the transformations in the streets of Paris at the turn of the century, acquired his archive after his death and organised the promotion of his work. On her return to New York in 1929, she followed his example and undertook a huge project to document the changes in the city. Experimenting with high- and low-angle shots and playing with contrast, she captured the co-existence of skyscrapers and houses from the past, advertising posters and shop windows. Her portraiture work was less lucrative than in Paris, so she actively sought funding to be able to carry out her project. She received help from the visual arts support fund in 1935 and in 1939 published *Changing New York*, with words by the critic, historian and writer Elizabeth McCausland, her partner of more than 30 years.

Berenice Abbott was also an influential teacher, the author of several photographic manuals and the inventor of sophisticated cameras, new techniques and patents. She is also known for her pioneering work in the field of scientific photography, where she managed to illustrate physical phenomena such as the magnetic field or the nature of light for educational purposes. These intriguing images with their abstract geometry showed complex mechanisms with great clarity.

1. Quoted in Hank O'Neal, *Berenice Abbott: photographe américaine* [American Photographer], P. Sers, 1982.

'A Nighttime View of New York',
1932,
gelatin silver print,
New York, Museum of Modern Art

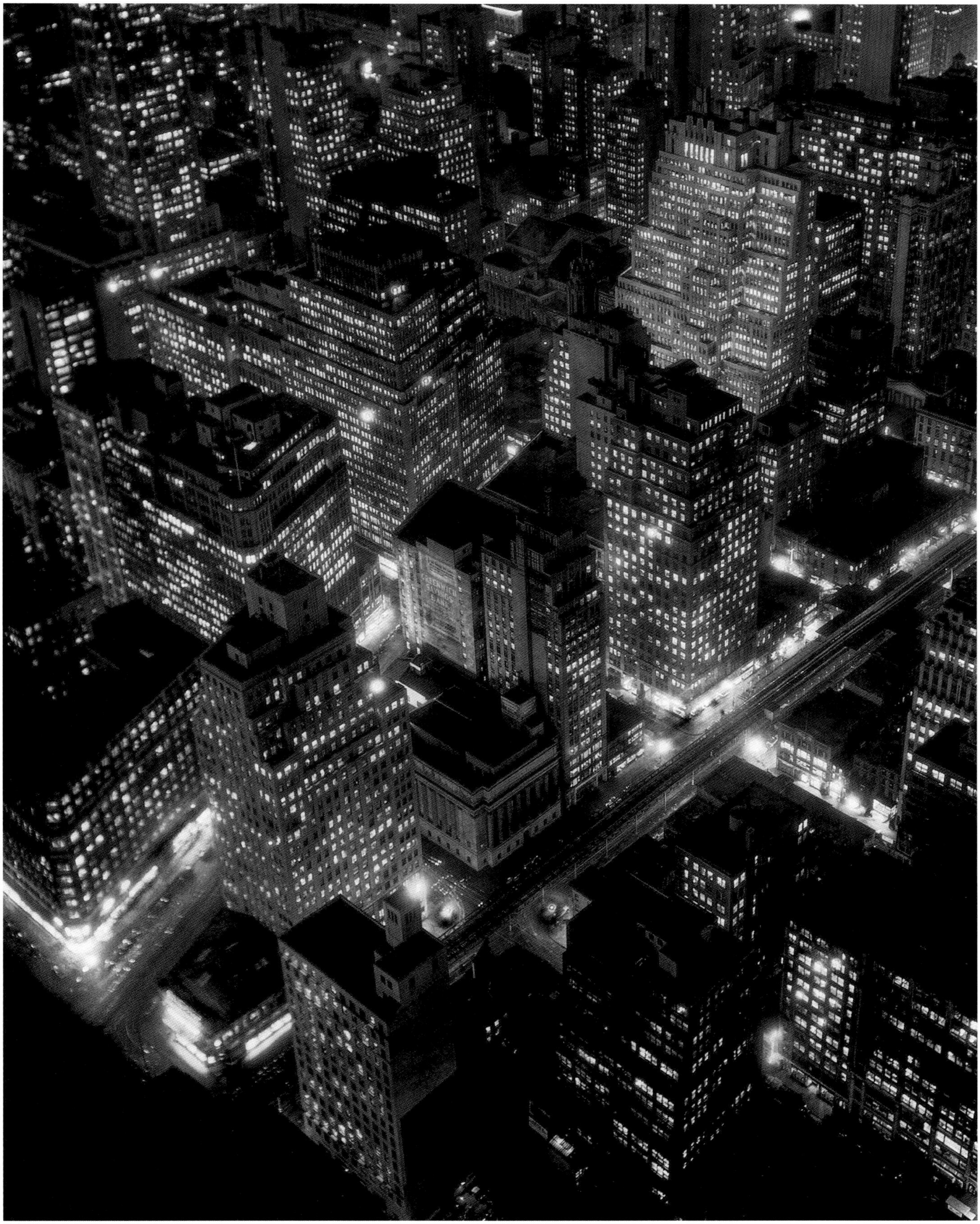

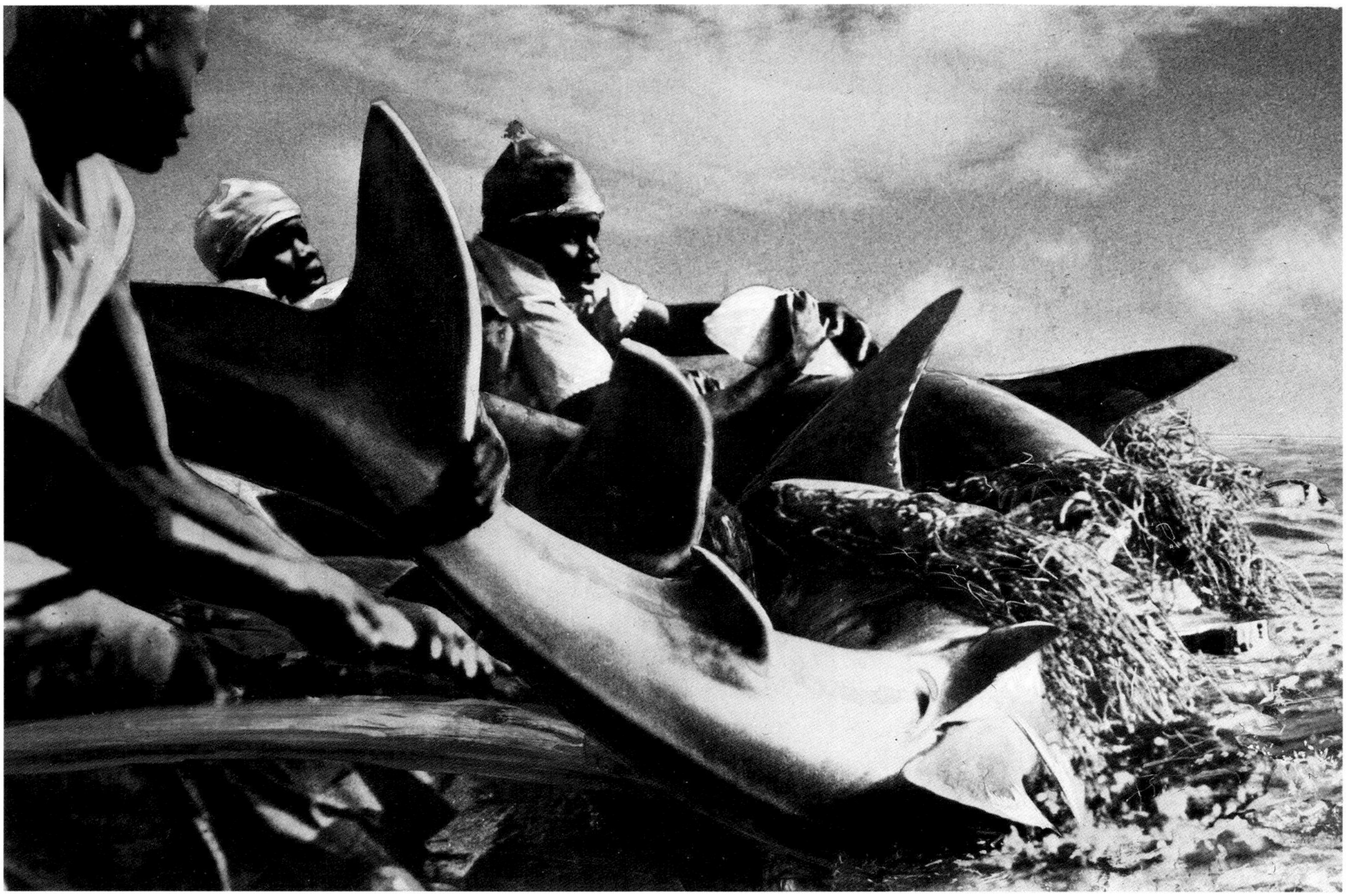

'Pêche au requin, Guinée' [Shark Fishing, Guinea]
1946–49,
duplicate print,
Lorient, Municipal Archives

ANITA CONTI

1899–1997, France

Nicknamed 'the lady of the sea', Anita Conti was the first female oceanographer and the creator of almost 40,000 photographs. She had an earlier career as a respected art book binder in the 1920s before turning to journalism and working for the Office Scientifique et Technique des Pêches Maritimes [Scientific and Technical Office for Marine Fishing]. In 1935, she took part in several expeditions on the first French oceanographic ship to draw up maps of fishing zones. During 1939, she spent 100 days on board the cod-trawler the *Viking* in the Barents Sea. With her Rolleiflex she both captured life on board the ship and created a scientific document. The only woman among 50 fishermen, she recorded their terrible working conditions.

During the war, she worked as a navy photographer on board minesweepers to document mine-clearing in the English Channel. She then went to the coast of West Africa, where she led an enquiry on the resources of the littoral and the traditional fishing methods controlled by the Algerian government. In 1952, she sailed on an expedition aboard the trawler *Bois Rosé* to the shoals of Newfoundland and Greenland and the following year published *Racleurs d'océans* [Ocean Scrapers]. Her second book, *Géants des mers chaudes* [Giants of the Warm Seas], which appeared in 1957, tells of her experience in Mauretania, Senegal, Guinea and Côte d'Ivoire. Her last book, *L'Océan, les bêtes et les hommes, ou l'ivresse du risque* [The Ocean, Beasts and Men, or the Thrill of Risk], published in 1971, sounded the alarm about the dangers of overfishing, which she fought against all her life in conferences and her writings. She argued for aquaculture, the elimination of waste and the use of fish normally thrown back into the sea, such as the cutlass fish.

Anita Conti's photographs were often taken under extreme conditions, on heaving seas and in bad weather. She used high-angle shots, showing activity on the bridge from the mast and rigging, or low-angle shots for her portraits paying homage to the courage and endurance of those who ply the seas.

LISETTE MODEL

1901, Austria–1983, USA

Born Elise Amelie Felicie Stern in Vienna, Lisette Model studied singing and composing. She moved to France with her mother and sister in 1922 and continued her musical career until 1933 before turning to photography. In 1935, she was published for the first time, when she was commissioned by *Regards* magazine to do a piece on the Promenade des Anglais in Nice. She took cheeky close-up views of often dozing tourists enjoying the sun. In Paris, she met the Russian painter Evsa Model, whom she married in 1937. She moved to New York in 1938, where she worked in the deprived Lower East Side. With her left-wing sympathies, in 1941 she exhibited with the cooperative Photo League, which promoted social documentary. The magazine *Harper's Bazaar* published her images of musicians at Sammy's Bar and Coney Island beach, where she famously made a portrait of a woman with a huge body and a radiant smile, a complete contrast with conventional norms of lean and athletic beauty. The Museum of Modern Art in New York acquired her photos for its collection, and her first solo exhibition was in 1943 at the Art Institute in Chicago. She acquired American citizenship in 1944. Suspected of being a communist, she lost all her magazine commissions during the McCarthy witch hunts of the early 1950s. From 1951 until the end of her life, she taught at the New School for Social Research in New York, where Diane Arbus was among her students. Known for her black-and-white street photos and fondness for unusual angles, she used high- and low-angle shots and cropping to create dynamic compositions. She would for example place her camera on the ground to photograph the feet of pedestrians passing by on the pavement, offering an unexpected view of the anonymous urban crowd from shoe-level. Her series *Reflections* took delight in fortuitous contrasts caused by the mirror effect of shop windows.

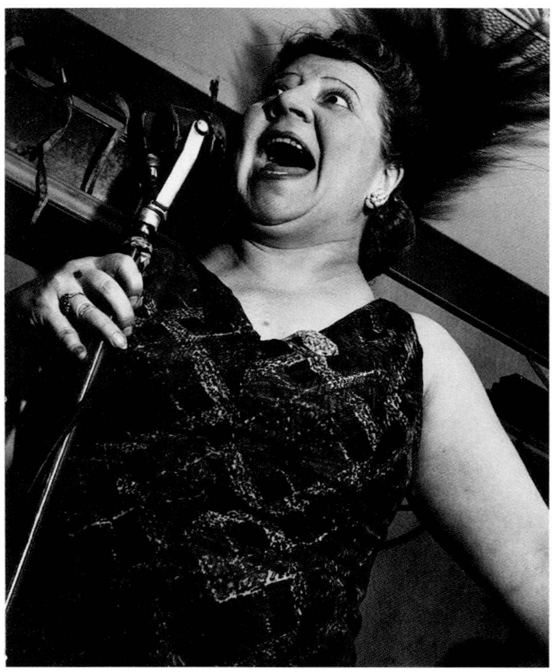

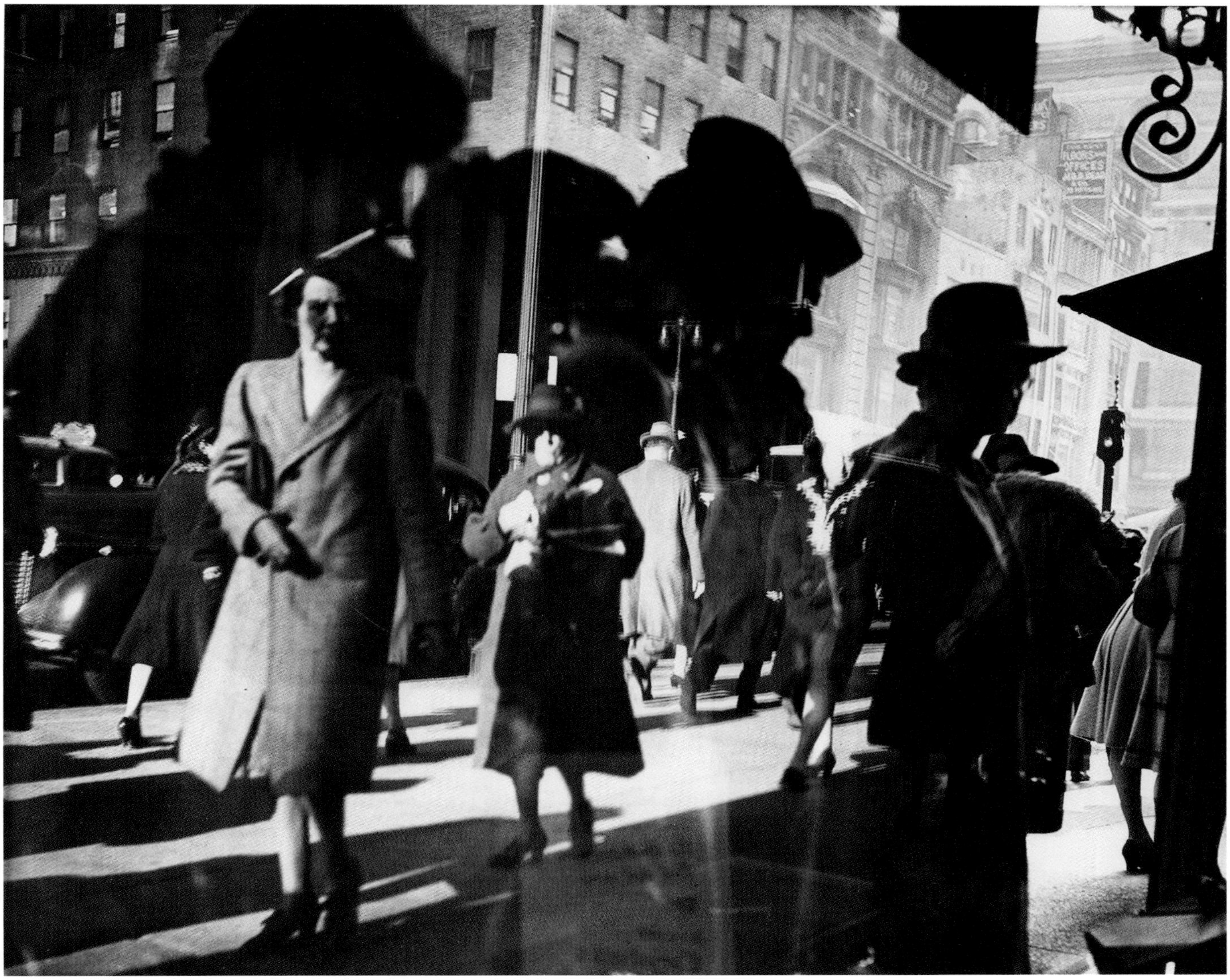

← 'Singer at the Café Metropole, New York',
1946,
gelatin silver print (1976),
Paris, Galerie Baudoin Lebon

↑ 'Reflections, New York City',
c. 1939–45,
gelatin silver print,
Paris, Galerie Baudoin Lebon

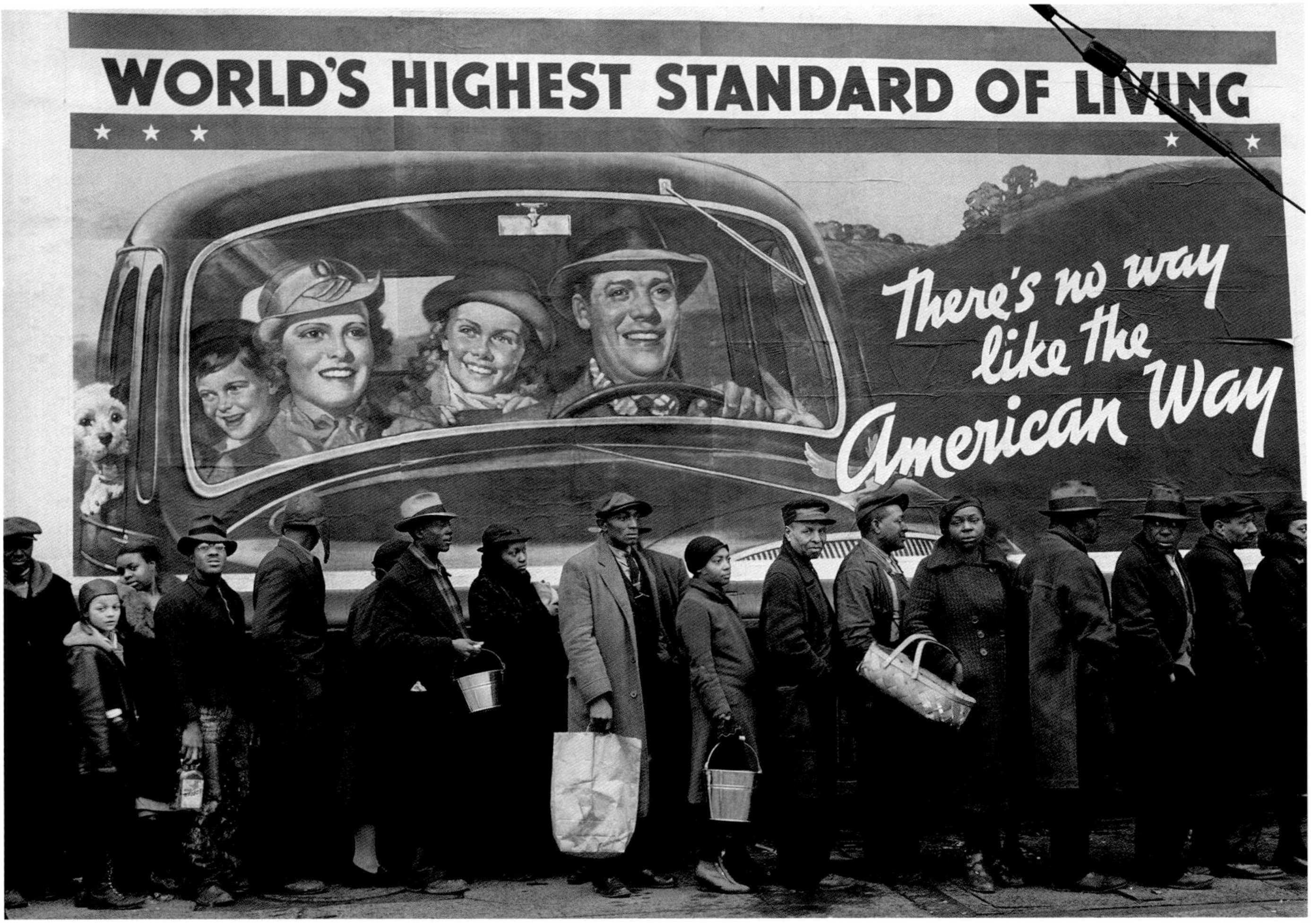

'Flood Victims, Louisville, Kentucky',
February 1937,
gelatin silver print (*c.* 1970)

MARGARET BOURKE-WHITE

1904–1971, USA

After studying zoology and photography, Margaret Bourke-White opened her first studio in her apartment in Cleveland. She became known for her views of architectural and industrial sites, which accentuated technological progress and engineering accomplishment. Her balanced modernist compositions won her commissions from industrial companies for their company reports. Her celebration of innovation fitted in with the editorial policy of the magazine *Fortune*, which used her photos in its very first issue in 1930. In the following year she published *Eyes on Russia*, a book on the industrial sites and economy of the USSR.

In 1936, she joined *Life* magazine and illustrated the cover of its first issue with a monumental image of the Fort Peck dam in Montana. She then developed a documentary style that gave more space to human figures. In 1937, with the writer Erskine Caldwell she published *You Have Seen Their Faces*, a study of underprivileged farmers in the American South which was produced as a spin-off of the documentary project of the Farm Security Administration. In 1941, she returned to the USSR with Erskine Caldwell, now her husband, and documented the bombing of Moscow by the Germans, an experience she related in *Shooting the Russian War*. From 1942, she was an American army correspondent on the European front. In 1945, she photographed German towns in ruins and the recently liberated concentration camps, especially Buchenwald. She continued working for *Life* in India after independence, in South Africa in the gold mines and in the early 1950s covering the war in Korea.

Her autobiography, *Portrait of Myself*, published in 1963, recounted her groundbreaking experiences in the fields of industrial photography, war reportage and documentary and showed her to be a vivid storyteller.

GRETE STERN

1904, Germany–1999, Argentina

From 1948 to 1951, Grete Stern composed nearly 150 amusing and subversive photomontages to illustrate the dreams submitted by the readers of the Argentinian magazine *Idilio* for interpretation in their series *Psychoanalysis Will Help You*, under the direction of the sociologist Gino Germani. In a surrealist vein, Grete Stern visualized the telescoping that appeared in their dreams, interrogating the restrictions imposed on women, the anxieties and power relations that crisscrossed the collective unconscious.

Trained as a graphic artist, Grete Stern moved to Berlin in 1927 and with her friend Ellen Auerbach opened a studio inspired by their childhood nicknames, ringl + pit, already creating portraits and adverts with a touch of humour. They promoted products such as hair lotion, gloves and cigarettes in their subtly fantastical still lives, combining them with cut-outs of mannequins and other objects.

Jewish and left-wing, Grete Stern left Germany after Hitler came to power and moved to London, where she made portraits of exiled intellectuals. She married the Argentinian photographer Horacio Coppola, and in 1936 they moved to Argentina, where she continued working in photography and graphic art. She photographed the urbanisation of Buenos Aires and ran the photography studio at the city's art museum. In the 1960s, she produced nearly 800 images on the culture of indigenous communities in the north of the country. She celebrated their craft skills but also took account of their deprived living conditions. A figure in the Argentine artistic scene, she introduced European avant-garde experimentation and invented a provocative and ironic style of photography.

'Sueño nº1, Articulos eléctricos para el hogar' [Dream No. 1, Electrical Appliances for the Home], *c.* 1950, gelatin silver print, private collection

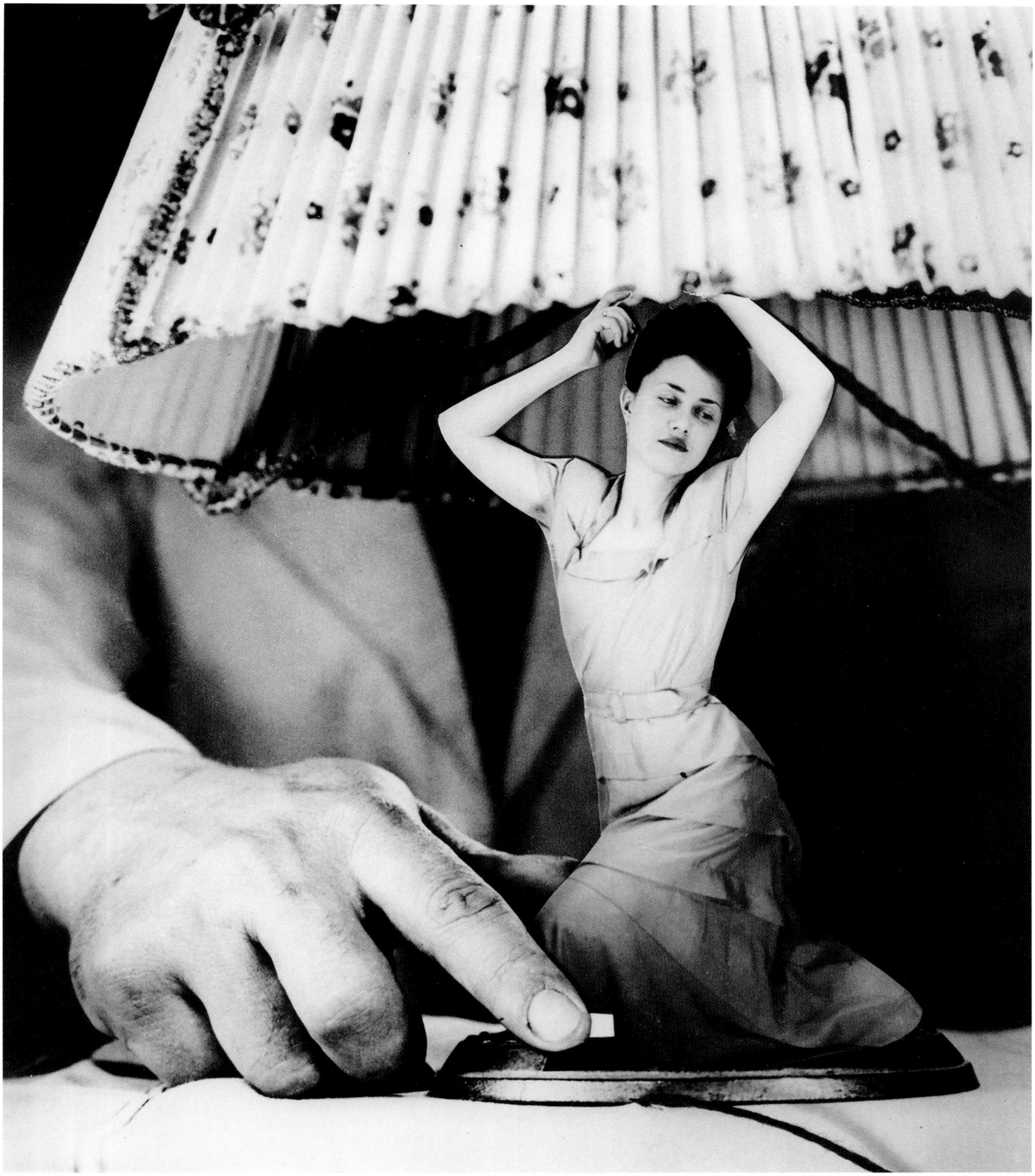

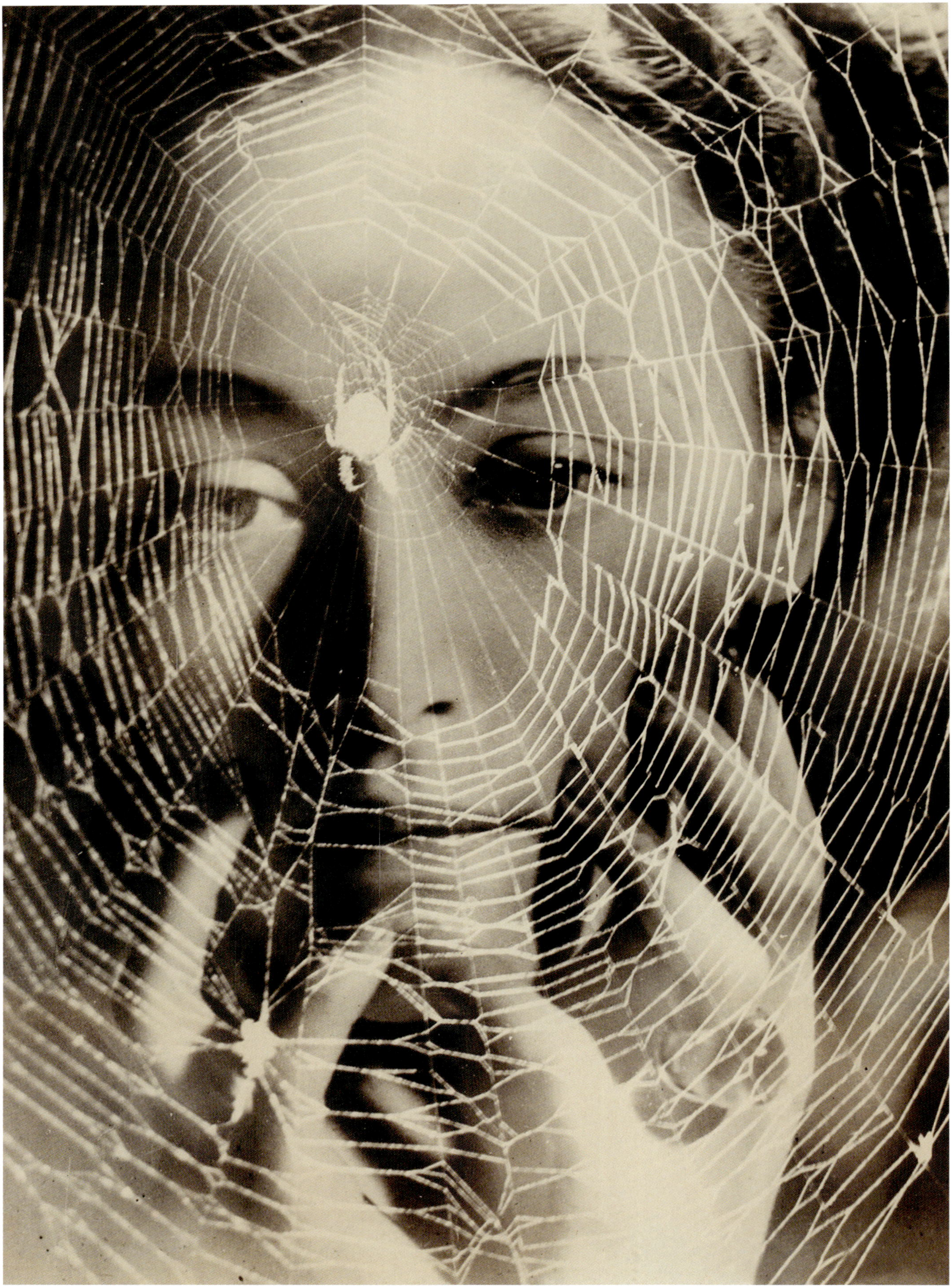

DORA MAAR

1907–1997, France

Born in Paris, Henriette Theodora Markovitch grew up between Argentina and France. She trained at the Ladies' Committee of the Central Union of Decorative Arts, then at the Académie Jullian, in the studio of André Lhote and at the Technical College of Photography and Cinematography of the City of Paris. She adopted the pseudonym Dora Maar in the late 1920s and in 1931, along with the cinema designer Pierre Kéfer, established a studio in Neuilly specialising in portraits and fashion shots. She later opened her own studio and worked on commission for women's magazines. She frequented avant-garde circles, exhibited with the surrealists in 1934 and 1937 and experimented artistically with film stills, double exposures, erotic nudes, photomontage, still life and street photography. Her hybrid creations displayed a surrealist fascination for the strange and dreams.

She was also interested in social issues, such as the poverty of the wastelands on the outskirts of Paris or life in deprived areas of London and Barcelona. Like Claude Cahun, she was one of the signatories of the manifesto of the revolutionary group Contre-Attaque [Counterattack].

In 1936, she became the lover and model of Pablo Picasso. She documented the successive stages in the realisation of the painting *Guernica*, which denounced the attack by Franco's bombers, produced film stills and took up painting again, inspired by cubism. When they split up for good in 1946, she fell into a depression and underwent psychoanalysis with Jacques Lacan. She moved to the Lubéron and made ink drawings of Provence landscapes before returning briefly to photography in an abstract vein in the 1980s. Her original work, sometimes overshadowed by her relationship with Picasso, shows that active women running thriving studios could succeed commercially and is testament to their contribution to the artistic adventure of the interwar period.

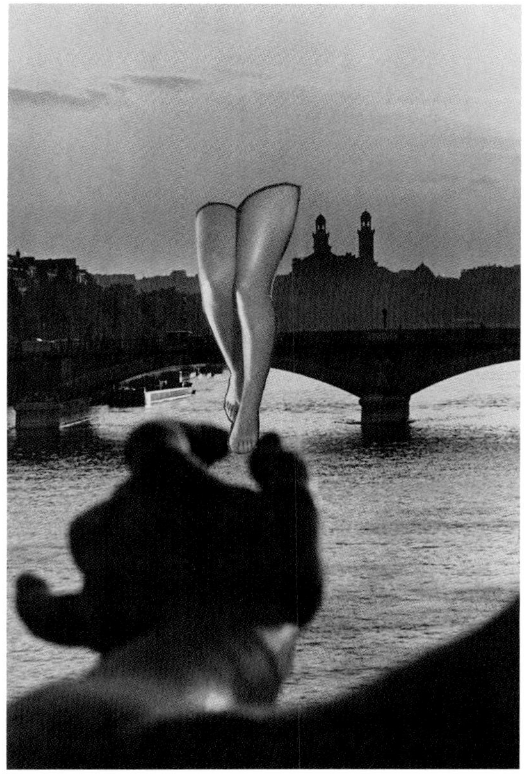

← 'Les années vous guettent' [The Years Are Catching Up with You], 1936, gelatin silver print, private collection

↑ 'Untitled', 1935, gelatin silver print, Paris, Centre Pompidou

JULIA PIROTTE

1907, Russian Empire (now Poland)–2000, Poland

Born Golda Perla Diament, Julia grew up in a Polish Jewish family of modest means. A member of communist youth movements, she was arrested for her political activities at the age of 17 and locked up for four years. In 1934, she managed to escape with the support of Red Aid International and tried to join her sister Mindla in France. Due to illness, she interrupted her journey in Belgium, where she worked in menial jobs, and married the trade unionist Jean Pirotte. She trained as a photographer and journalist in Brussels.

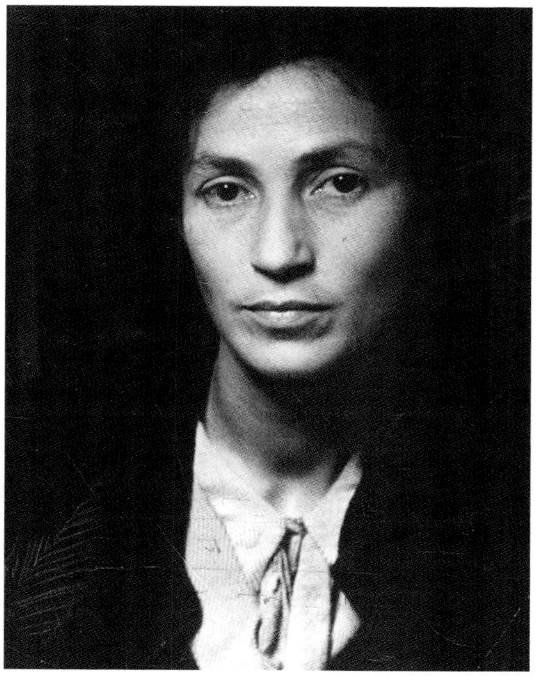

She left Belgium after the Nazi invasion in May 1940 and took up residence in Marseille, where she found work in an aircraft factory. She also took portraits on a private beach and was a photographer for the local press. She joined the Resistance as a liaison agent working alongside snipers and partisans – a group recruited from the immigrant workforce. She forged false papers and was a courier of arms and pamphlets. She recorded operations in the maquis and made portraits of several members of the Resistance, including her sister, who was arrested in 1942, deported to Germany and guillotined at Breslau prison on 24 August 1944. During the war, she also photographed the inhabitants of the Old Port and Jewish women and children interned in the camp at Bompard. She participated in the liberation of Marseille and covered the insurrection.

On returning to Poland in 1946, she documented the reconstruction of the country and the return of emigrant workers for the journal *Żolnierz Polski*. She was at Kielce after the pogrom which killed 42 Jews and bore witness to the ongoing antisemitism after the Holocaust. In 1948, she covered the World Congress of Intellectuals in Defence of Peace in Wroclaw. She travelled to Israel in 1957 to try out the kibbutz way of life. Exhibited since the 1980s, her work constitutes a historical chronicle of the fight against fascism and for social justice.

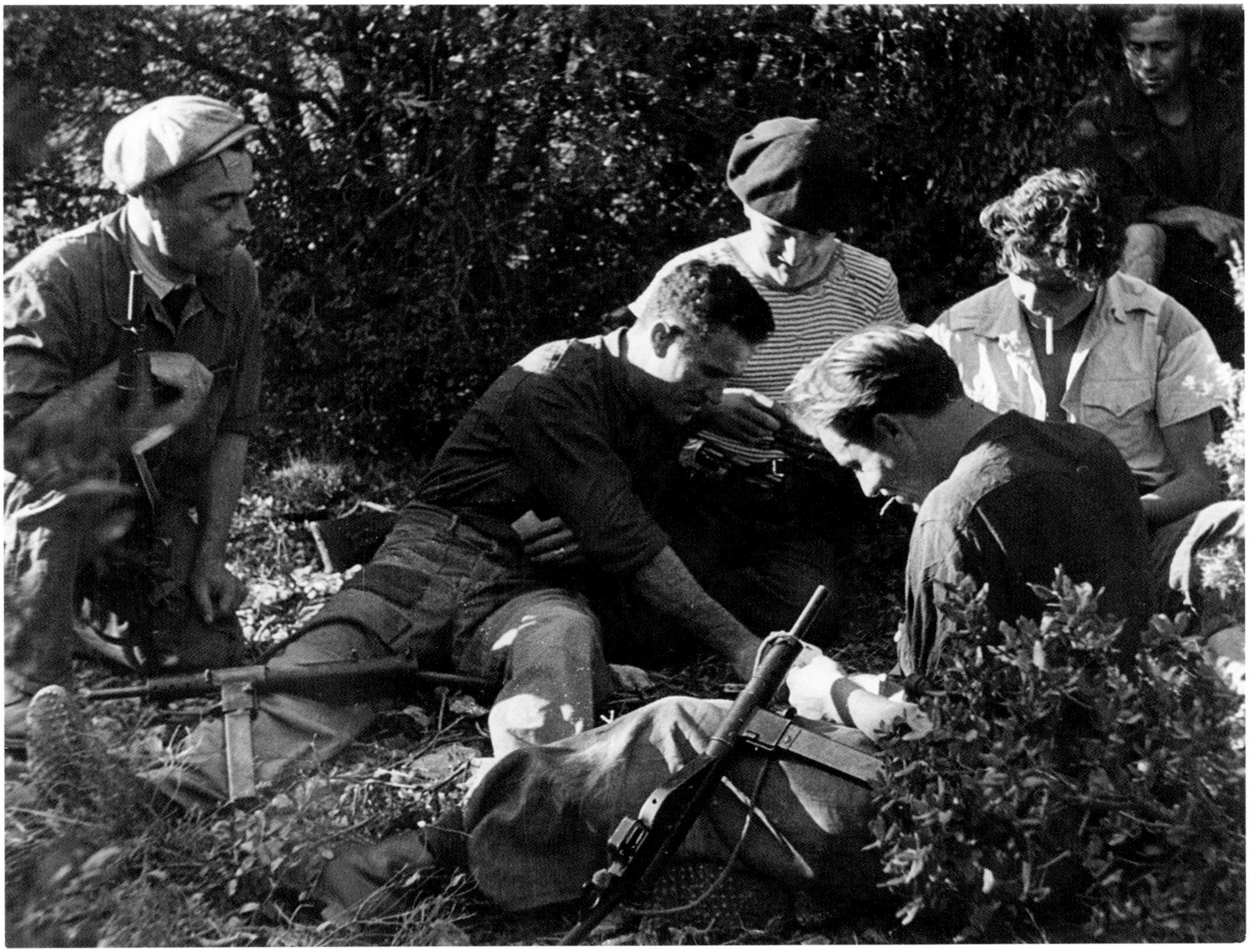

← ‘Mindla Diament, soeur de l’artiste. France’ [Mindla Diament, Sister of the Artist. France],
before 1944,
gelatin silver print,
Paris, Mémorial de la Shoah

↑ ‘Maquisards près de Venelles à Sainte Victoire’ [Resistance Fighters Near Venelles at Sainte Victoire],
1944,
gelatin silver print,
Paris, Musée de l’Armée

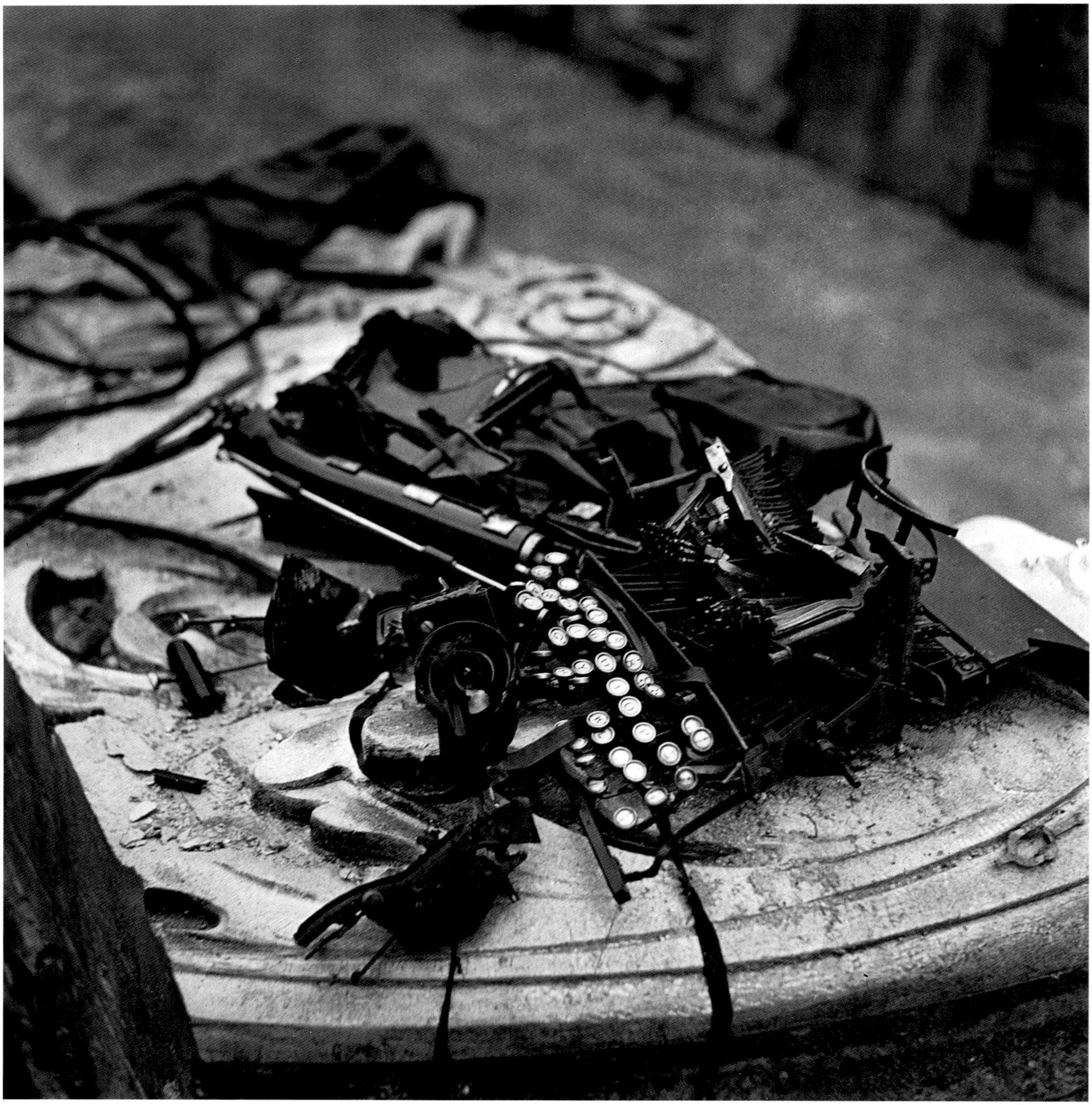

↑ 'Remington Silent, London, England',
1940,
gelatin silver print,
Lee Miller Archives

→ 'Self-Portrait with Headband, Lee Miller Studios, Inc., New York, USA',
c. 1932,
gelatin silver print,
Lee Miller Archives

LEE MILLER

1907, USA–1977, UK

In March 1927, Lee Miller's face inspired the cover of *Vogue* magazine. Her direct gaze was accentuated by the cloche hat covering her forehead, the lights of Manhattan twinkling in the background. A superstar model, she was the epitome of elegance and modernity. She left for Paris in 1929, where she learned photography from her compatriot Man Ray, and became his lover and muse. She joined him in his surrealist experiments and helped him perfect the technique of solarisation. She ran her own studio in New York from 1932 to 1934 and became known for her celebrity portraits, her fashion pictures and her adverts.

She married the Egyptian businessman Aziz Eloui Bey in 1934 and moved to Cairo; she left her husband in 1937 to return to Paris, where she met the British surrealist painter Roland Penrose. She moved in with him in London in 1939 and worked for British *Vogue*. She documented the war effort of women and daily life under the Blitz. She began to write her own reports to accompany her photos, recounting her experiences with verve and humour, in the first person. She went to Normandy after D-Day, covered the bombing of Saint-Malo, the liberation of Paris, the Alsace campaign and the discovery of Dachau concentration camp. An image showing her naked in the bath in Hitler's apartment in Munich – an act symbolising the need to purify herself and purge herself of the images that haunted her – caused a scandal. Some spectators considered this an inappropriate surrealist provocation. She later continued to work for the illustrated press and created numerous portraits of artists from her circle of friends.

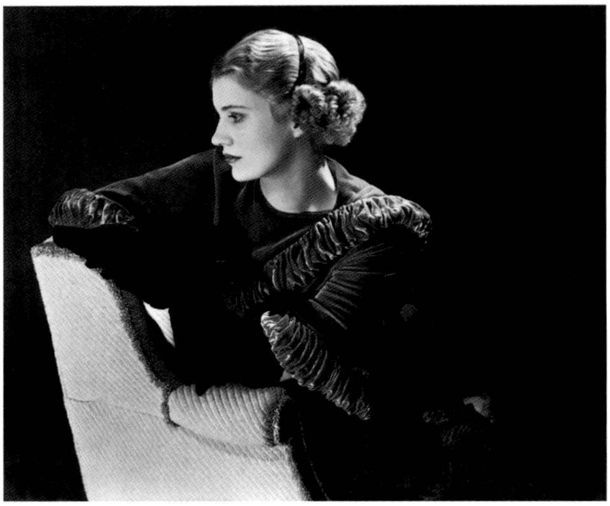

The profuse career of Lee Miller illustrates the opening up of opportunities that characterised this period: photography was still a young medium, and women could try their hand at a wide range of things. From surrealism to reportage, from portraiture to fashion, from writing to technical manipulation, from Europe to Egypt, Lee Miller was never limited to a single field. She became a famous portraitist in New York, where she tried to achieve the best possible quality for her prints by putting in the effort in the darkroom; she was also one of the bylines of *Vogue*, recognised for her photographs and her lively and elevated writing. Her life was characterised by experimentation, risk-taking and sheer audacity.

EDITH TUDOR-HART

1908, Austria–1973, UK

Dangerous – Edith Tudor-Hart was that in more ways than one. Born in Vienna, she grew up in a leftist Jewish family who ran a bookshop in a working-class part of town. A Montessori teacher, she lived in London in 1925 to gain her degree, where she made the acquaintance of her future husband. She trained in photography at the German school of the Bauhaus and began publishing her pictures in the press. She was active in the Communist Party and was a witness to the precarious existence of the unemployed and the workers in her native city. Threatened because of her political engagement and her Jewish origins, she was arrested in May 1933. She went into exile in London and continued to document the conditions of the underprivileged, South Wales miners living in overcrowded lodgings in London's East End.

Her political engagement did not only feed into her photographic work. Edith Tudor-Hart led a double life as a spy working for the Soviet Union. As a headhunter, she would have been one of those who recruited Kim Philby, the mole in the British Secret Service and a member of the famous Cambridge group of five working for the KGB; and Anthony Blunt, an art historian who worked for Queen Elizabeth. Under surveillance by the intelligence services, she destroyed part of her archive in the early 1950s.
In 1949, she published a reportage on a school founded by a fellow Austrian for children experiencing difficulties and continued her research into childhood, health and education, reconnecting with her first vocation. Children figured highly in her work, often occupying the centre of the image at a time when the defence of their rights was gaining international traction. Her portrait of a little girl looking enviously at the window of a baker's was intended for the cover of a book that was never published. The proposed title quoted the nursery rhyme refrain 'rich man, poor man', crystallising the inequalities she spent her life combatting.

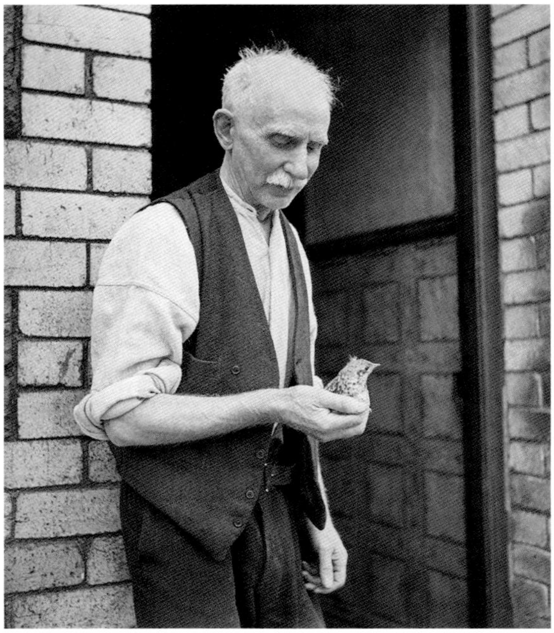

↑ 'Untitled, Tyneside',
c. 1937,
London, FOTOHOF Archive

→ 'Gee Street, Finsbury, London',
c. 1936
gelatin silver print (2004),
London, FOTOHOF Archive

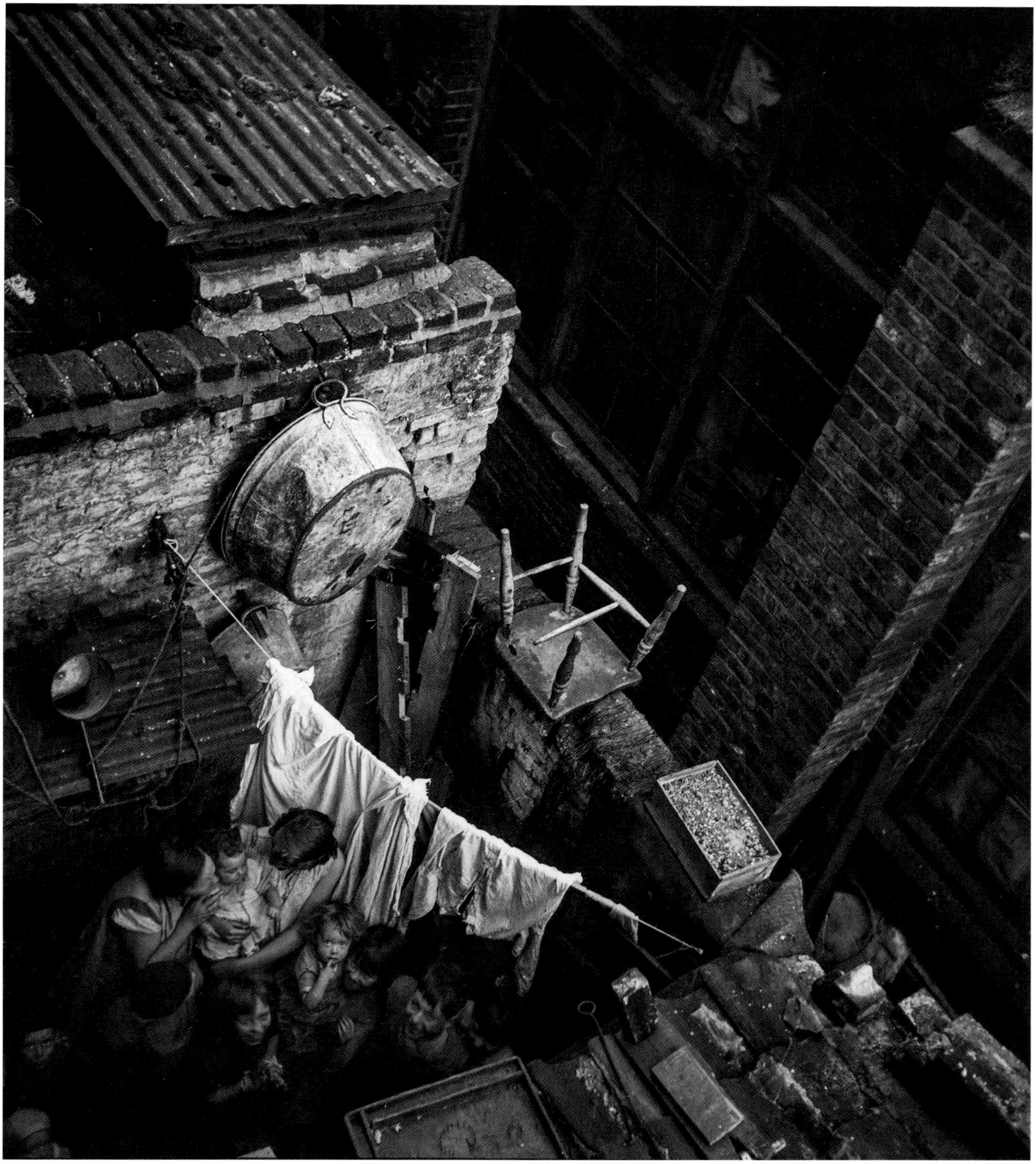

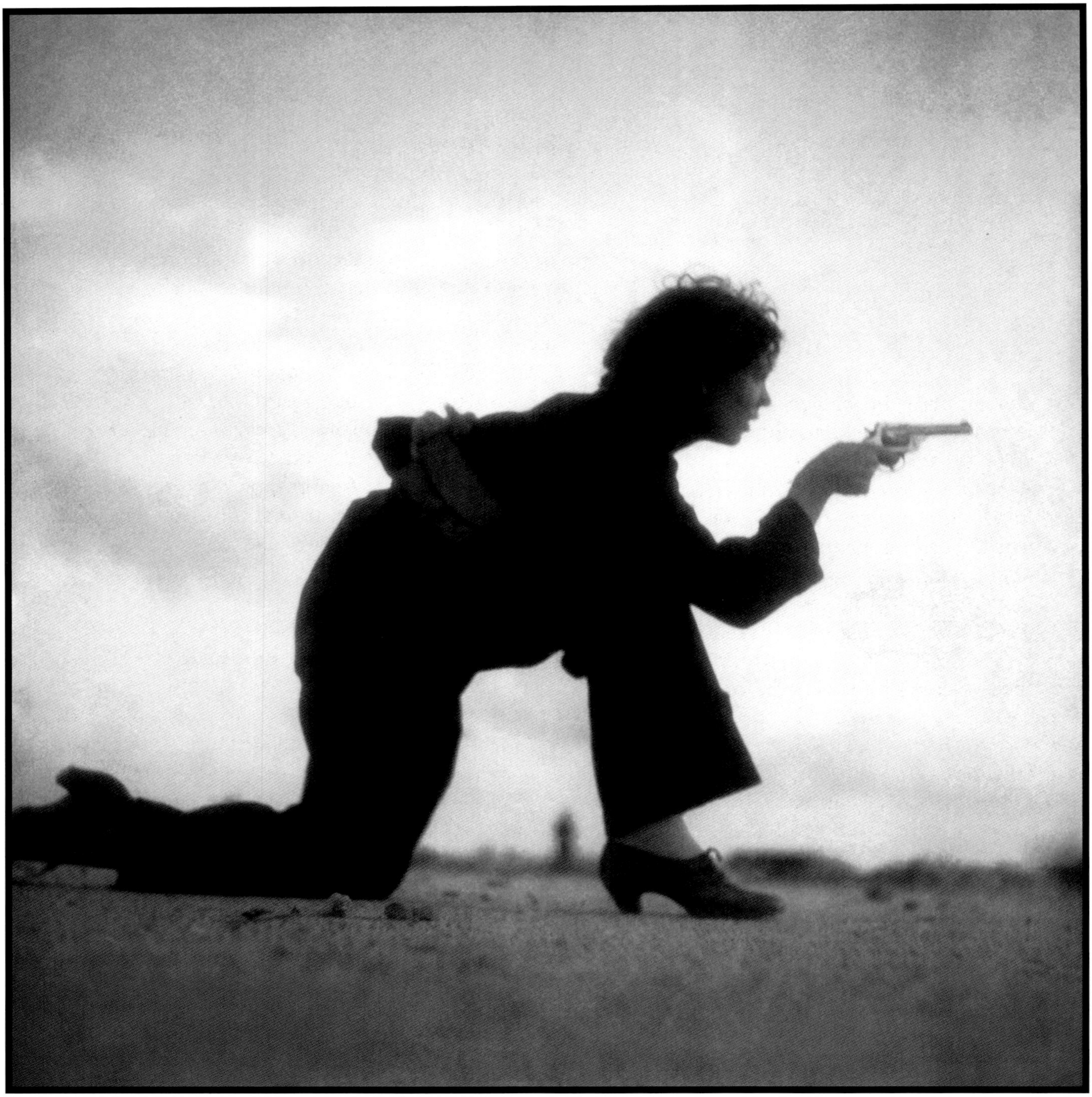

GERDA TARO

1910, Germany–1937, Spain

Gerta Pohorylle was born into a Jewish family in Stuttgart and engaged in the struggle against the rise of Nazism. Arrested in March 1933, she fled to Paris after she was freed. Penniless, she worked cash-in-hand and joined groups of activist refugees who were illegally distributing pamphlets to Germany. She met the Hungarian photographer Endre Ernö Friedmann and began working for the Alliance Photo agency. In early 1936, she came up with a bold strategy for selling their pictures better: from then on, she called herself Gerda Taro while her partner adopted the name Robert Capa, presenting himself as a famous American reporter. Given the increasing antisemitism of the time, abandoning their original names protected them from stigmatisation and marked the beginnings of the legend that is associated with their partnership. Gerda Taro – literally – made a name for herself at a time when the notion that a photographer was an author in their own right began to gain currency.

Together, they went to Spain, like many artists and intellectuals, to lend their support to the republican cause after General Franco's coup d'état. She photographed women's military groups being trained, battles at the front, but also life at the rear, the fate of refugees and the terror of air raids. A militant anti-fascist, Gerda Taro hoped that her images would alert public opinion to the menace of authoritarian parties. She worked ceaselessly despite the risks she incurred. Her photographs were published in the international press, sometimes attributed to her partner or with no mention of her name.

On 25 July she met her death at the battle of Brunete, run over by a tank as the troops drew back. Her death was keenly felt in the leftist circles in Paris, who gathered in Père-Lachaise cemetery to celebrate her role as a heroine of the fight against fascism. As the first female photojournalist killed in action, she inspired several novels. Her work was reconstituted at the end of the 2000s thanks to the discovery of the 'Mexican suitcase', a stash of negatives which allowed certain pictures signed by Capa to be reattributed to her.

'Republican Militiawoman Training on the Beach, Outside Barcelona',
August 1936,
gelatin silver print,
Magnum Photos Archive

EVE ARNOLD

1912, USA–2012, UK

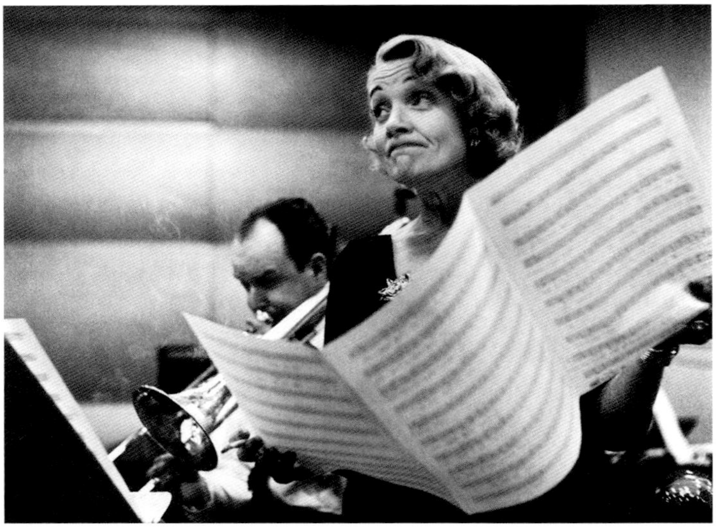

Known for her portraits of Marilyn Monroe, Eve Arnold left behind some of the most intimate images of the star, showing her learning her lines or behind the scenes during filming. She photographed numerous celebrities and always tried to get behind the mask of glamour that was traditionally displayed to the public and uncover a more sincere and authentic gaze. This quest formed the framework of her first book, an autobiographical work published in 1976 with the eloquent title *The Unretouched Woman*. In it she revisited her career as a reporter and chose a singular narrative line, describing the novelty of her experience in a professional world largely dominated by the male gaze.

Wherever she went, she always tried to present a different face of women, far removed from stereotypes and the regular conventions of attractiveness. She also revealed the mundane domestic lives of women, offering close-up views of the precise activities that made up their day, the small, anodyne tasks that usually went unseen.

Born Eve Cohen in Philadelphia to Ukrainian Jewish immigrant parents, she grew up in modest circumstances and began a career as an estate agent. She moved to New York in 1943 and worked for a photographic processing firm in New Jersey. Her first reportage, on African American fashion parades in Harlem, was published in *Picture Post* in 1950. She joined Magnum Photos the following year and travelled to Russia, China, South Africa and the Middle East, where in 1971 she made a film about women and the hijab, *Behind the Veil*. From 1963, she lived in London and collaborated regularly with the *Sunday Times Magazine*. From the late 1970s, she concentrated on displaying her archive through exhibitions and the publication of dozens of books.

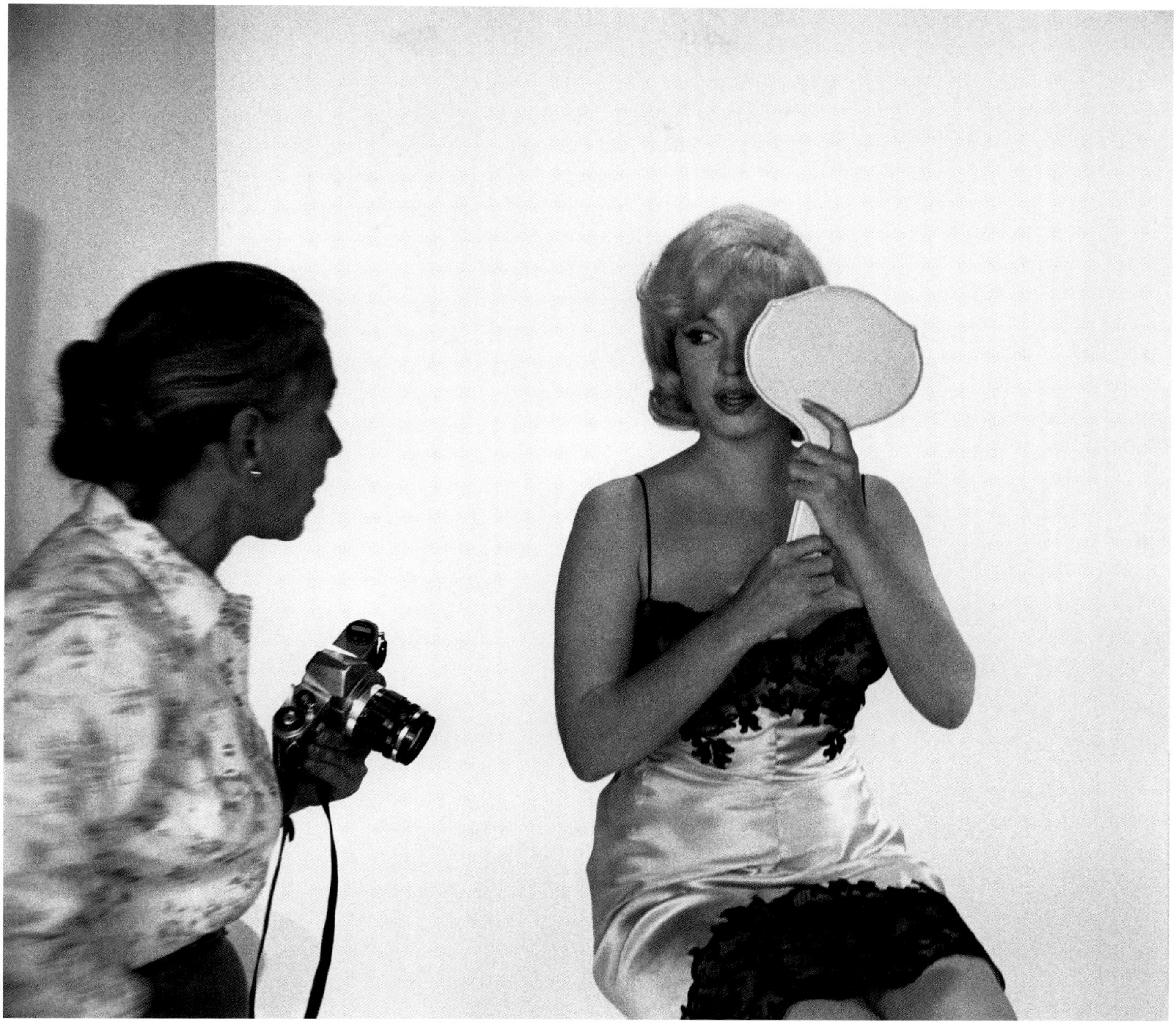

↖ 'Marlene Dietrich at the Recording Studio of Columbia Records, Who Were Releasing Most of Her Songs She Had Performed for the Troops, New York City', November 1952, Magnum Photos Archive

↑ 'Marilyn Monroe During the Filming of *The Misfits*', 1960, Magnum Photos Archive

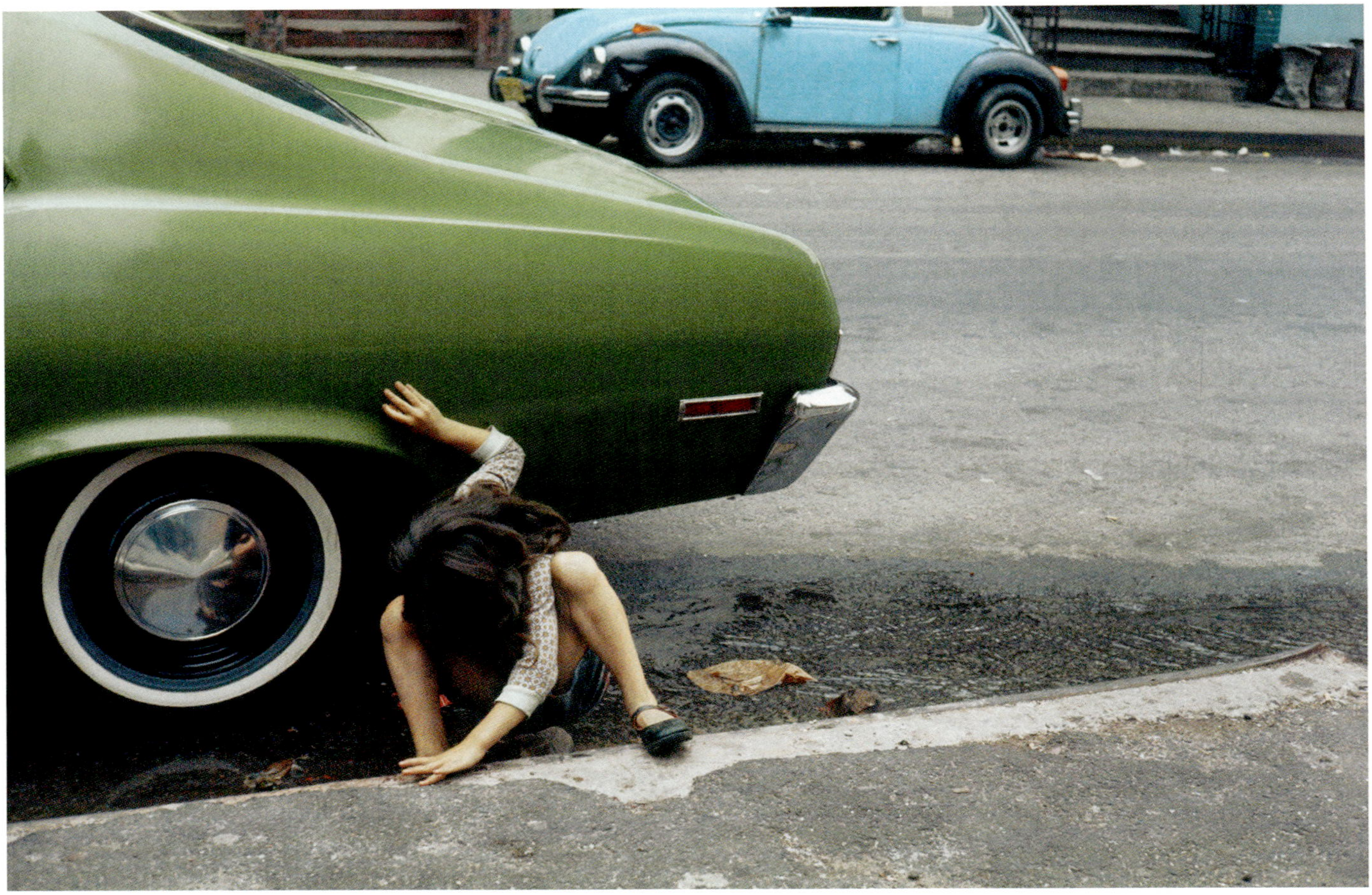

↑ ‘New York’,
1980,
Cologne,
colour print,
Thomas Zander Gallery

↗ ‘New York’,
1940,
Cologne,
gelatin silver print,
Thomas Zander Gallery

HELEN LEVITT

1913–2009, USA

Born in Brooklyn, Helen Levitt took her first steps as an apprentice to a portrait photographer in the Bronx in 1931. Between 1938 and 1939, she worked as Walker Evans' assistant. She became known for her photos of working-class areas of New York and exhibited at MoMA in 1943. The heroes of her images are the children who populated this city transformed into a vast playground. Illuminating the hard frame of the rundown streets, crouching or leaping, their graceful silhouettes perform an improvised dance. At pavement level, at their height, Helen Levitt shows the extent to which they appropriate their urban surroundings and turn them into a poetic space. With their proud gazes and radiant smiles, they adopt a range of different characters and cover the walls with mysterious messages in chalk. 'Button for the secret passage, press here,' one message reads. Their enigmatic signs defined the contours of their city within a city.

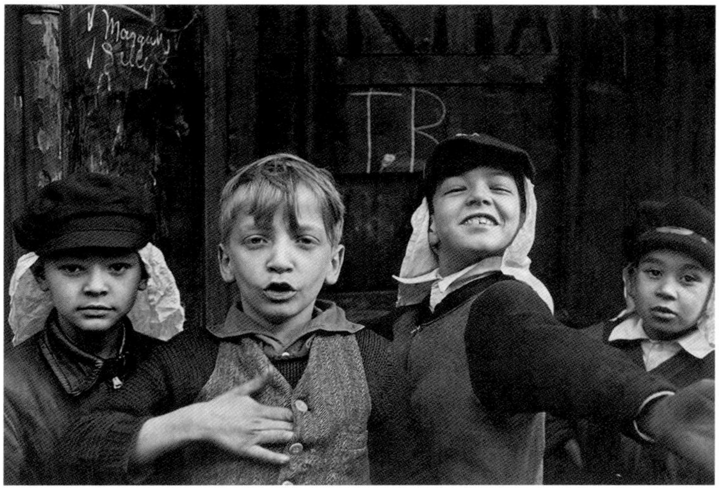

Helen Levitt also turned her hand to filmmaking and made the documentaries *The Quiet One* (1949) and *In the Street* (1952) with the writer James Agee and the painter Janice Loeb. She turned to colour with the support of the Guggenheim Foundation, which gave her grants in 1959 and 1960, and she displayed her work as a projection at MoMA in 1974, helping to broaden the spectrum of photographs considered acceptable in galleries beyond the traditional black-and-white.

To head off the pitfalls of humourless condemnation or sentimental celebration, Helen Levitt employed a 'way of seeing' – to adopt the title of her 1965 book – which was both attentive and amused, keeping a respectful distance from these young models. Some of them openly taunt the camera in a cheeky way while others bar her access, gathering around to protect their treasure. Rather than showing children as lovable objects, she saw them as genuine subjects experimenting with a form of imagination and freedom that always seemed to spill beyond the frame of her photographs.

JANINE NIÉPCE

1921–2007, France

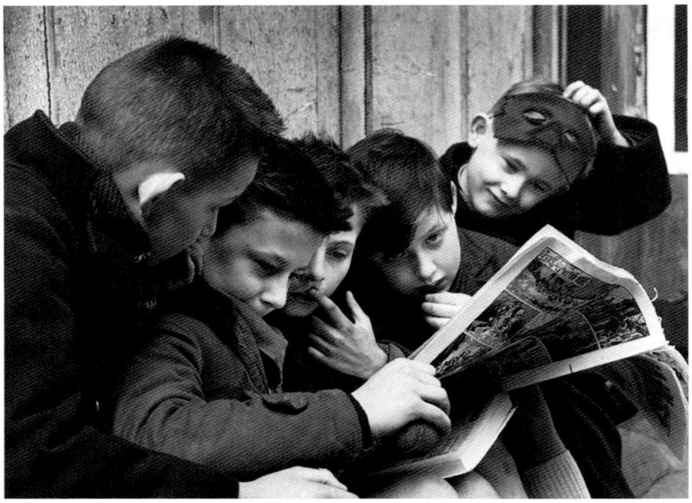

Janine Niépce shared a name with one of the early inventors of photography, the creator of the first heliographs around 1826. From this distant relation she inherited an evocative surname, as much a hindrance as a help to her, perhaps, as she traced her own path. With this involuntary baggage she studied history of art at the Sorbonne during the war, developed films for the Resistance and worked as a liaison agent in the liberation of Paris. She became a reporter and from 1955 travelled with the Rapho agency, covering social subjects in France and later, after 1963, abroad.

A humanist photographer, she had an eye for the unusual and surprising and captured scenes on the street or in everyday life full of empathy and picturesque and nostalgic elements. Many of her images show children absorbed in reading comics.

She was also one of those privileged to witness the feminist movement of the 1970s, documenting demonstrations, information campaigns about contraception, the struggle for abortion rights and women's access to the job market, especially in traditional male professions. She herself succeeded in carving out a place in an often macho professional sphere and would commonly respond to inopportune remarks: 'A child is heavier than a photographer's equipment, housework is just as tiring as this hard profession.'[1] The author of almost 20 books and a member of the Feminist Archives association, she set about communicating the precious documentation that she had accumulated. Frequently reproduced, her images of political events and her portraits of figures such as Simone de Beauvoir and Gisèle Halimi helped forge the collective memory of feminist grievances.

---

1. Afterword to *France*, Arles, Actes Sud, 1992, with a text by Marguerite Duras.

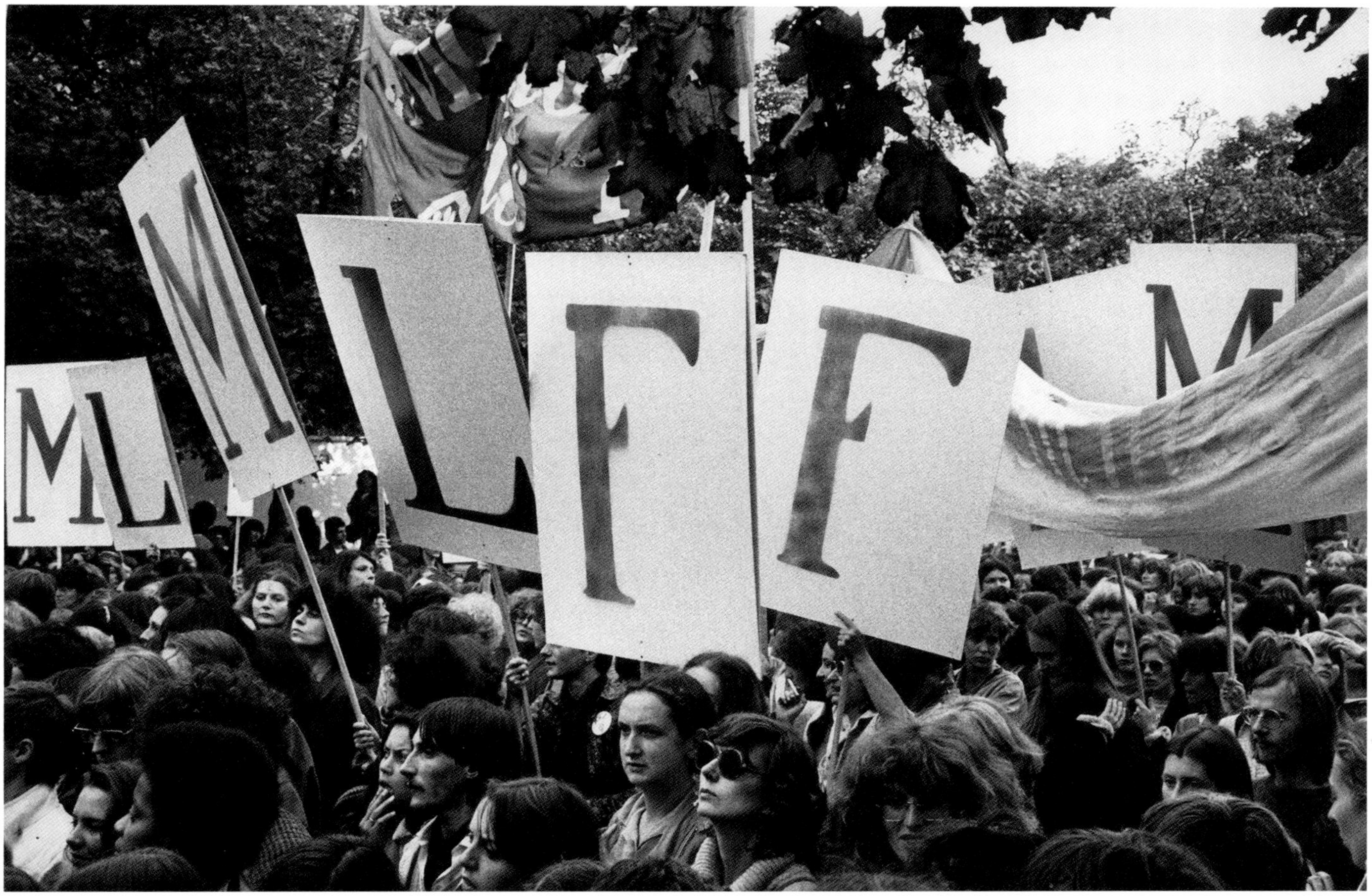

↖ 'La Vogue des bandes dessinées, France'
[The Fashion for Comic Books, France]
1956,
Roger-Viollet Collection

↑ 'Manifestation en faveur de l'avortement libre, Paris' [Demonstration in Favour of Free Abortion, Paris],
1979,
Roger-Viollet Collection

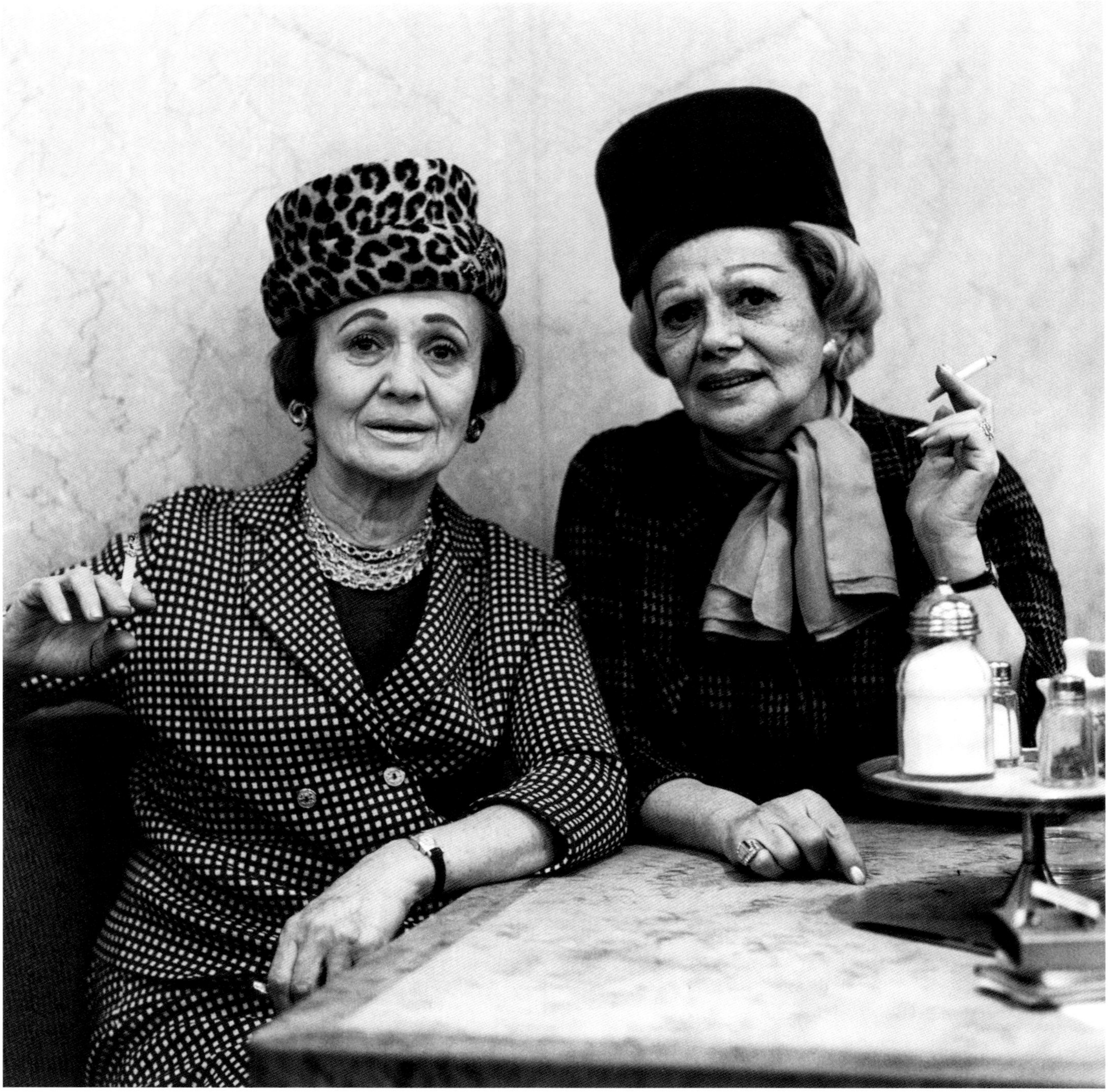

'Two Ladies at the Automat, N. Y. C. 1966',
1966,
gelatin silver print,
San Francisco, Fraenkel Gallery

DIANE ARBUS

1923–1971, USA

Diane Arbus trained with Lisette Model and devoted herself completely to photography after 1956. In 1963 and 1966, she received two grants from the Guggenheim Foundation to carry out her emblematic projects, *American Rites, Manners and Customs* and *The Interior Landscape*. Nudists, cross-dressers, twins, children, peri-urban couples, circus performers... Published in magazines such as *Esquire* and *Harper's Bazaar*, her black-and-white, square-format photographs questioned the codes and conventions of American culture, revealing the dissonance and strangeness at the heart of the most familiar scenes. Her direct, uncompromising images were shown at MoMA in New York in 1967 in the exhibition New Documents, which honoured a generation of photographers. Diane Arbus took her own life at the age of 48 in 1971. A year later, she was given a retrospective at the same museum.

For the critic Susan Sontag, the 1967 exhibition marked an 'anti-humanist' turning point by lining up 'an assortment of monsters and borderline cases', emphasising the crushing isolation of the individuals in her 'Grand-Guignol'. According to Sontag, Diane Arbus replaced the consoling compassion of postwar photography with a frigid coldness, an antidote to the notion of life as success: 'it is her way of saying shit to *Vogue*, shit to fashion, shit to everything pretty'.[1]

Conversely, Robert Hughes emphasised the originality of a work characterised by 'the flat, documentary exactness, the stiff poses, the unforgiving hardness and clarity', eschewing all condescending generalisations to restate the necessity of a radical empathy.[2] For him, denying her models our concern amounts to relegating them further to the margins of society and refusing them a place in our community.

By shining a light on the precarity of norms, Diane Arbus disturbs the optimism and the consumerist imagery of America triumphant. Celebrated and integrated into the history of photography, her work coincides with the emergence of another vision of the country, more sombre, oppositional and subversive, which cut across literature, music and independent cinema, contributing paradoxically to its cultural hegemony.

1. Susan Sontag, 'Freak Show', *New York Review of Books*, 15 November 1973, reissued as 'America Seen through Photographs, Darkly' in *On Photography*, London, Penguin, 1979, pp. 32–48.
2. Robert Hughes, 'To Hades with Lens', *Time Magazine*, 13 November 1972.

LISETTA CARMI

1924–2022, Italy

Lisetta Carmi took up photography in the early 1960s, abandoning her career as a pianist after a trip to Apulia with the ethnomusicologist Leo Levi. She committed herself to political social documentary, exploring the world of work or the lives of children being cared for in Gaslini hospital in Genoa. In the port of Genoa, she witnessed the harsh working conditions of the dockers. With the support of the Italian Federation of Port Workers, her exhibition toured the country and travelled as far as the Soviet Union. In 1966, she published a collection of photos of the monumental cemetery of Staglieno and a book of images of people on the streets of Paris, accompanied by words by Alain Robbe-Grillet. Her 1966 portrait of the poet Ezra Pound at home won the Niépce prize for Italy.

Between 1965 and 1971, she gained the confidence and friendship of transvestite prostitutes living in a house in Genoa's former Jewish ghetto. In 1972, Sergio Donnabella founded the publishing house Essedi with the aim of publishing a book based on her photos, which hadn't found a publisher up until then. But it proved too incendiary for the bookshops, who refused to sell it, and only a few hundred copies of the 3,000 printed escaped being pulped. Over time, she gave up photography to devote herself to her spiritual quest and opened an ashram in Apulia.

The rediscovery of her work on transvestites led to the publication in 2022 of an expanded edition, including colour images. Lisetta Carmi denounced the stigmatisation of transvestites by a society that 'uses them, pays them, judges them'. Her portraits gave visibility and dignity to ostracised people whose very existence threatens the fundamentals of the social order: 'I believe that the judgement that we make on others is almost always a judgement that we make on ourselves. What we are afraid of in others is also inside us. And we always defend ourselves by attacking that part of us that we reject.'[1]

1. Back cover blurb of *I travestiti*, Rome, Essedi, 1972.

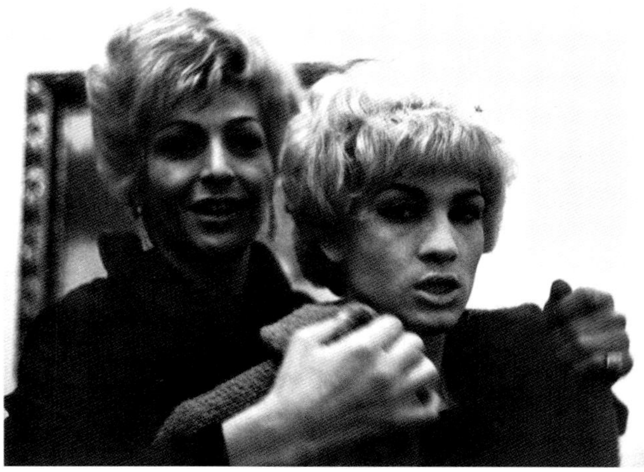

↑ 'I travestiti, Novia e la bella Elena' [The Cross-dressers, Novia and the Lovely Elena],
1965–67
Genoa, Galleria Martini e Ronchetti

→ 'I travesti, Lola Montez' [The Cross-dressers, Lola Montez],
1965–70,
Genoa, Galleria Martini e Ronchetti

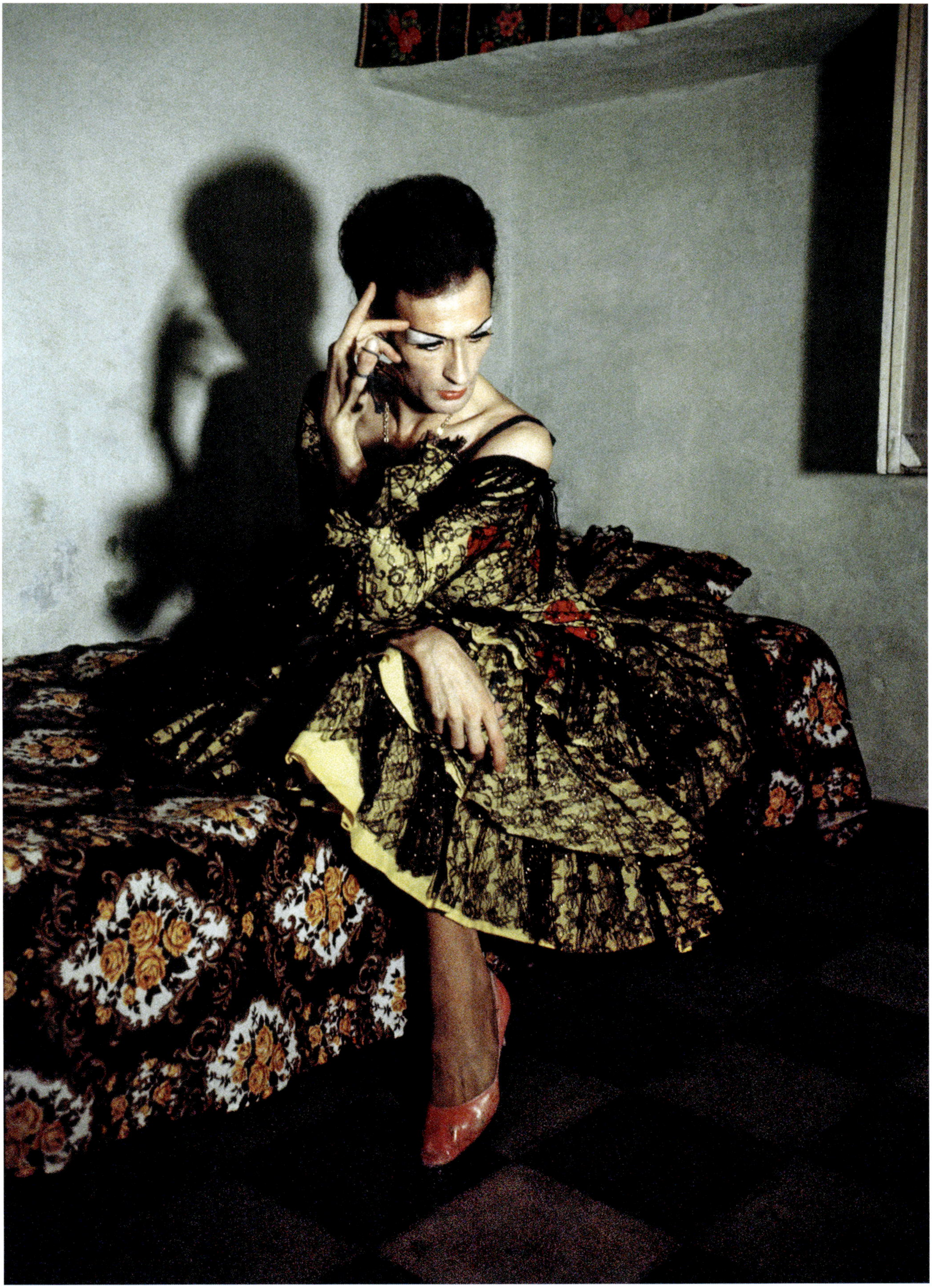

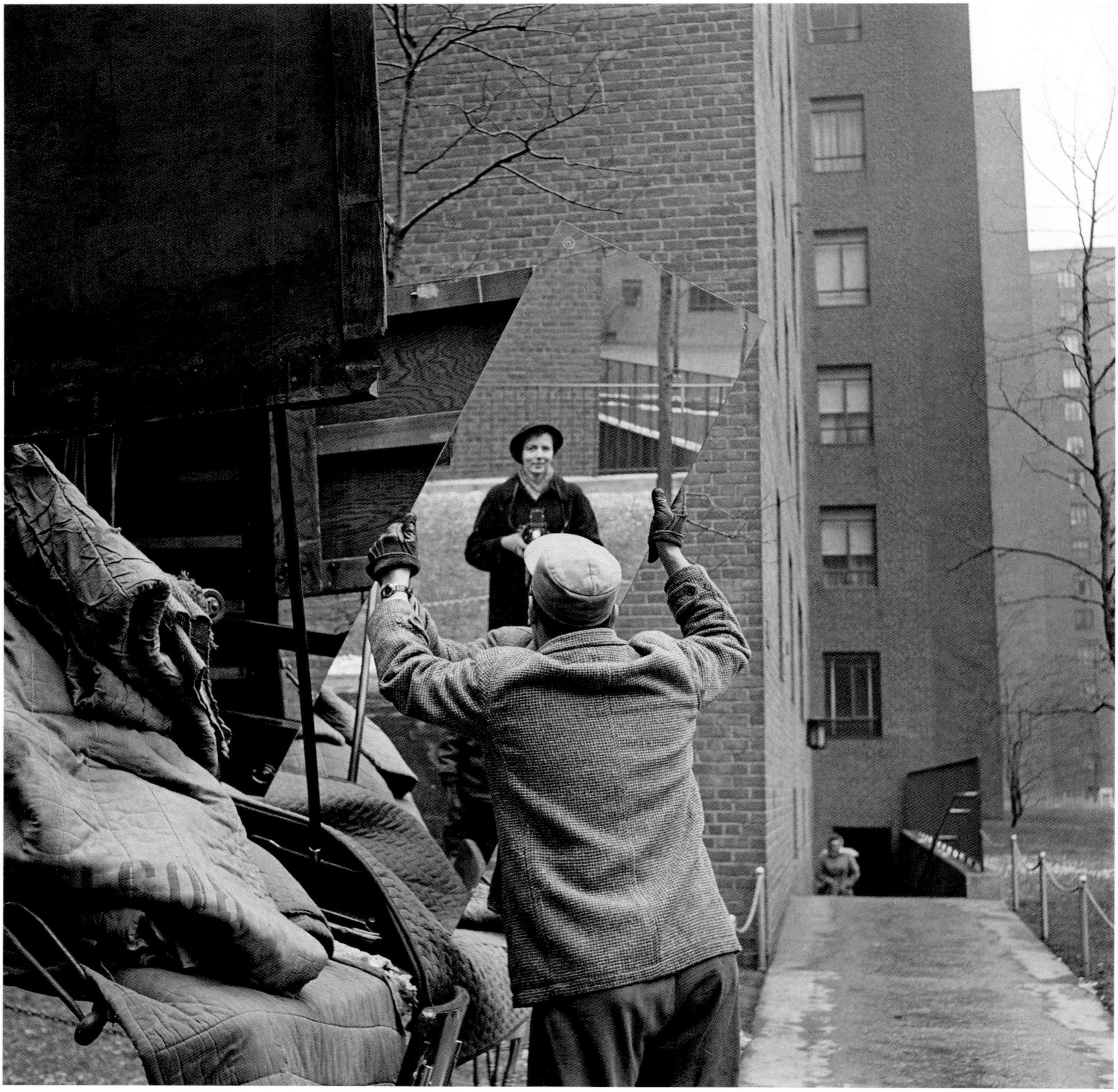

↑ 'Self-Portrait',
1955,
New York, Howard Greenberg Gallery

→ 'Chicago',
16 May 1957,
New York, Howard Greenberg Gallery

VIVIAN MAIER

1926–2009, USA

The 'nanny photographer' Vivian Maier has excited much interest since the end of the 2000s with the discovery of her work, which was never shown in her lifetime. It came about when the collector John Maloof acquired her vast photographic archive, when the storage facility in which it was kept was obliged to sell it in 2007 because of a default on payment of rent. This discovery marked the beginning of the process of reconstructing her mysterious life story. Vivian Maier had made thousands of prints of striking modernity, echoing the works of some of the great figures of street photography. Who was this prolific and enigmatic woman who had ended up alone and penniless having processed nearly 100,000 negatives in the utmost secrecy? In 2013, Maloof produced the film *Finding Vivian Maier*, cleverly feeding the mythology and the speculation around her work, from which he was profiting handsomely.

Vivian Maier grew up between France and the USA. She worked as a nurse in New York and Chicago, while practising photography with the aid of a cheap camera, a Box Brownie, then after 1952 a Rolleiflex. She developed and printed her own snaps, playing with geometry, shadows and reflections of urban scenes. She also used colour and travelled abroad. Did she see herself as an artist and did she want her images to be seen? In a biography published in 2017, Pamela Bannos dismissed the legend of the 'Mary Poppins of photography', dreamed up by certain men for their own profit, and defended the coherence of her technical and formal work. Her posthumous celebrity remains ambiguous, however, especially as she appears in a large number of self-portraits, at the edge of a mirror or a shadow, a fleeting, elusive presence.

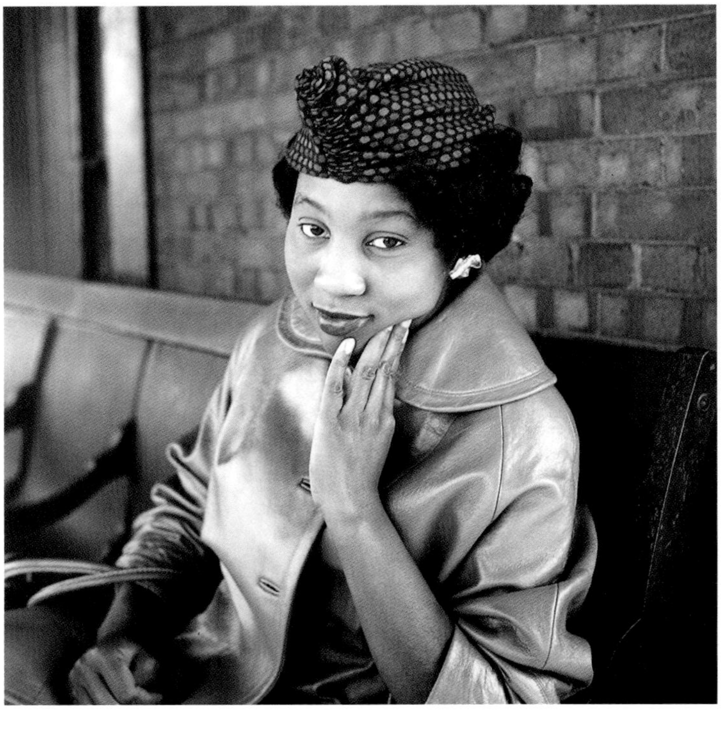

AGNÈS VARDA

1928, Belgium–2019, France

Agnès Varda began in the 1950s as a set photographer working for the Avignon Festival and Jean Vilar's Théâtre National Populaire. She turned her hand to documentary photography, stage setting and portraiture, in Rue Mouffetard in Paris, but also in China and Cuba. From 1954, she exhibited her work in the courtyard of her house in Rue Daguerre, an appropriate address, since it was named after one of the 19th-century pioneers of the photographic process.

Her photographic work is overshadowed by her fame as a film director. The only female figure in the New Wave, she made her mark in a cinema world dominated by machismo. From short films to documentaries via installations, her protean work explores places, such as the city of Los Angeles; people, such as the actress and singer Jane Birkin; or political subjects, such as the consumer society and homelessness. A signatory of the 'Manifesto of the 343' calling for the legalisation of abortion in 1971, she became a feminist and in 1976 produced a film on the women's movement, *L'Une chante, l'autre pas* [One Sings, the Other Doesn't]. She turned her gaze on her own life in *Les Plages d'Agnès* [The Beaches of Agnès] and that of her husband, the film-maker Jacques Demy, in two documentaries. The rediscovery of her photos began in the 2010s with an exhibition of images used to construct an animation film about her trip to Cuba in 1962. Produced in the year of her death, the series *À deux mains* [Two Handed] shows tender and familiar gestures between pairs of friends. On the oiled tablecloth on the kitchen table their hands are surrounded by heart-shaped garlands of tiny potatoes. These faceless portraits express a form of love that owes little to romantic ardour, nestled instead in the domestic décor of everyday life.

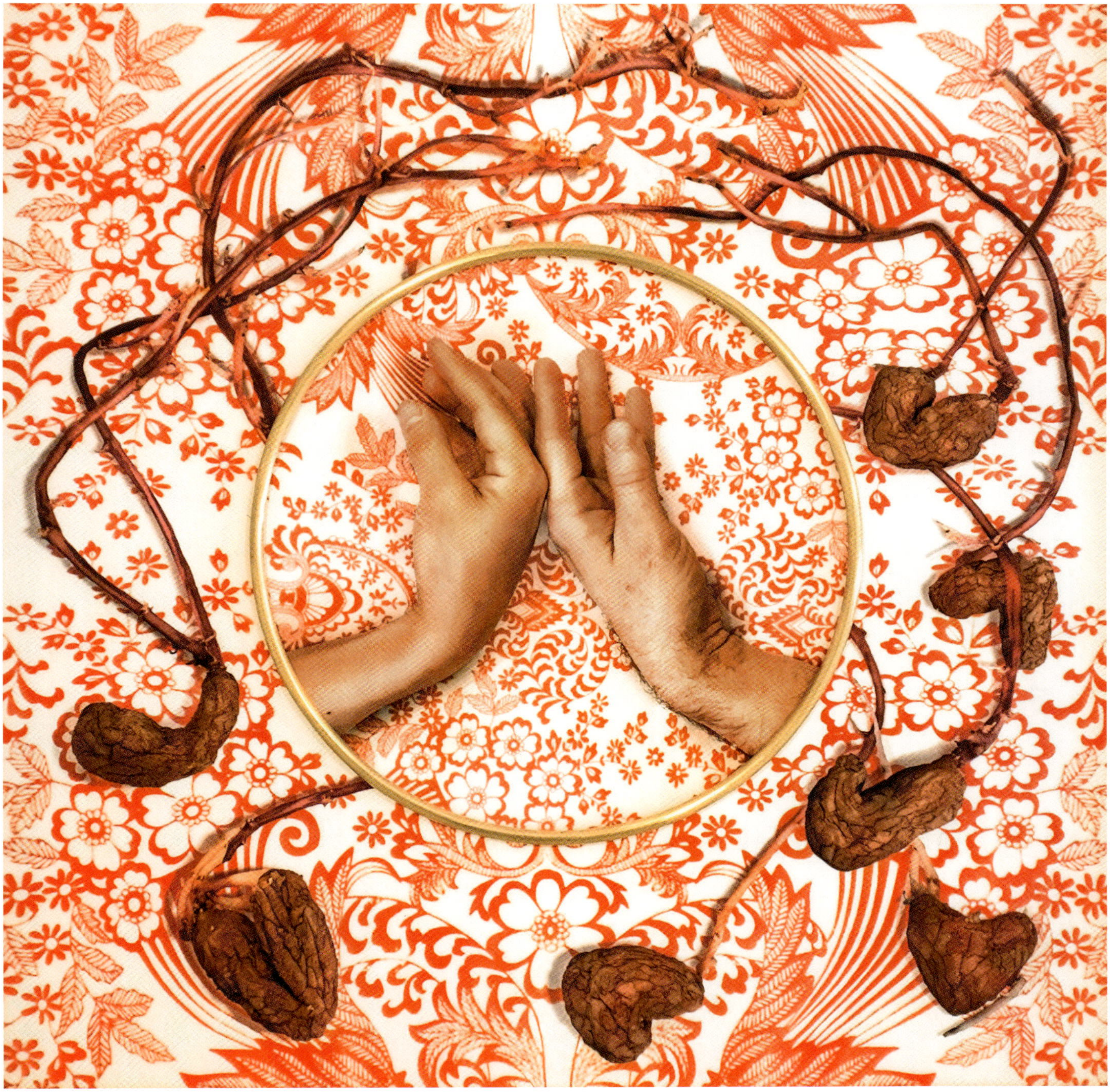

'Les Mains complices: Koo et Hans Ulrich'
[Hands Together: Koo and Hans Ulrich],
2019,
photographs and digital montage,
Estate of Agnès Varda

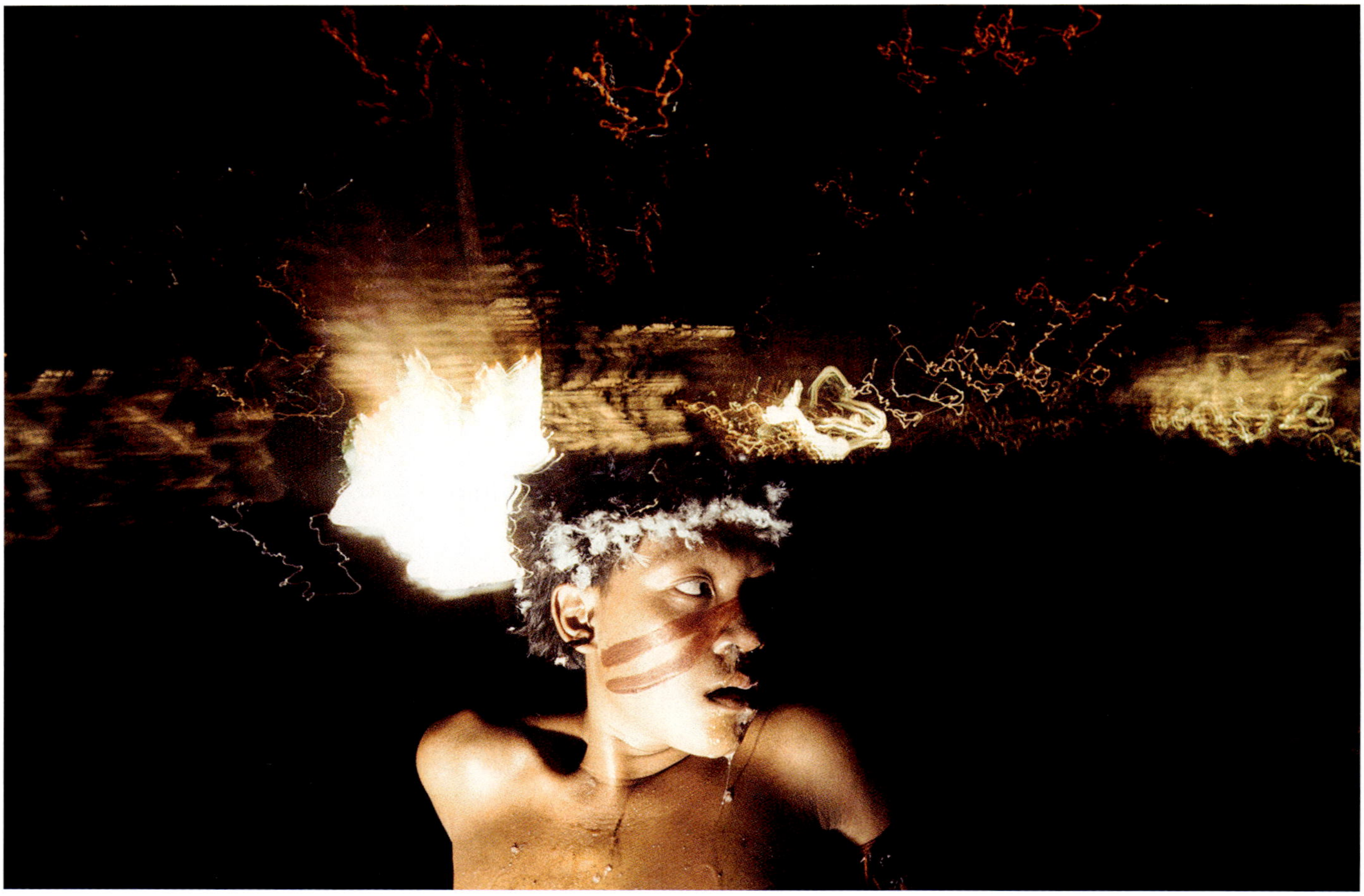

'Antônio Korihana thëri sob o efeito do alucinóbeno yãkoana, Catrimani – da série O reahu' [Antônio Korihana thëri Under the Effects of the Hallucinogen Yãkoana, Catrimani – from the Series *O Reahu*], 1972–76,
pigment print from a slide,
Brazil, Galeria Vermelho

CLAUDIA ANDUJAR

1931, Switzerland

Claudia Andujar grew up in Transylvania and sought refuge in Switzerland during the Second World War. Her father, a Hungarian Jew, was murdered in Dachau along with most of her family. After the war, she emigrated to the USA and began her career as a photojournalist in 1955 in Brazil. She discovered the existence of the Yanomani Indians in 1971 while conducting a reportage on the Amazon for the magazine *Realidade*. Supported by a grant from the Guggenheim Foundation, she was able to conduct in-depth work on their culture and ritual practices. She took portraits and experimented with various forms of manipulation, playing with changes of light or infra-red to try to reproduce their experience of the world. This led to her suggesting to the Yanomani that she might represent their shamanic visions and mythology through her pictures.

Towards the end of the 1970s, the Brazilian military government built the Trans-Amazonian highway, which brought with it increased deforestation, gold mining, agricultural colonisation and the spread of epidemics. The threat hanging over the lives of the Yanomani echoed Claudia Andujar's experience of genocide in her own family during the Second World War. She became a political activist and founded the Commission for the Creation of the Yanomani Park in 1978, which set out to define the indigenous tribe's territory; this was finally recognised in 1992. She participated in a vaccination campaign by taking portraits that created a record of each of the patients. The Yanomani activist Davi Kopenawa considered her to be a 'true friend' and ally who helped him to use 'the bow and arrow of speech, his mouth and his voice to defend his people'.[1]

---

1. David Kopenawa, quoted by Valentina Tong in Luce Lebart and Marie Robert (eds.), *Une histoire mondiale des femmes photographes* [A Global History of Women Photographers], Paris, Textuel, 2020, p. 299.

CLAUDE BATHO

1935–1981, France

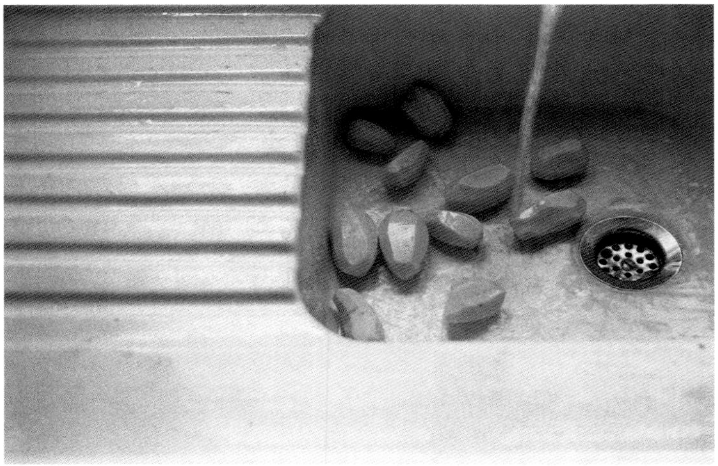

A sponge resting on the edge of the bath, its softness contrasting with the smooth coldness of the ceramic surface: this mundane detail of a non-subject and non-event grabbed the attention of Claude Batho. For her, these insignificant fragments of everyday life and these 'very simple instants' deserved to be immortalised. Flipping journalistic convention, Claude Batho derived the material for her work from such intimate and anecdotal details, highlighting activities that normally passed unnoticed: potatoes being washed in a sink, beans being hulled, a pile of laundry waiting to be ironed… Everywhere, a diffuse light gives her interior scenes a tangible materiality, caressing the texture of the wallpaper or accentuating the matte smoothness of an oilcloth.

The photograph of the sponge was a manifesto of her poetic approach to domestic life and childhood, so much so that it was used on the cover of her 1982 monograph, published a year after her premature death. The pared-down title is a simple, straightforward statement: *Claude Batho photographe* [Claude Batho Photographer]. The sponge and bath are repeated at a metatextual level by a print of the same image hanging from a line. Like many photographers, Claude Batho made her bathroom into a makeshift laboratory: her life and work were inseparable. The book was published by Éditions des Femmes, directed by the feminist Antoinette Fouque, who had published an earlier work in 1977, *Le Moment des choses* [The Moment of Things]. The eminently personal photographs of Claude Batho clearly struck a chord with the experience of many female readers, casting a new light on activities normally dismissed but rehabilitated by feminist debates.

↖ 'Pommes de terre dans l'évier' [Potatoes in the Sink],
1980,
Paris, La Galerie Rouge

→ 'L'Éponge et son image' [The Sponge and Its Image]
gelatin silver print,
Paris, La Galerie Rouge

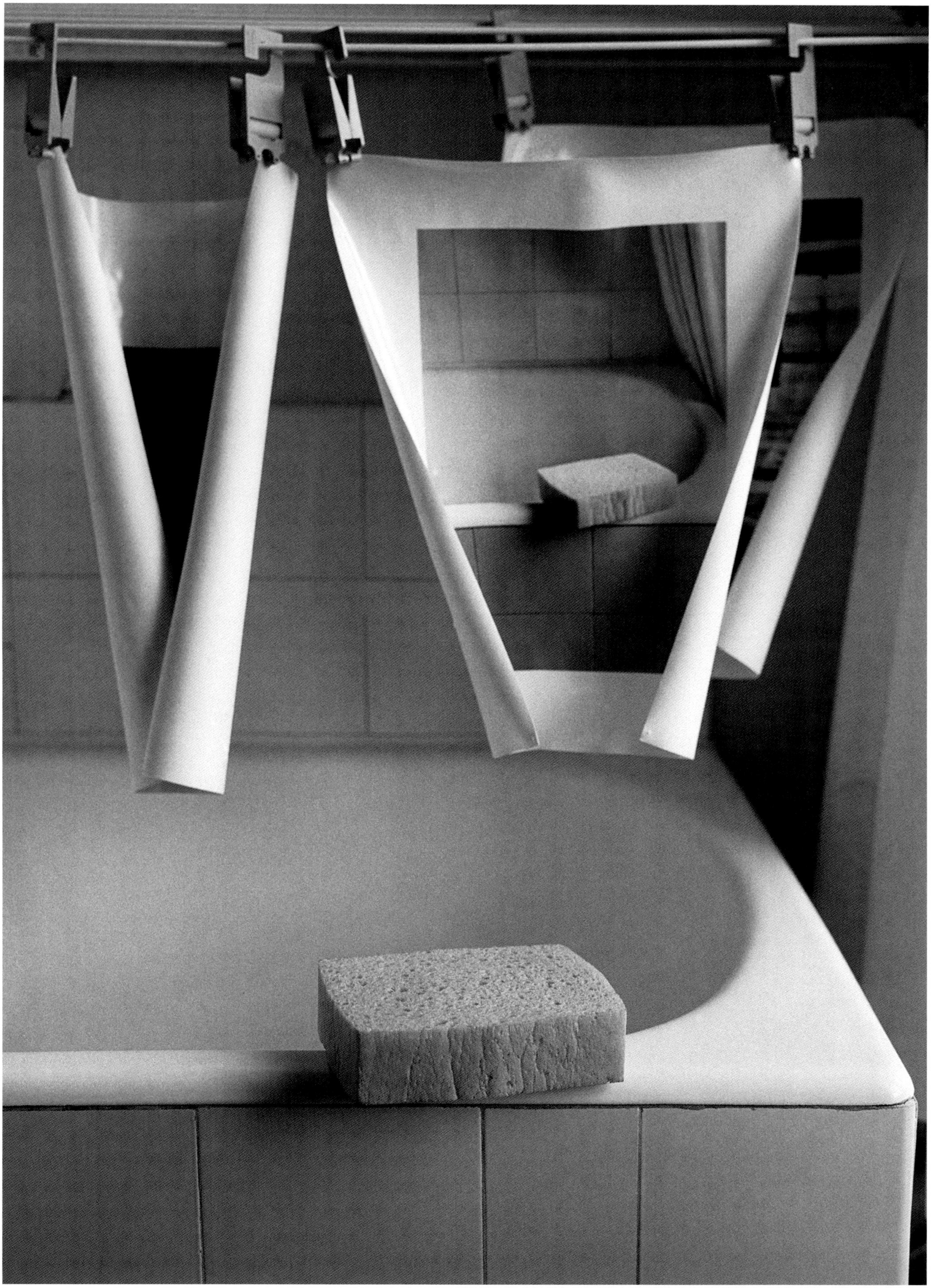

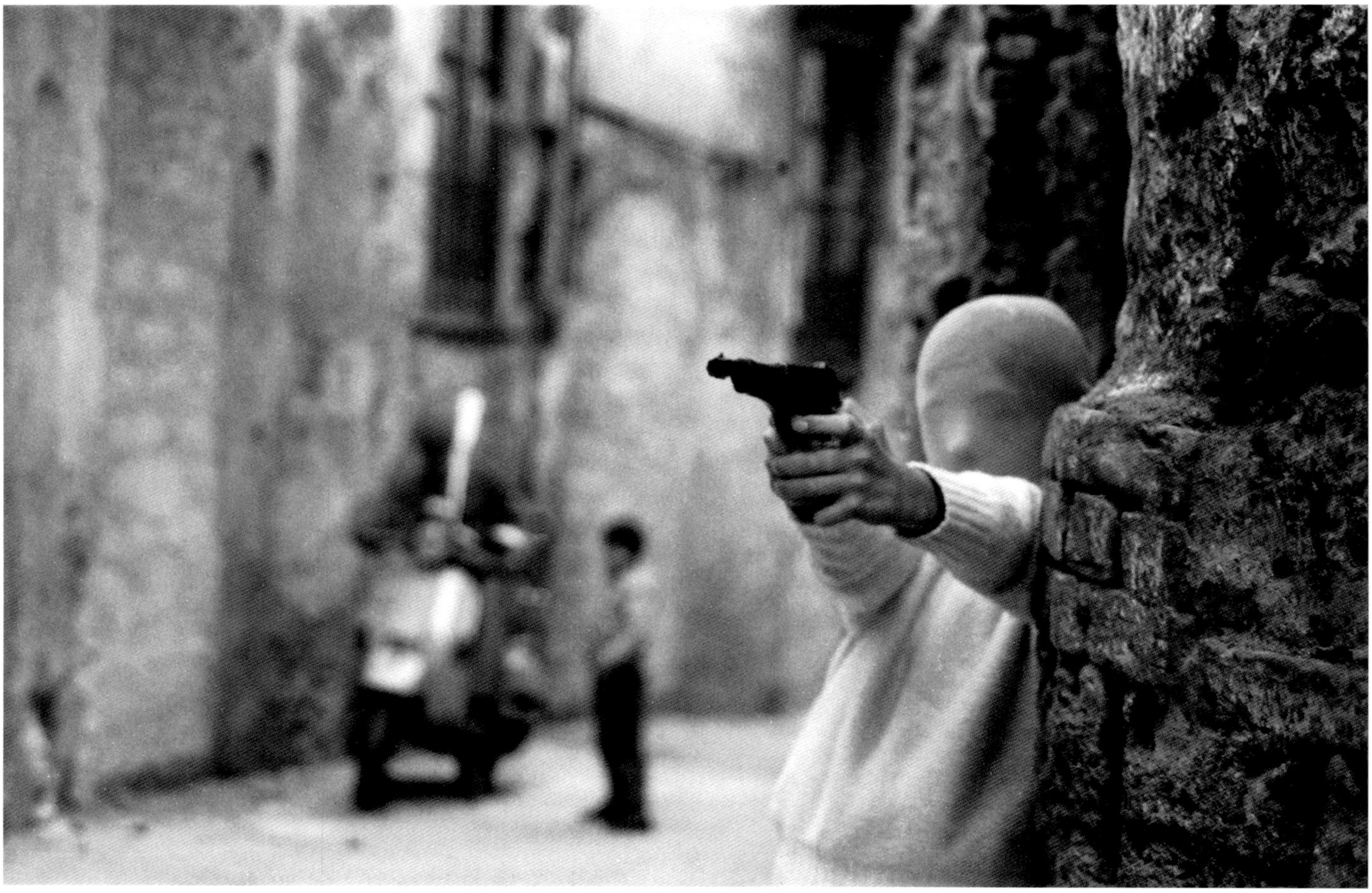

↑ 'Vicino alla Chiesa di Santa Chiara, il gioco del killer, Palermo' [Next to the Santa Chiara church, the Killer Plays, Palermo],
1982,
Letizia Battaglia Archivo

→ 'Rosaria Schifani, vedova dell'agente di scorta Vito, ucciso insieme al giudice Giovanni Falcone, Francesca Morvillo ed I suoi colleghi Antonio Montinaro e Rocco di Cillo, Palermo' [Rosaria Schifani, Widow of the Escort Agent Vito, Killed with the Judge Giovanni Falcone, Francesca Morvillo and Colleagues Antonio Montinaro and Rocco di Cillo, Palermo],
1992,
Letizia Battaglia Archivo

LETIZIA BATTAGLIA

1935–2022, Italy

Married at the age of 16 and divorced at 35, Letizia Battaglia began her career as a photojournalist in the early 1970s while raising her three girls. In Palermo and more widely in Sicily, at great risk to herself, she documented the murders and extortions of the Mafia. Originally a freelancer, she worked as director of photography of the newspaper *L'Ora* between 1974 and 1990. In a patriarchal society and a male-dominated profession, she took unflinching shots of bodies left lying in the middle of the road, the sometimes routine settling of accounts and the reign of terror. She made portraits of the widows and families of victims who took the risk of testifying, showing how this violence also affected women and children. In the 1980s, she courageously pinned up her images in the streets of the Corleones' Mafia fiefdom to confront the authors of these crimes with their responsibility and to break the *omerta*.

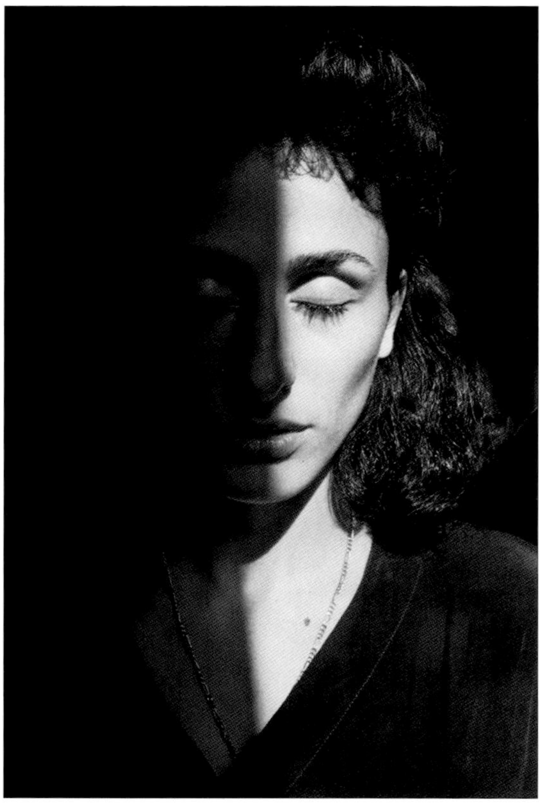

In the mid 1980s, she joined the Ecology Party, sat on the Palermo town council and continued her fight against corruption. One of her daughters, Shobha Battaglia, took on her mantle and continued her work on the Mafia. In 1991, Letizia participated in the creation of the feminist revue *Mezzocielo* and set up her own publishing house the following year. Two of her images were used as evidence of the compromising of the former Italian prime minister Giulio Andreotti at his trial in 1993. In 2017, she opened the International Photography Centre in Palermo, which ensured long-term distribution and transmission of her images and those of her colleagues. Letizia Battaglia's work reverses the masculine mythology of the power of arms and codes of honour and explicitly denounces the bloody violence of the mob which flourishes on the fertile ground of poverty and injustice.

MARIANNE WEX

1937–2020, Germany

After her early work as a painter, Marianne Wex turned to photography and compiled a vast repertoire of the forms of body language. Between 1972 and 1977, she snapped members of the public out and about in Hamburg and collected images cut from magazines or adverts. She built up a collection of 5,000 photographs sorted into categories based on the postures they showed: arms or legs crossed, hands in pockets, head on elbows, swaying hips, couples holding each other round the waist… Male and female figures were separated into two strands, which highlighted the gestures common to each gender. Her collection presented this typology of performance by gender the better to subvert it. For example, in the section 'an experience', she invited models to mimic the gestures of the opposite sex. Her sociological and feminist study showed how sexist hierarchies impregnated everyday life and the unconscious. Assembled on large cardboard panels, the images were exhibited in West Berlin from 1977 before providing the content of a book that came out in 1979 with the title *Let's Take Back Our Space: Female and Male Body Language as a Result of Patriarchal Structures.* The photographs were juxtaposed with statues from various periods, from Antiquity to the 19th century, adding a historical dimension to the subject.

Her work was rediscovered in 2009 on the back of an exhibition in England, finding an unexpected echo in the activism of a new generation of feminists preoccupied with questions surrounding the body. Marianne Wex seemed to perfectly illustrate the concept, much bandied about in the 2010s, of 'manspreading'. Designating the habit of sitting legs-apart on public transport, reducing the space available for other passengers, the expression refers to the disproportionate space accorded to men in the public environment, reflecting structural inequalities.

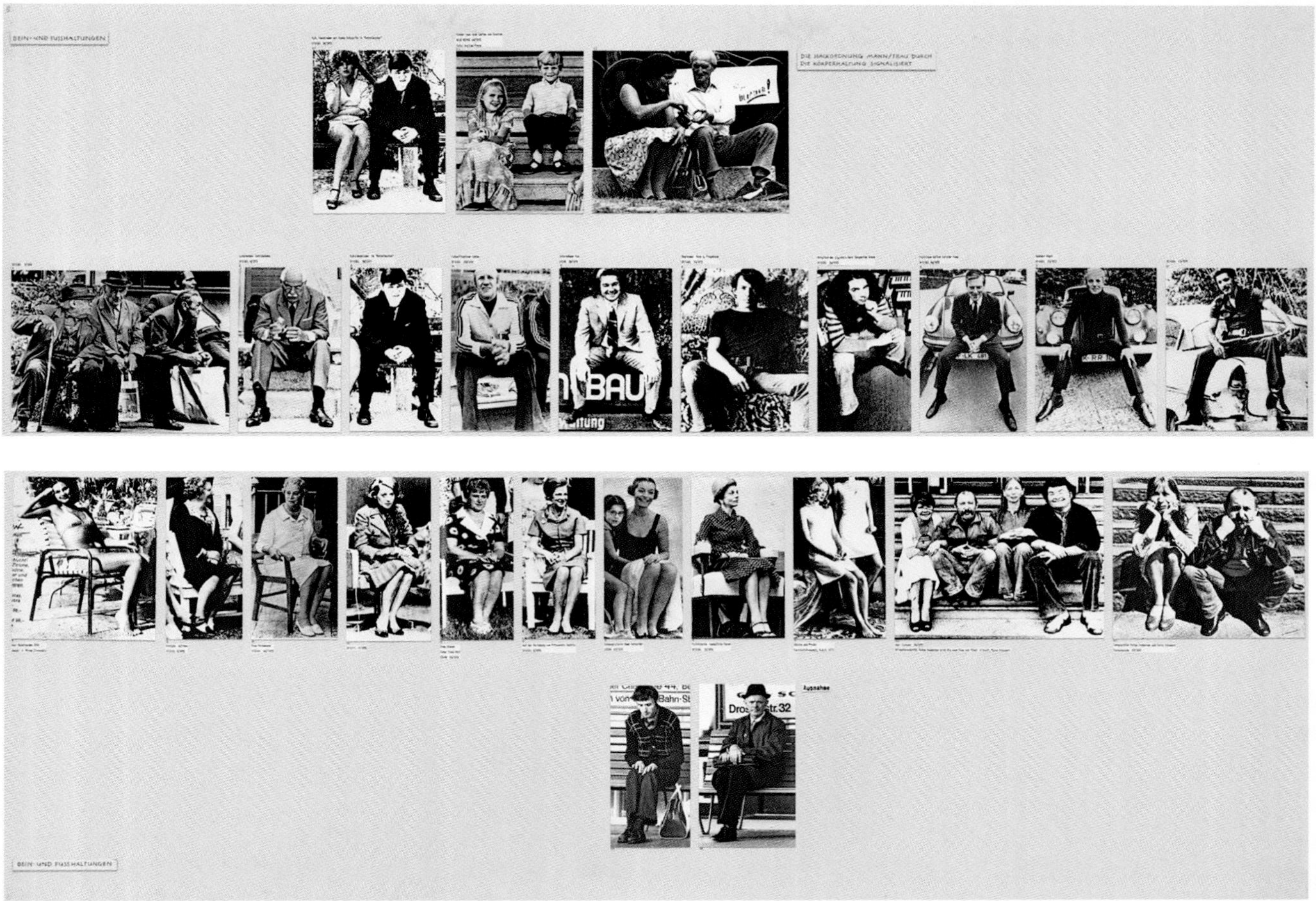

'Let's Take Back Our Space: "Female" and "Male" Body Language as a Result of Patriarchal Structures (Leg and Foot Positions)',
1977–2008,
archive print,
Berlin, Tanya Leighton Gallery

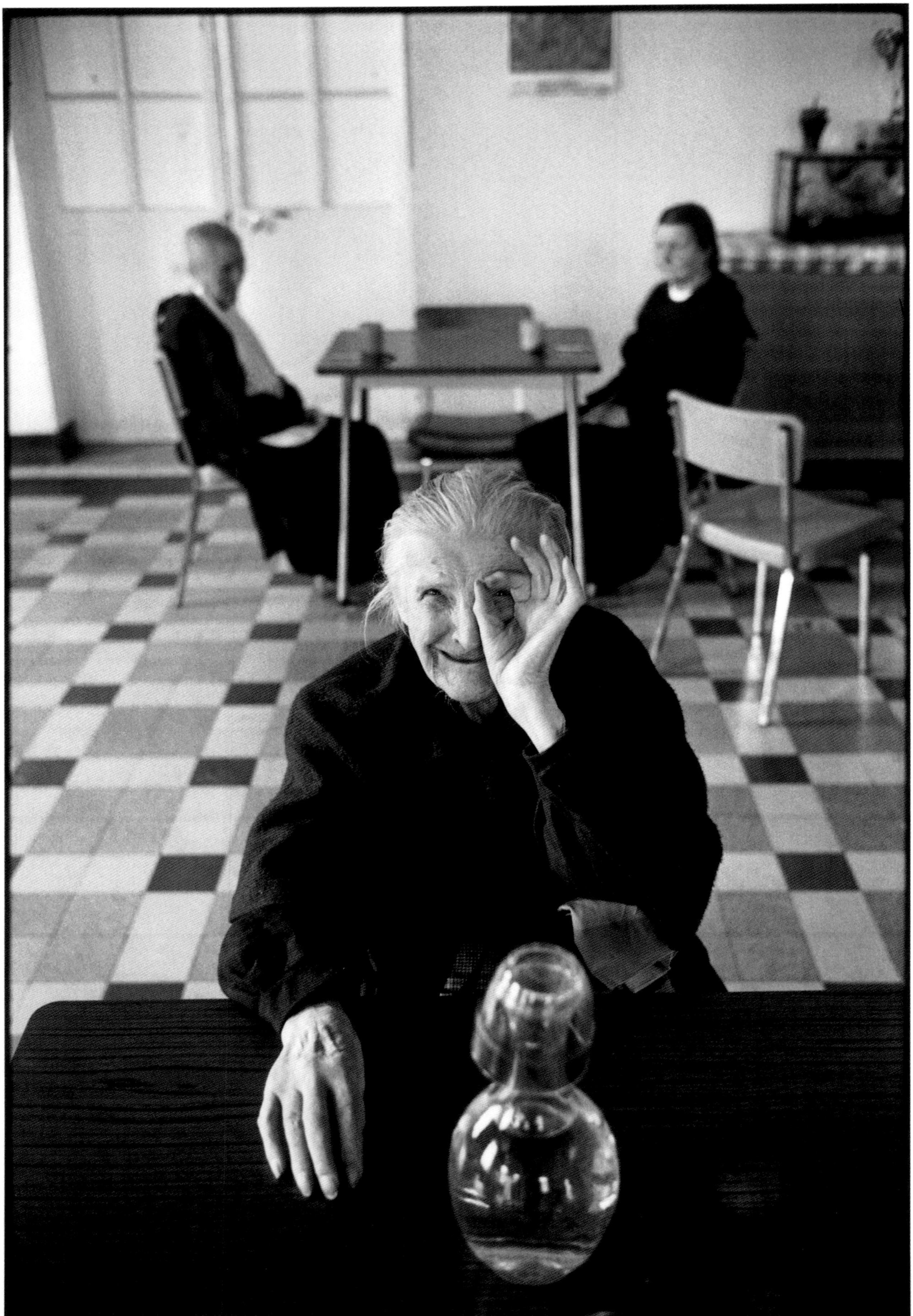

MARTINE FRANCK

1938, Belgium–2012, France

After studying art history in Madrid and then at the school of the Louvre, Martine Franck was profoundly affected by her first trip to the Far East in 1963–64 with her friend Ariane Mnouchkine. On their return, the latter founded the Théâtre du Soleil [Theatre of the Sun], and Martine Franck would be its faithful witness, photographing all of their productions. She worked as an independent photographer and published reportages on artists and writers in magazines such as *Life* and *Vogue*. In 1966, she met Henri Cartier-Bresson, a famous figure 30 years her senior, and married him in 1970. That same year, she signed up with the Vu agency before becoming one of the founders of Viva in 1972, then joining Magnum in 1980.

Martine Franck explored her favourite themes with a sensitive and empathetic eye: lonely old people, in partnership with the charity for the elderly Petits Frères des Pauvres; the inhabitants of the island of Tory off the north-west coast of Ireland; or Tibetan child monks (*tulkus*). She also documented the demonstrations of the Women's Liberation Movement in the 1970s, the making of the first issue of their 'menstrual' *Le Torchon brûle* [The Dishcloth Burns], then, in 1991, conducting a study of women at work, from engineers to train drivers, commissioned by the Secretariat of the Rights of Women. She herself succeeded in carving out a place in a professional world biased towards men, alongside – and sometimes in the shadow of – her illustrious husband, who owed her a great debt. In 2003, she founded the Henri Cartier-Bresson Foundation and worked to promote his archive. Her own collection, today held in the Foundation, demonstrates her unfailing commitment to her subjects. As she put it, talking of one of her portraits: 'In the beginning it is all about the conversation. Sometimes we might spend hours, days just observing, without saying a word, without "disturbing". What I am trying to capture is the light in the eye, the gestures, a moment of listening or concentration – precisely when the model is not talking.'[1]

1. Statement gathered by Daniel Marchesseau, *Martine Franck photographe* [Martine Franck Photogrpaher], Paris, Musée de la vie romantique/ Adam Biro, 2002, p. 27.

'Hospice, Ivry-sur-Seine',
1975,
Magnum Photos Archive

SARAH MOON

1941, France

Sarah Moon grew up between France and England and made her debut as a model in the 1960s. She adopted her pseudonym when she took on her first job as stand-in photographer for the *Express* at the end of the decade. Self-taught, she developed her practice throughout the 1970s. She became known through her work for top fashion houses such as Cacharel, Dior and Chanel and for the magazine *Vogue*. She built up close relations with her models, having also had experience on the other side of the lens, and she ventured outside the confines of her studio to use Paris as the backdrop to her images.

Hovering between real and imaginary, her world is dreamlike and melancholic. Animals, still lives and ghostly silhouettes are haloed in soft focus. A dull light suffuses her sharp black-and-white contrasts and the flat fills of colour. Adept in using a Polaroid, she foregrounded the fragility of the photographic paper, accentuating the impression of the figures fading away and revealing the contours of the frame.

She was very much part of photographic networks and she lived for 48 years with the editor Robert Delpire and produced documentaries such as *Henri Cartier-Bresson, point d'interrogation* [Question-mark] in 1994. She authored films inspired by the stories of Andersen – *The Little Mermaid, The Steadfast Tin Soldier* and *The Little Match Girl* – and Perrault – *Bluebeard* and *Little Red Riding Hood*, whose adventures she had already illustrated for an album in 1963. Liberally interpreting these archetypal characters, she mixed, fixed and animated images. Her evanescent visions, haunted by some latent anxiety, interrogate the fears and prohibitions of childhood.

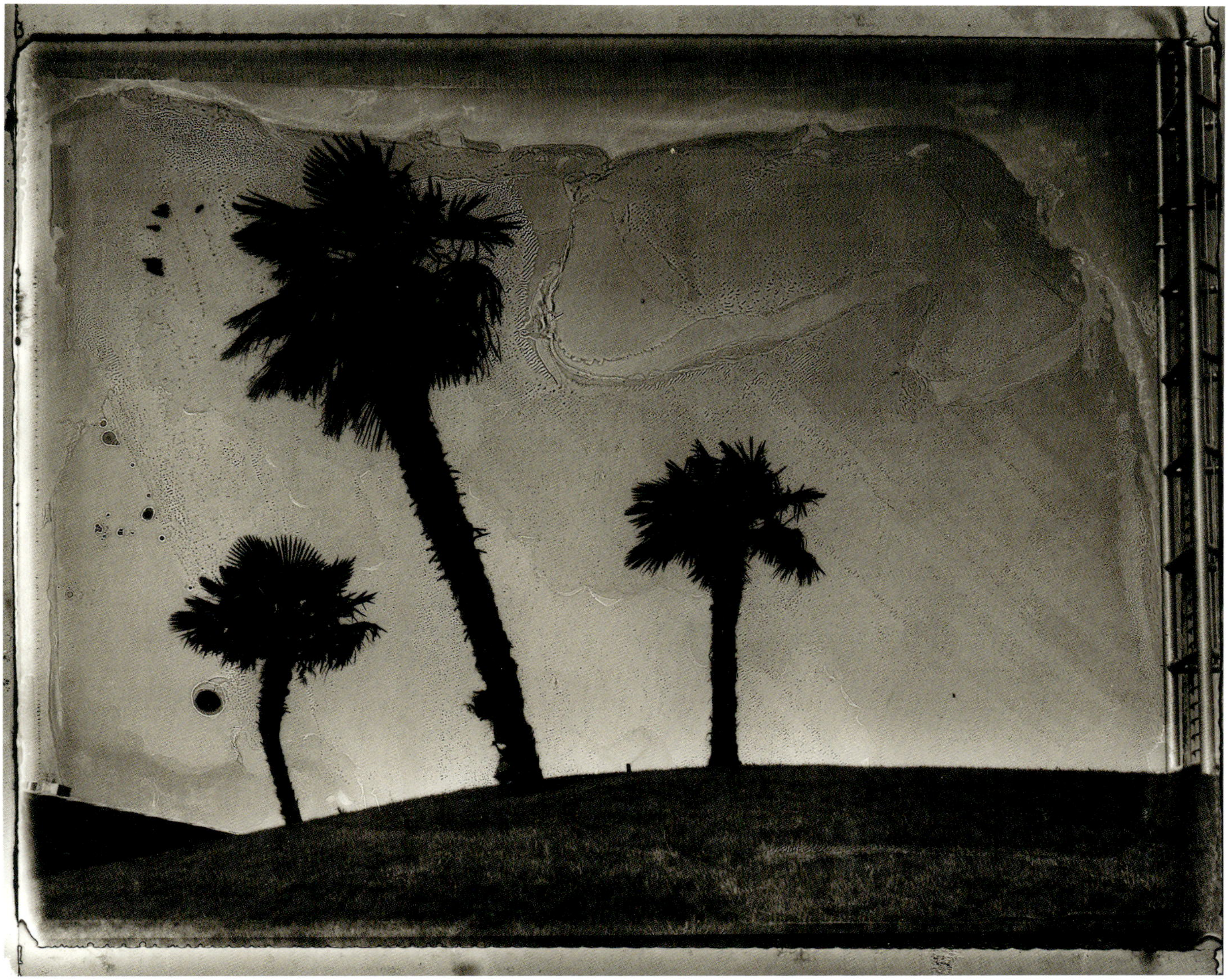

'Le Rond-point des trois palmiers'
[Roundabout of the Three Palm Trees],
photograph transferred with engraving,
artist's collection

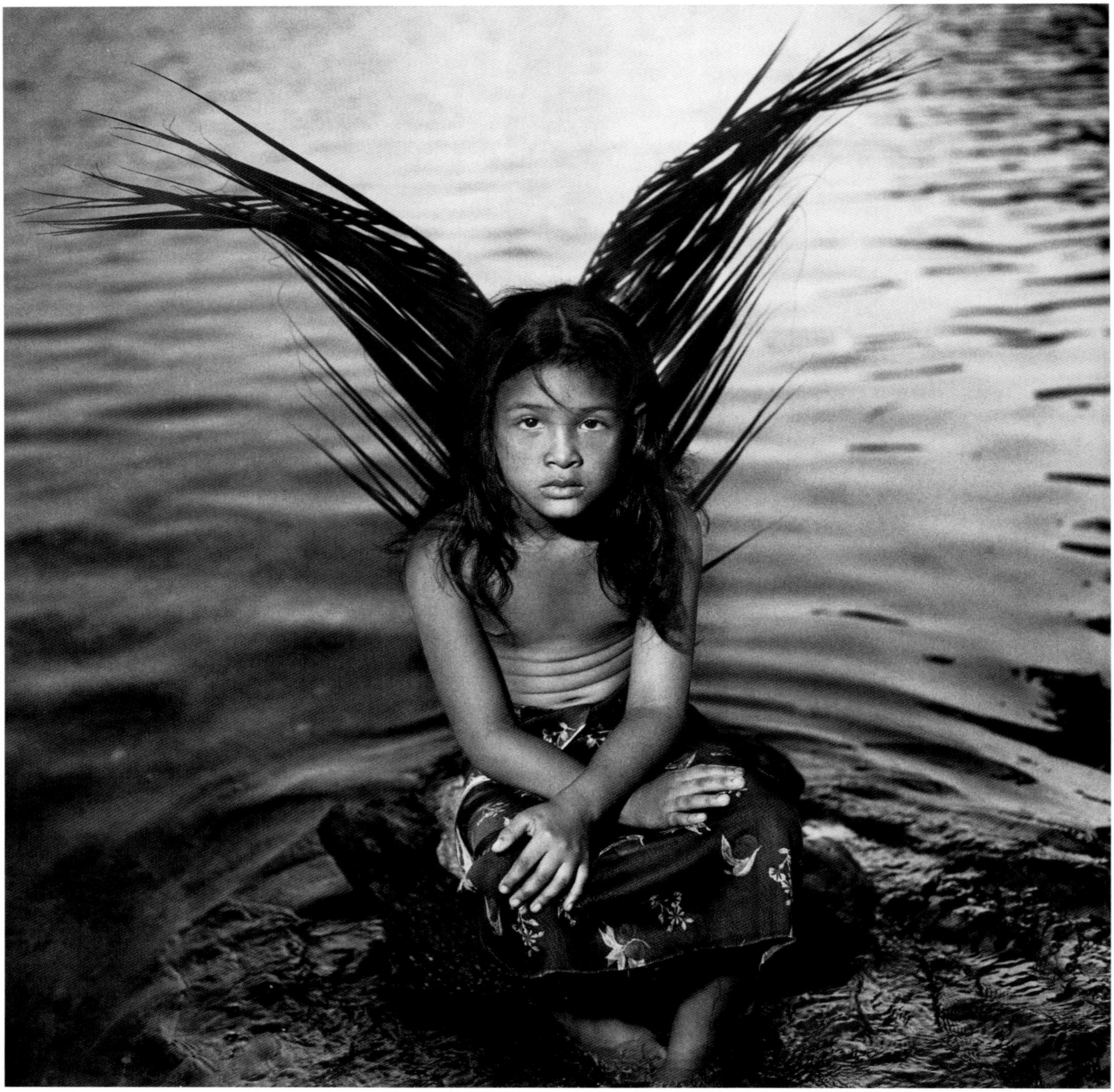

↑ 'Palm Ángel, Emberá, hijos del río' [Palm Ángel, Emberá, the children of the river], 1998, gelatin silver print, Paris, La Galerie Rouge

↗ 'La Servidumbre, Edita, Panamá' [Servitude, Edita, Panama], *c*. 1978–80, gelatin silver print (2009), Paris, La Galerie Rouge

SANDRA ELETA

1942, Panama

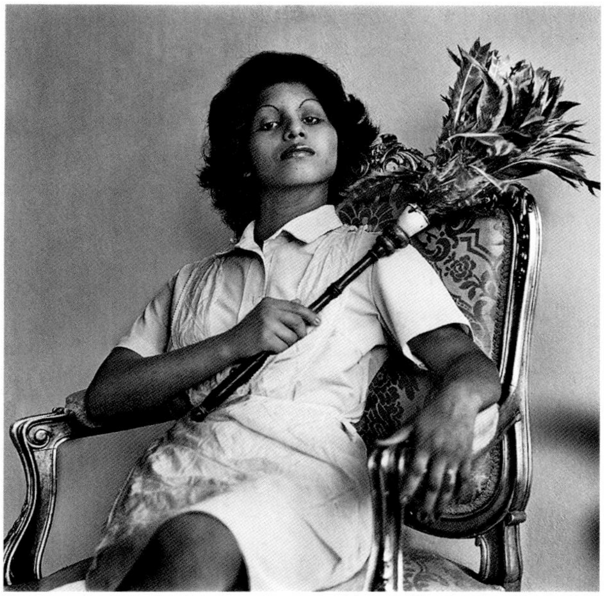

Brandishing her feather duster like a sceptre, a chambermaid proudly stares down into the lens. This provocative portrait is from the series *Servitude*, a study of domestic work in Franco's Spain and in Panama during the military dictatorship. Created by Sandra Eleta between 1975 and 1989, these pictures cast light on a traditionally invisible profession. Domestic servants are required in effect not to be noticed: cleaners operate in secret, sometimes at night, when the rooms are empty. The fruits of their labour remain unseen, by definition: no one pays attention to the cleanliness of a room, only dirt catches the eye.

Here, the young woman squats on her chair and observes us with a proprietorial air, staking her claim to places she knows better than anyone, even though she occupies a subordinate position. This subversive and ironic gaze expresses the critical relationship between domestics and their employers in these sumptuous mansions, where previous generations had adopted more modest poses and, if anything, took pride in belonging to their grand houses. Sandra Elata herself came from a well-off family and she interrogated the class relations and power dynamic that ensured the perpetuation of this luxurious way of life.

Sandra Eleta was fond of long-term projects and the black-and-white square format. Between 1977 and 1981, she photographed the town of Portobelo, which was peopled by the descendants of African slaves, and she founded a group of local female artists as well as a cooperative for the promotion of heritage. She also documented the populations of the indigenous Guna and Emberá as well as the community of artists at Solentiname in Nicaragua. A cross between ethnography, documentary and poetic contemplation, Sandra Eleta's work offers a nuanced testimony of Panama's creative and cultural traditions.

ABIGAIL HEYMAN

1942–2013, USA

In 1974, Abigail Heyman published *Growing Up Female: A Personal Photo-Journal*, which combined images exploring the American condition with handwritten fragments evoking her own journey.[1] On the cover, the title was written in pencil, expressing the intimate nature of this project, which fell somewhere between autobiography and sociological enquiry. Abigail Heyman drew her photographic rule of thumb from the famous feminist slogan 'the personal is political': far from being isolated or unimportant, her personal experience resonated with that of many women and was part of the creation of a collective subject. Childcare, domestic tasks and sexuality were among the sometimes taboo themes that deserved to be aired in public so that all were able to speak up and reclaim their rights.

Abigail Heyman worked as a freelancer for various magazines and was for a while associated with the Magnum agency, then involved in the creation of Archive Pictures. She taught at the International Center of Photography in New York. She also took photos of weddings and in 1987, published a book entirely devoted to this subject, the fruit of seven years' work.[2] She attended around a hundred weddings without ever having the role of 'official' photographer in order to preserve her autonomy and be able to adopt an oblique view, characterised by humour and tenderness, at these moments when social and familial identities became crystallised. She eschewed the clichés of happy photogenic groups and invented an anti-photography of marriage, revealing the power relations and the expectations inherent in this social ritual.

A committed feminist, Abigail Heyman drew on her activism to develop a method that transformed photography into a collective consciousness raising, making women the subjects of their own histories. In 1978, she addressed younger generations with a book for children containing portraits of women exercising a wide variety of professions, sometimes in domains traditionally associated with men, with a view to expanding the perspective of girl readers, since making something visible is to make it possible.[3]

1. *Growing Up Female: A Personal Photo-Journal*, New York, Holt Rinehart & Winston, 1974.
2. *Dreams & Schemes: Love and Marriage in Modern Times*, New York, Aperture Foundation, 1987.
3. *Butcher, Baker, Cabinetmaker: Photographs of Women at Work*, New York, Crowell, 1978.

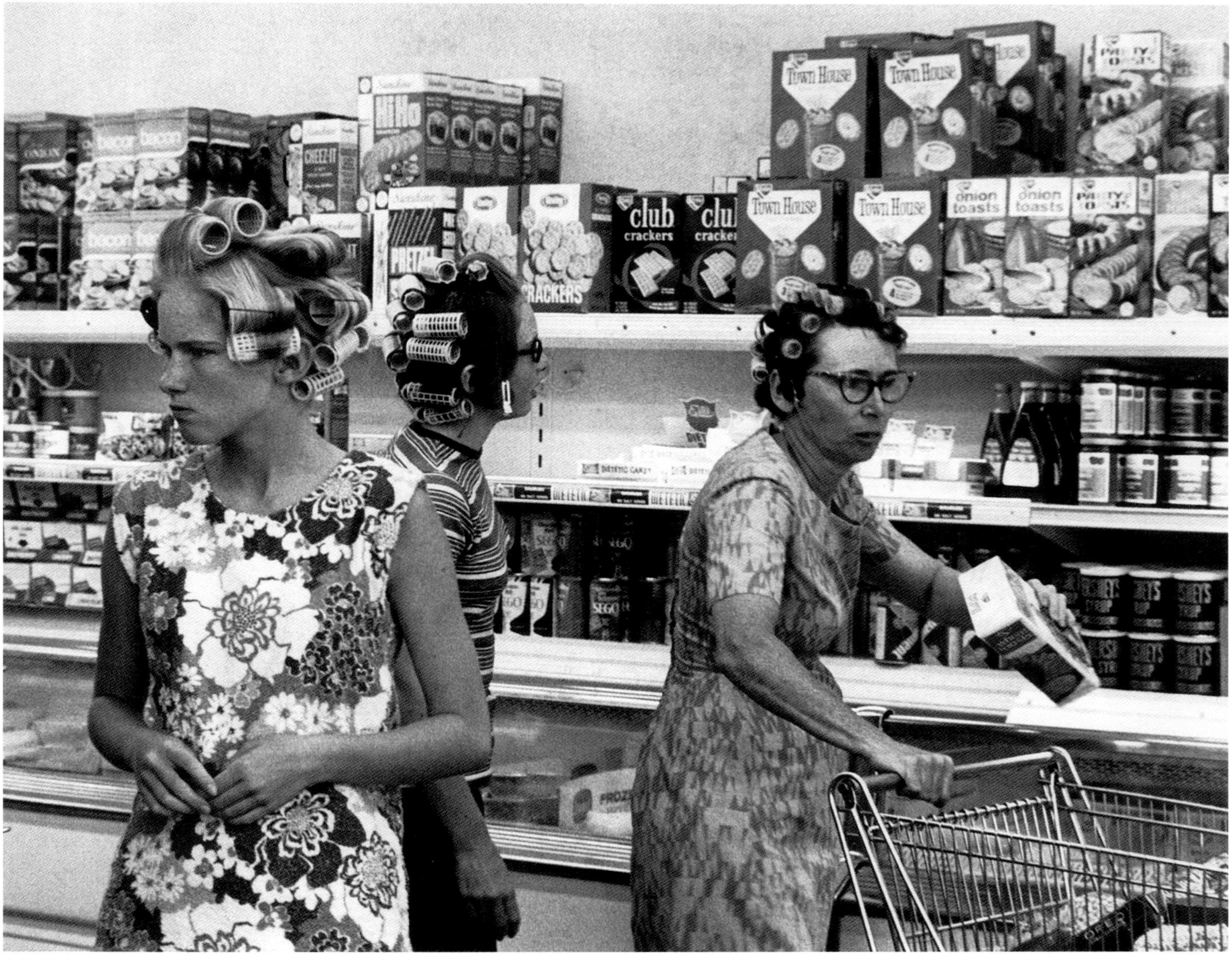

'Supermarket',
1971,
gelatin silver print,
Abigail Heyman Archives

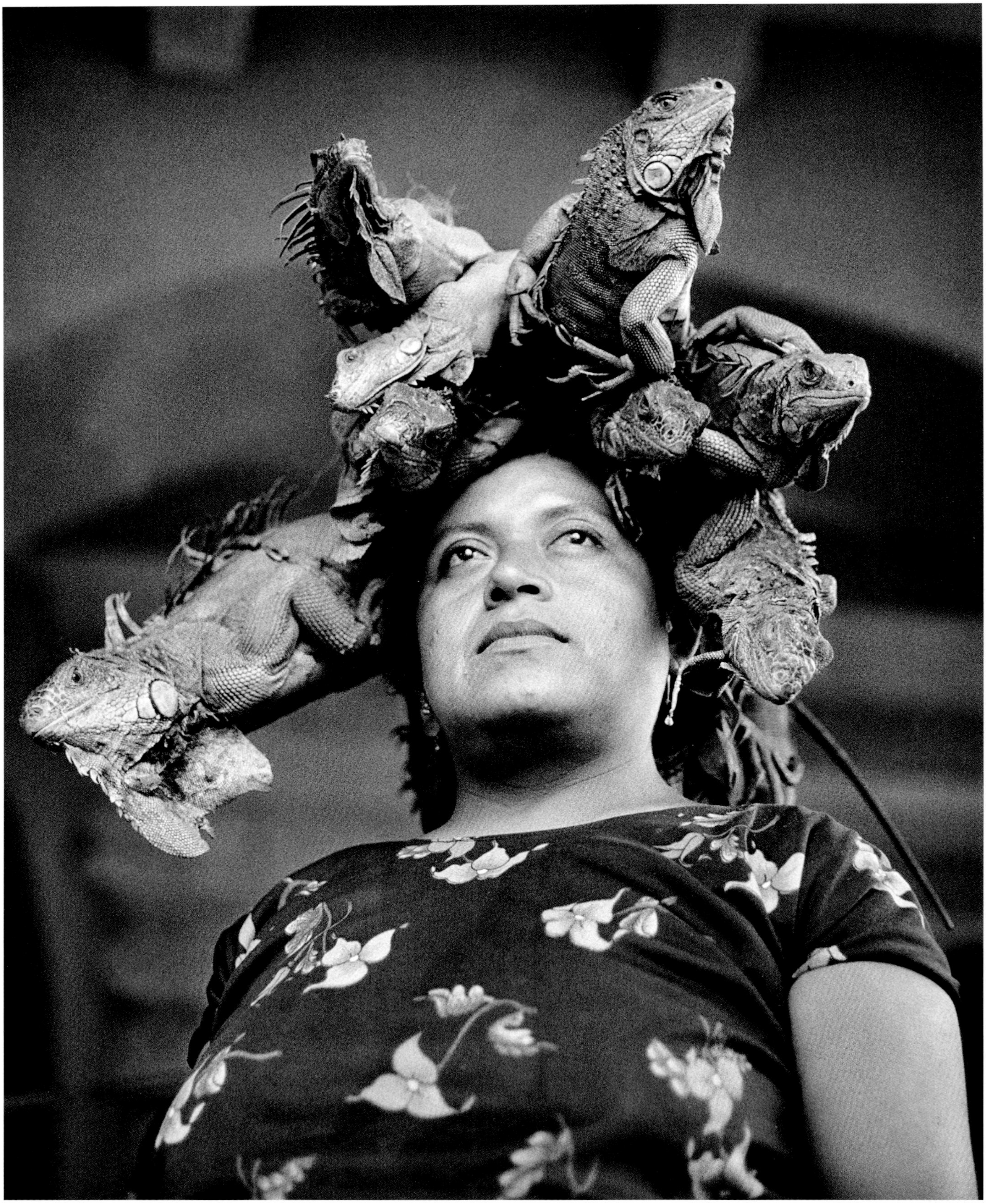

GRACIELA ITURBIDE

1942, Mexico

Graciela Iturbide began studying cinema at the age of 27, when she already had three children and was in the throes of a divorce, thus breaking with her conservative upbringing. She turned to photography when she met Manuel Álvarez Bravo, who encouraged her on this path. She became his assistant and travelled all over the country with him. Deeply affected by the loss of her daughter, who died at the age of six in 1970, she documented child funerals in the cemeteries of Mexico, where the graves were decorated with paper cutouts and flowers, and photographed the Day of the Dead ritual.

In 1978, she received a commission from the National Ethnographic Archive to document indigenous groups, such as the nomadic Seri in the Sonora desert in the north-west of Mexico. The following year, she began a decade-long study of the Juchitán people in the south of the country. Embedded in their community, she tried to avoid the pitfalls of exoticism as peddled in touristic clichés. She published *Juchitán de las mujeres* [Juchitán of the Women] in 1989, highlighting the central political role played by women in this community. Her high-contrast black-and-white photographs showed the intermingling of traditional rituals and modernity, illustrating the salience of pre-Hispanic cultural ideas. Her portrait of a woman with her head crowned by reptiles, captured one market day, shows the irruption of strangeness and magic into everyday life. Avoiding downbeat condescension, she defended indigenous and popular cultures by unveiling their mystery and poetry.

Various commissions took her to Cuba, Germany, India, Madagascar, Hungary, France and the USA. In 2019, she published a book containing her photographs of birds, a recurring motif in her work. From poultry in shops to skies filled with enigmatic clouds, these sometimes lyrical sometimes prosaic photographs interrogated our relationship with the living world.

'Nuestra Señora de las Iguanas, Juchitán, Oaxaca' [Our Lady of the Iguanas, Juchitán, Oaxaca],
1979,
gelatin silver print,
Santa Monica, ROSEGALLERY

PAZ ERRÁZURIZ

1944, Chile

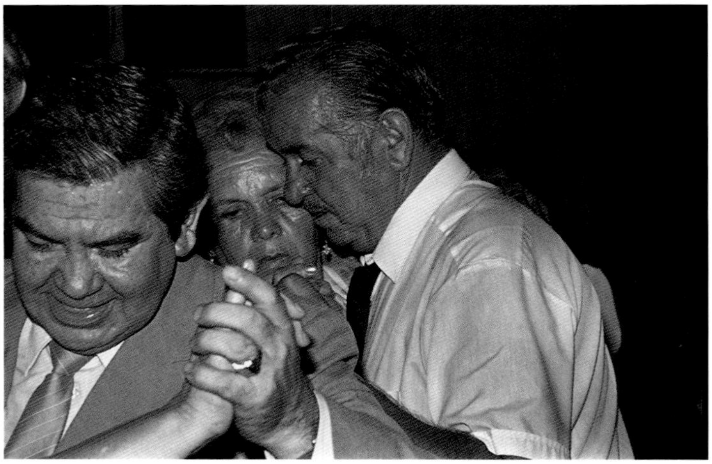

Paz Errázuriz taught herself photography while working as a teacher. Her first publication, however, was a children's book conceived with her students and her two children. Sacked because of her union membership in the wake of General Pinochet's coup in 1973, she saw her house requisitioned. She devoted herself to photography full time and set up a darkroom in her bathroom, her only way to guarantee the security of her work. In 1981, she participated in the creation of the Association of Independent Photographers (AFI), which aimed to protect reporters from political repression and to distribute their images. She followed the *mujeres por la vida* [women for life], who assembled to defend the rights of women and to denounce the disappearance of their loved ones, abducted by the military dictatorship.

Her work explores the margins of society, exposing situations of exclusion or stigmatisation to do with poverty – she photographed destitute people sleeping on the streets – or with health or disability, through her work on mental illness and old people. She was also interested in the spectacle of bodies in performance, in the circus or sport, with her series on boxers and wrestlers. Her iconic book *Adam's Apple*, published after the end of the dictatorship in 1990, paid homage to the courage of transvestites living off prostitution, decimated by AIDS and poverty. In the face of the violence of the authoritarian regime, she offered an engaged portrait of people defying norms to denounce social injustice.

Her late 1980s series *Tango* focused on elderly couples visiting dance clubs. The tight framings accentuated their concentrated or laughing expressions, absorbed in the music, and showed the sensitivity and empathy of Paz Errázuriz's approach.

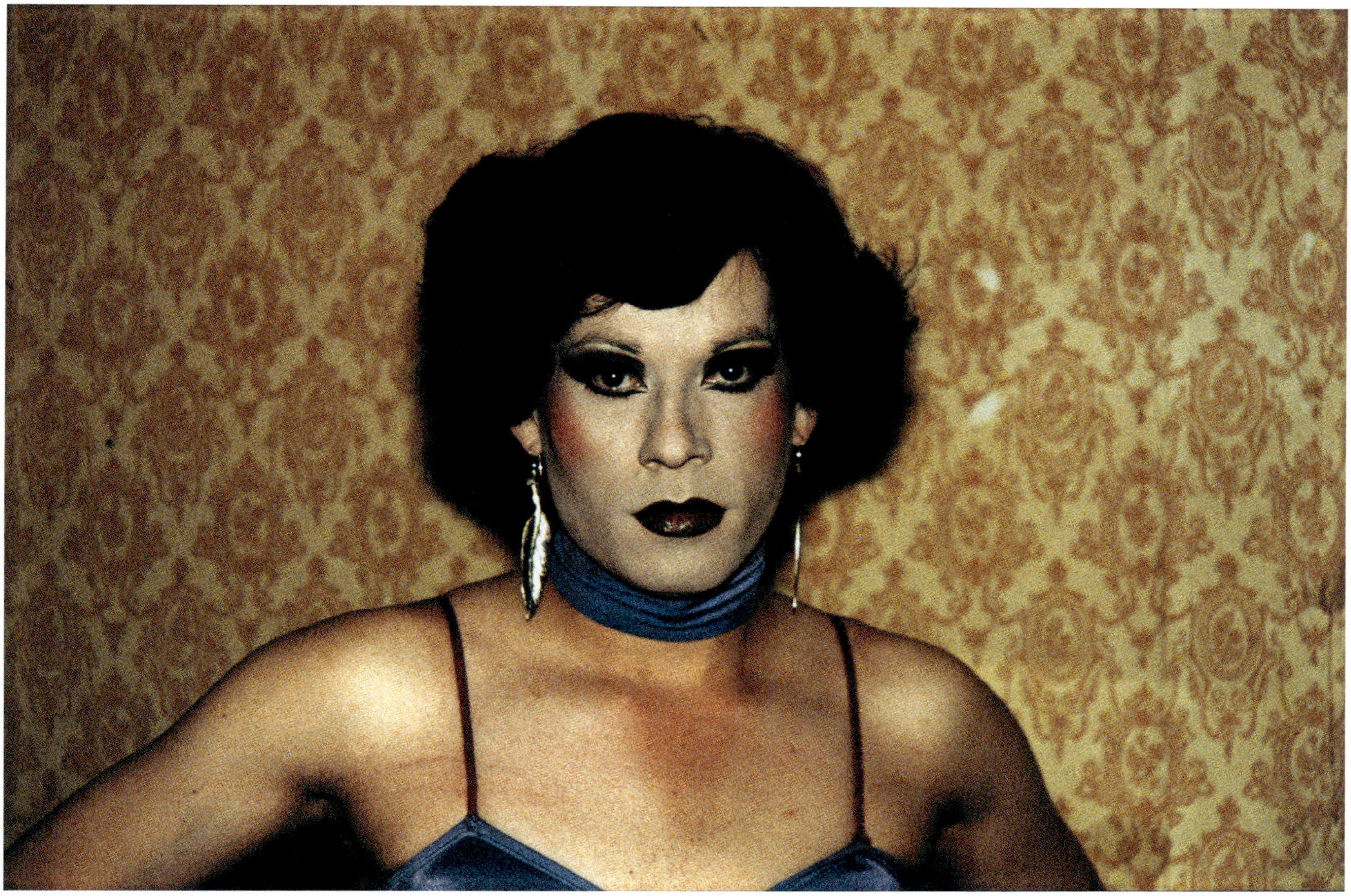

↖ 'Tango',
1988,
gelatin silver print,
artist's collection

↑ 'Evelyn, La Palmera, Santiago',
Adam's Apple series,
1982–86
digital colour print,
artist's collection

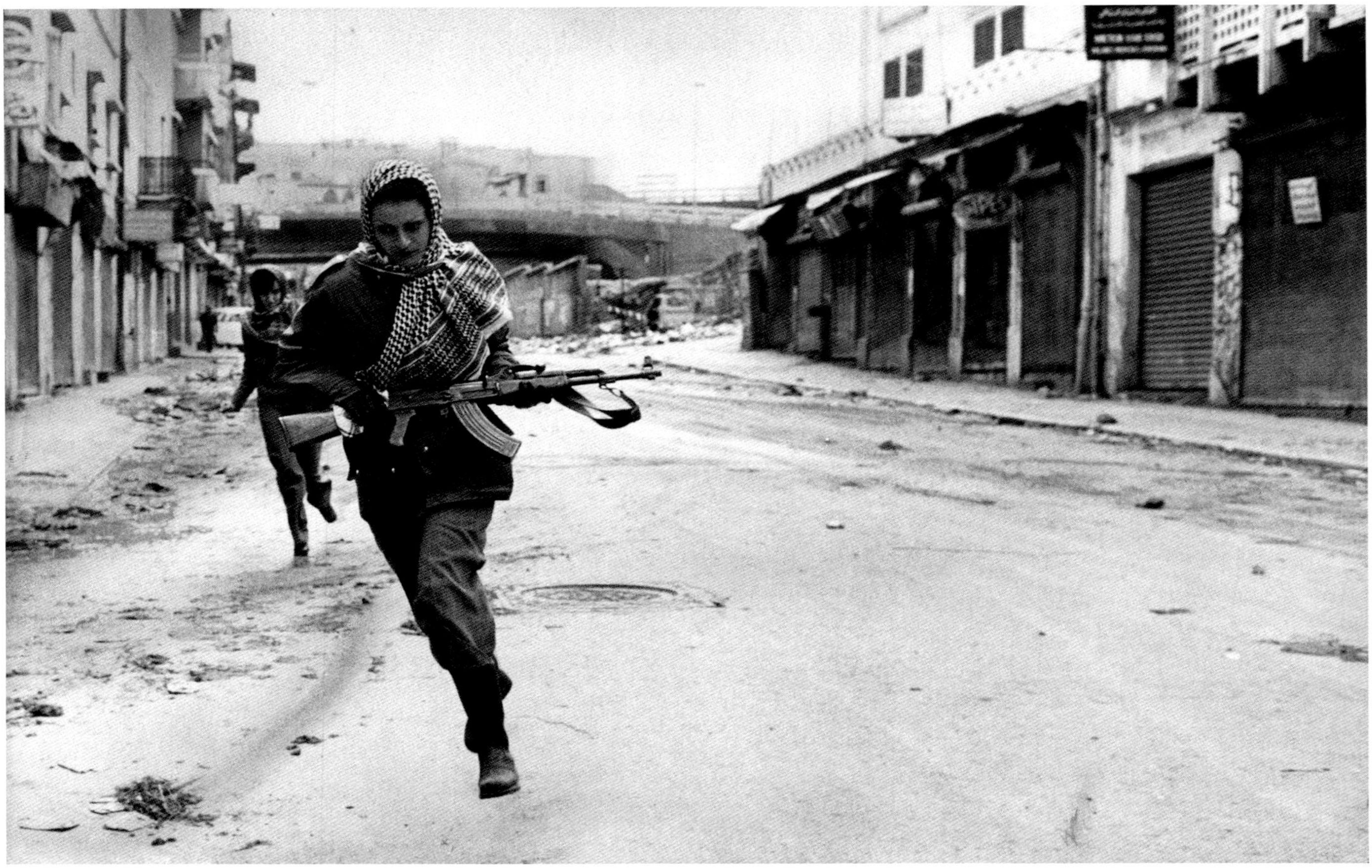

↑ 'Une combattante palestinienne pendant la guerre civile, Beyrouth, Liban' [A Palestinian Fighter During the Civil War, Beirut, Lebanon], 1976, Catherine Leroy Endowment

→ 'Des civils fuient Saigon à l'arrivée des forces nord-vietnamiennes, quelques jour savant la fin de la guerre du Viêtnam' [Civilians Flee Saigon at the Arrival of the North Vietnamese Forces, a Few Days Before the End of the Vietnam War], 20 April 1975, Catherine Leroy Endowment

CATHERINE LEROY

1944, France–2006, USA

In 1966, at the age of 21, Catherine Leroy went off to cover the war in Vietnam. Self-taught, she managed to carve out a place in a milieu dominated by men and made a parachute jump with American troops on the airborne operation 'Junction City' in 1967. She was seriously wounded while following a Marine unit. In 1968, she documented the month-long Têt offensive launched by the North Vietnamese. She was briefly imprisoned, and her account made the cover of *Life* magazine on 16 February. Her colour images revealing the losses suffered by the American forces, published by *Look* magazine in May, coincided with the shift in press and public opinion against the war in the wake of the pacifist movement of veterans. The anti-war activism culminated in 1969 at Woodstock, where she photographed the singers Joan Baez and Janis Joplin. In 1972, she co-produced the documentary *Operation Last Patrol*, following the journey of a veterans' association to Miami to protest against the deadlock in the conflict at the Republican Party convention.

She returned to Vietnam to document the fall of Saigon and the end of the war in 1975. She moved to Beirut and the following year she received the Robert Capa gold medal, which rewards the courage of reporters, for her work on the civil war. Her reportages, distributed by the Gamma and later Sipa agencies, took her to Somalia, Libya, Kenya, Gabon, Afghanistan, Pakistan, Japan, China, Egypt, Iraq, Iran, Jordan, Gaza and Ireland. In 2002, she created a website dedicated to correspondents of the Vietnam war, which led to the publication of an anthology in 2005. The creator of shocking images, Catherine Leroy is a highly regarded figure in the very male genre of war photography.

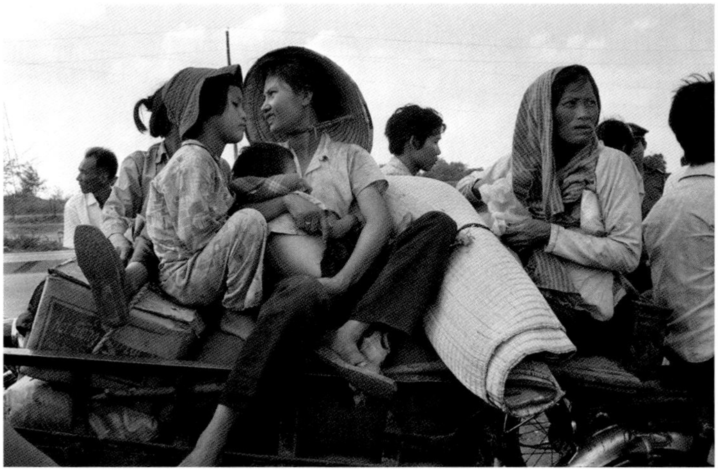

CHRISTINE SPENGLER

1945, France

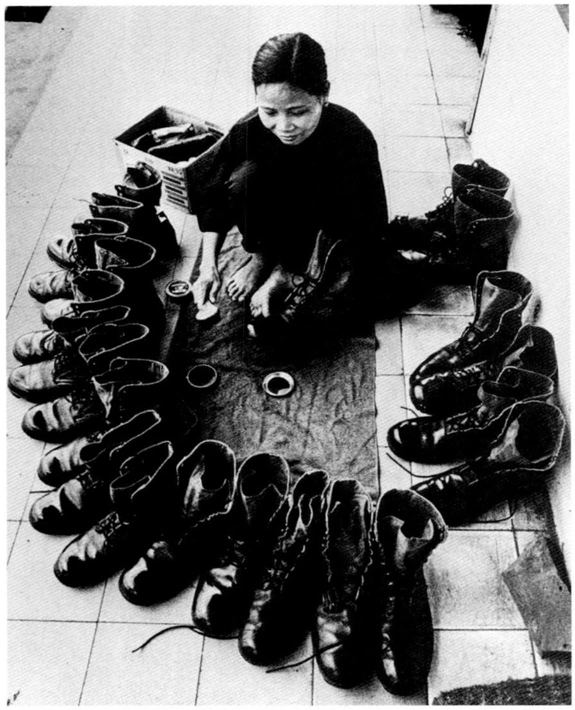

Christine Spengler studied French and Spanish literature and wanted to become a writer. She turned to photography on a trip to Chad in 1970, where she took portraits of Toubou fighters. Her images of Northern Ireland published in the foreign press marked the beginning of her international recognition. The following year she went to Vietnam, where she sold her photographs to the Associated Press agency. In Cambodia she captured the bombing of Phnom Penh by the Khmer Rouge. In 1976, she worked with the Sygma agency and covered the Polisario Front in the Western Sahara for *Time* magazine. Her reportages took her to Iran in 1979, then to El Salvador and Nicaragua in 1981. She covered the Libyan civil war in 1982.

Alongside this work, she created dreamlike or theatrical settings, clashing visuals evoking the saturated colours of the Spanish Movida and the heritage of her mother, the surrealist artist Huguette Spengler. Deeply affected by her brother's suicide, in the 1980s she created little funeral altars in memory of the deceased members of her family, adorned with pearls and coloured cloths. In 1985, at the Rencontres d'Arles, she showed a projection combining her war reportages and her photomontages. Other compositions figure portraits or details, such as a hand, an eye or a mouth, isolated and surrounded by jewels, shells and flowers.

She continued with her reportages and worked in Afghanistan in 1997, Kosovo in 2000 and Iraq in 2003. Rather than restricting herself to soldiers, she turned her attention to the fate of female combatants, children and civilians to show different facets of the conflicts. Her autobiography, *Une femme dans la guerre* [A Woman at War], published in 2006, recounted her engagement with communities scarred by grief and violence.

↑ 'Le Départ des Américains, Viêtnam' [The Departure of the Americans, Vietnam], 1973, artist's collection

→ 'Londonderry, funérailles de l'IRA, Irlande du Nord' [Londonderry, IRA funeral, Northern Ireland], 1970, artist's collection

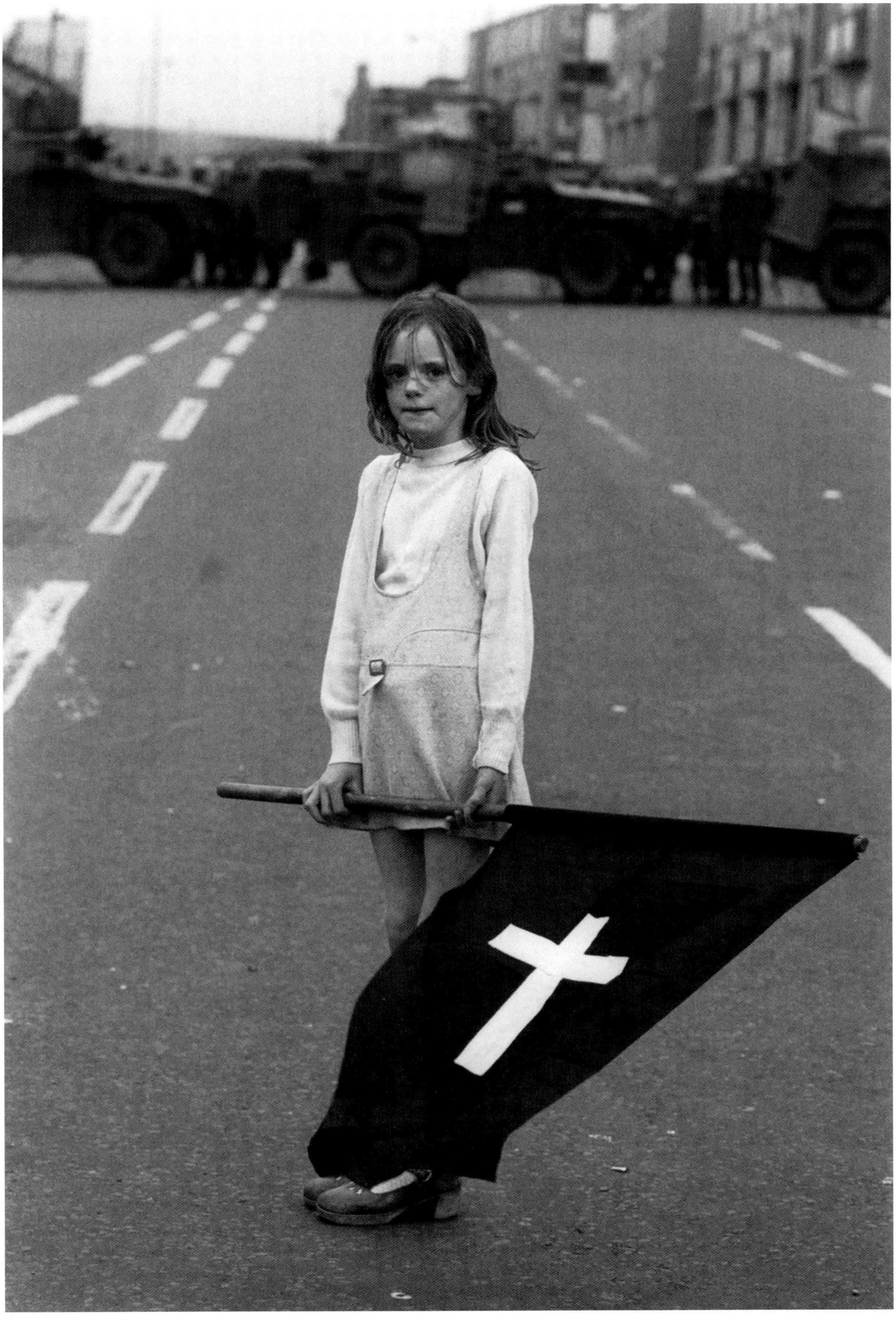

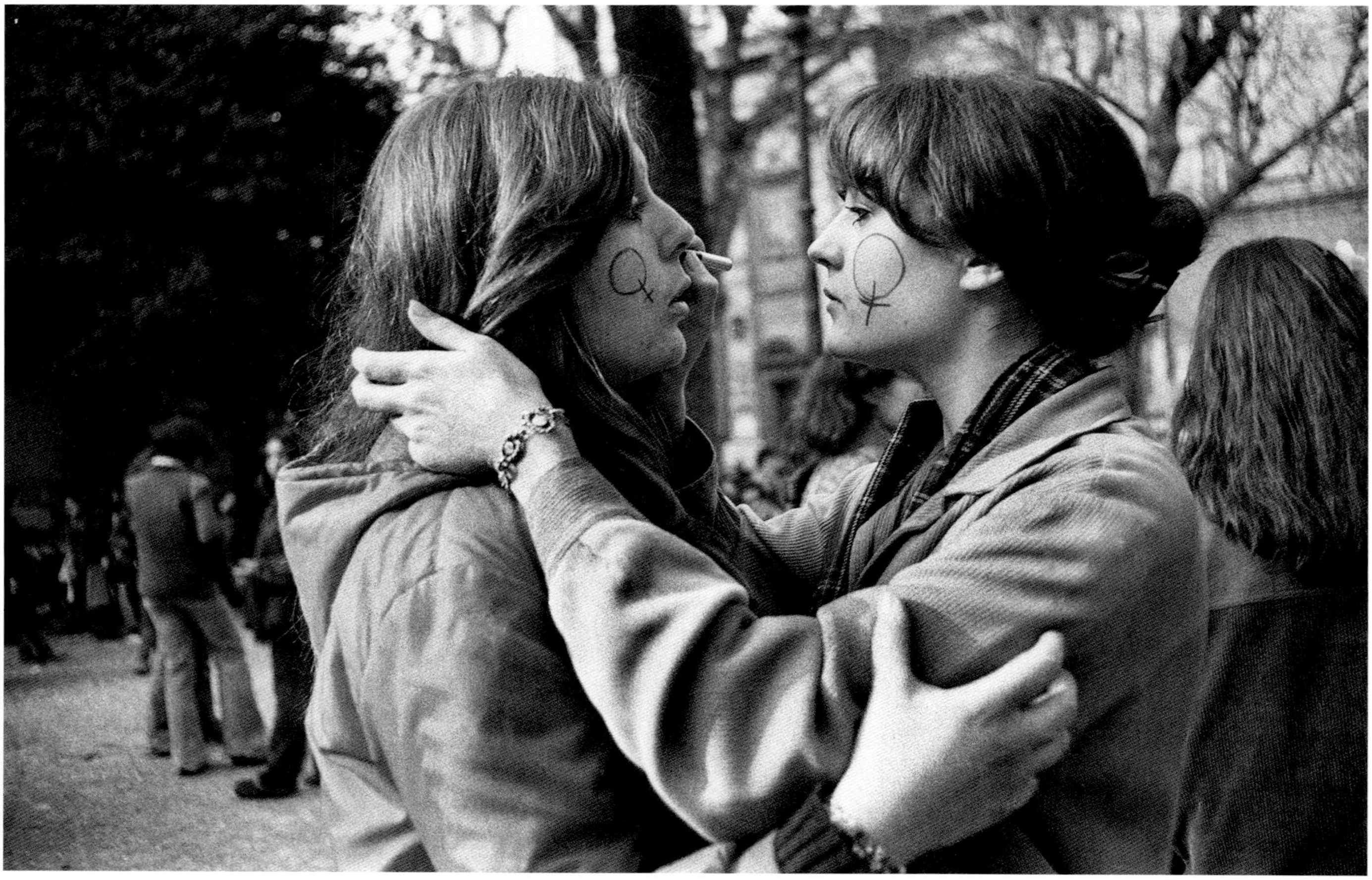

↑ 'Roma' [Rome],
8 March 1977,
artist's collection

→ 'None (Torino), Stabilimenti Indesit'
[None (Turin), Indesit Factory],
1983,
artist's collection

PAOLA AGOSTI

1947, Italy

Paola Agosti began her career as an independent photographer in 1969. She made reportages in Europe, South America, the USA and Africa, as well as portraits of figures from the political or cultural worlds. With her inside view of feminist activism, in 1976 she published *Riprendiamoci la vita* [Let's Take Back Our Lives], a masterful study of mobilisation in its various forms. She adopted a different way of looking when she was photographing women. Rather than taking a superior view, she worked 'with', by immersion, relying on empathy and connection. 10 years later, she published *La donna e la macchina* [Woman and Machine], a book on female workers in industries from car factories to cotton mills. Her images question whether liberation is compatible with capitalist production. She took an interest in products specifically aimed at women, such as washing machines purported to alleviate domestic chores in order to increase women's productivity, or typewriters, the indispensable tool for secretaries.

In 1977, she undertook a large study of the peasant communities of Piedmont, inspired by a book by the writer Nuto Revelli, *Il mondo dei vinti* [The World of the Vanquished]. She assembled a 'visible record' of the cultural heritage and the dignity of these 'forever forgotten' people left on the sidelines by economic progress. Extending this project, she crossed the Atlantic to Argentina, where there was a community descended from immigrants from Piedmont who had arrived around the end of the 19th century, settling in Buenos Aires and in rural regions.

The author of around 15 books, Paola Agosti chronicled the transformations of Italy in the second half of the 20th century, marginalised rural communities in the diaspora as well as artists and activists in the women's movement.

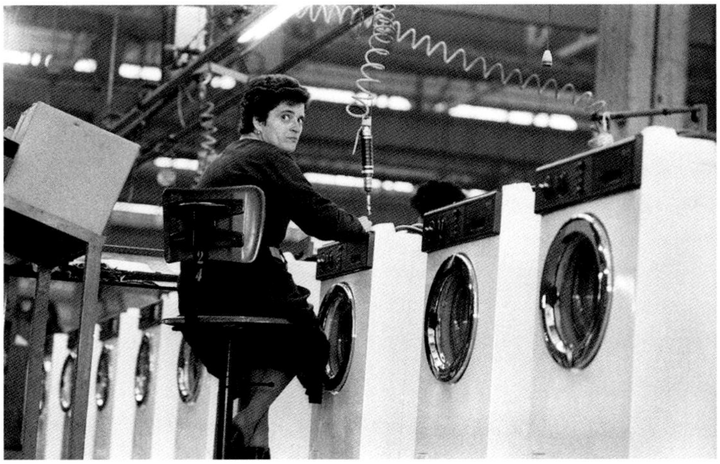

ISHIUCHI MIYAKO

1947, Japan

Chosen to represent Japan at the 2005 Venice Biennial, Isiuchi Miyako's work is intimate and poetic, marked by a nostalgic meditation on the passage of time. Her first series were characterised by high-contrast, grainy, black-and-white prints representing the weight of years gone by. The first, in 1976, was on her hometown of Yokosuka, which was adjacent to an American naval base. She grew up there in a small lodging house with a beaten earth floor, sharing a communal bathroom with the other inhabitants of the building, which had been erected after the war. Her book *Apartment*, published in 1978, explored the cramped spaces of these dilapidated, overcrowded blocks. She created a fictional building pieced together from multiple different locations; her work crystallised the collective experience of a country struggling to reconstruct itself and contain the aspirations of the generation born after the conflict. In a similar vein, *White Night*, in 1981, evoked the rooms of former night clubs.

In 1988, on the occasion of her 40th birthday, she began her series *1-9-4-7*, photographing the hands and feet of women born the same year as her. The soles of the feet, normally invisible, were displayed in all their glory, crisscrossed with wrinkles, an anonymous testimony to the ageing of the body. After the death of her mother, between 2000 and 2005, she began compiling a colour repertoire of the objects she owned, creating a portrait in absentia using shoes or gloves that still bore the imprint of the deceased. In 2007, she began the series ひろしま*/hiroshima*, an inventory of objects that had survived the atom bomb and were preserved in the Peace Memorial Museum, in particular women's clothing that had been in contact with their irradiated skin. The title, written in Hiragana characters, used a system of writing that had long been employed by Japanese women. Displayed against luminous backgrounds, they formed a physical testimony of the atomic annihilation.

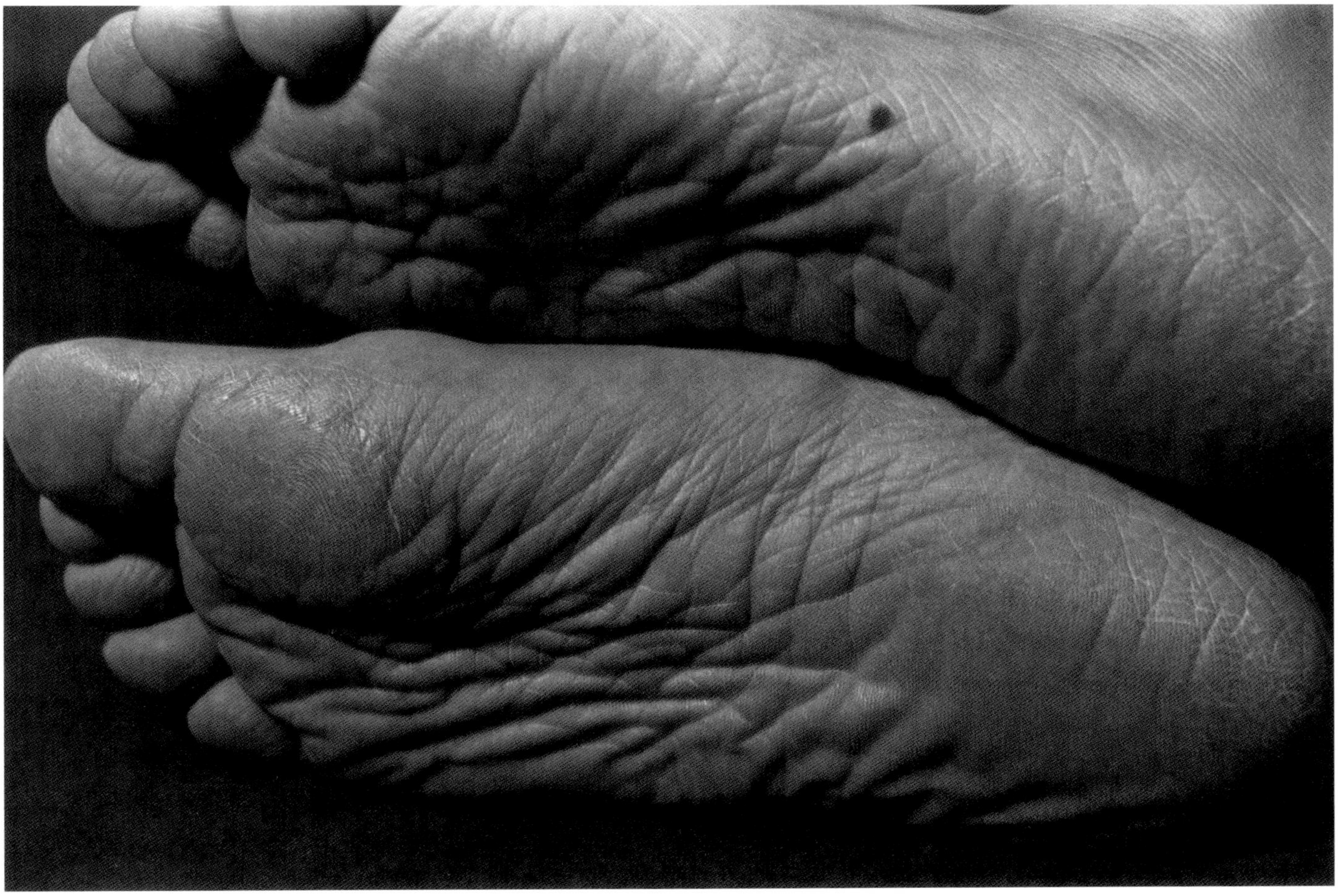

‘1. 9. 4. 7 #49’,
1988–89,
Osaka, The Third Gallery Aya

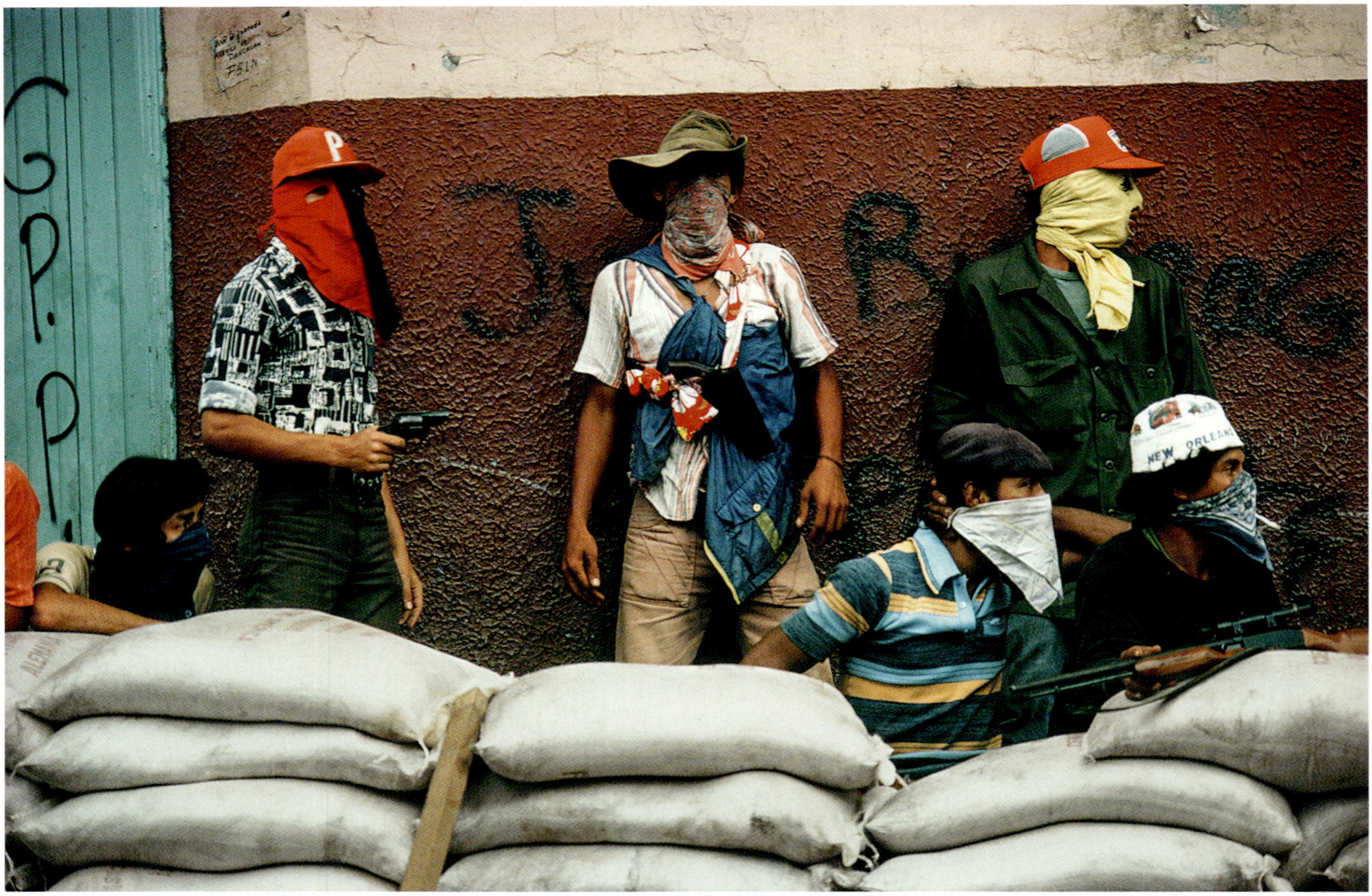

↑ 'Muchachos Await the Counterattack by the National Guard, Matagalpa, Nicaragua',
1978,
colour print (2019),
Magnum Photos Archive

↗ 'Little Italy, Dee and Lisa on Mott Street, New York',
1976,
gelatin silver print (2018),
Magnum Photos Archive

SUSAN MEISELAS

1948, USA

Susan Meiselas trained in visual education at Harvard and first used photography for educational purposes, setting up studios in schools or local communities. She made her mark in 1976 with the publication of *Carnival Strippers*, a study of travelling striptease shows in the north-east of the USA. Rather than rehash the glamorous or depressing clichés surrounding this profession, she chose to let the women she met speak for themselves through long testimonies.

A member of the Magnum Photos agency, she produced some of the best-known images of the Sandinista revolution in Nicaragua in 1978–79. Throughout the 1980s, she conducted reportages, co-produced films and supported photographers, principally in Central and South America. She never limited herself to the role of a simple reporter and from 1991 undertook a huge project collecting documentary material on the visual memory of the Kurdish people and their diaspora, displayed in the form of a travelling exhibition, an interactive website and a book. A pioneer of collaborative practice, she used the image as a tool of dialogue and sharing.

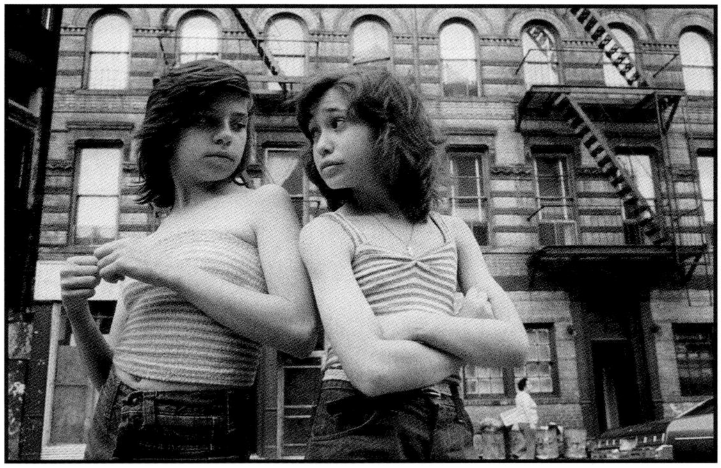

Women's words have been at the heart of her work from the 1970s, when she documented the coming of age of girls in Prince Street, the street below her home in New York, to 2016, when she organised writing and collage workshops in a home for female victims of violence in the UK. She thus offered women the opportunity to take possession of their images and express themselves in their own way, to organise their living space as well as their story. The title of the project, A Room of Her Own, cites the famous essay by Virginia Woolf, which talked of the difficulty women face in finding a place to create in the absence of a dedicated room and mental space, time and recognition. Photography provided one such possible place to express and transmit these occluded stories.

SOPHIE RISTELHUEBER

1949, France

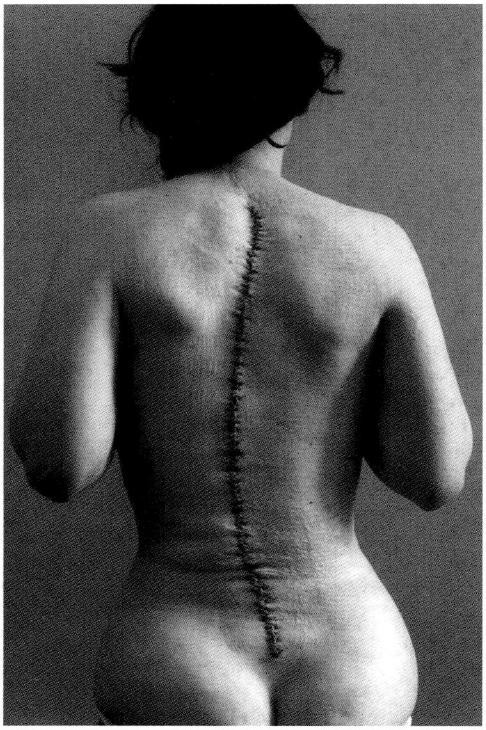

Rather than the shock of the new, Sophie Ristelhueber was fascinated by the aftermaths of events, the traces left in their wake. From her early years in 1980s Beirut, she chose to photograph gutted buildings, the abandoned and lifeless remains, rather than live combat. This 'day after' photography anatomised the surgery that the war performed on urban or natural landscapes. She followed the same process in 1992 after the Gulf War, showing the marks of conflict in the Kuwaiti desert, combining aerial views and close-ups in a disconcerting jumble of different scales. In Iraq in 2001, she captured a landscape bristling with the charred tree trunks of a palm grove decimated by fire. On the West Bank, she showed roads blocked by rocks and debris, the violence inflicted on the land echoing that experienced by its inhabitants.

These contemplative images of destruction revealed the traces left in the long-term collective memory. In 1994, this reflection was embodied, literally, in an intimate work showing in close-up the scars left by suture marks on the skin of patients in a Parisian hospital.

Though she started out working in the press and publishing and co-produced a film on the psychiatric asylum of San Clemente with Raymond Depardon, she later went against the flow of media images, which she sometimes used as her material. In 2006, she composed montages representing bomb craters using videos of car bombings in Iraq and her own images. The crevasses in the 2019 series *Sunset Years* are no longer ones deliberately inflicted by men but the result of a wider destruction of our planet, from the cracks in the dried-out shores of the Dead Sea to the tarmac on Parisian roads blistering in the heat.

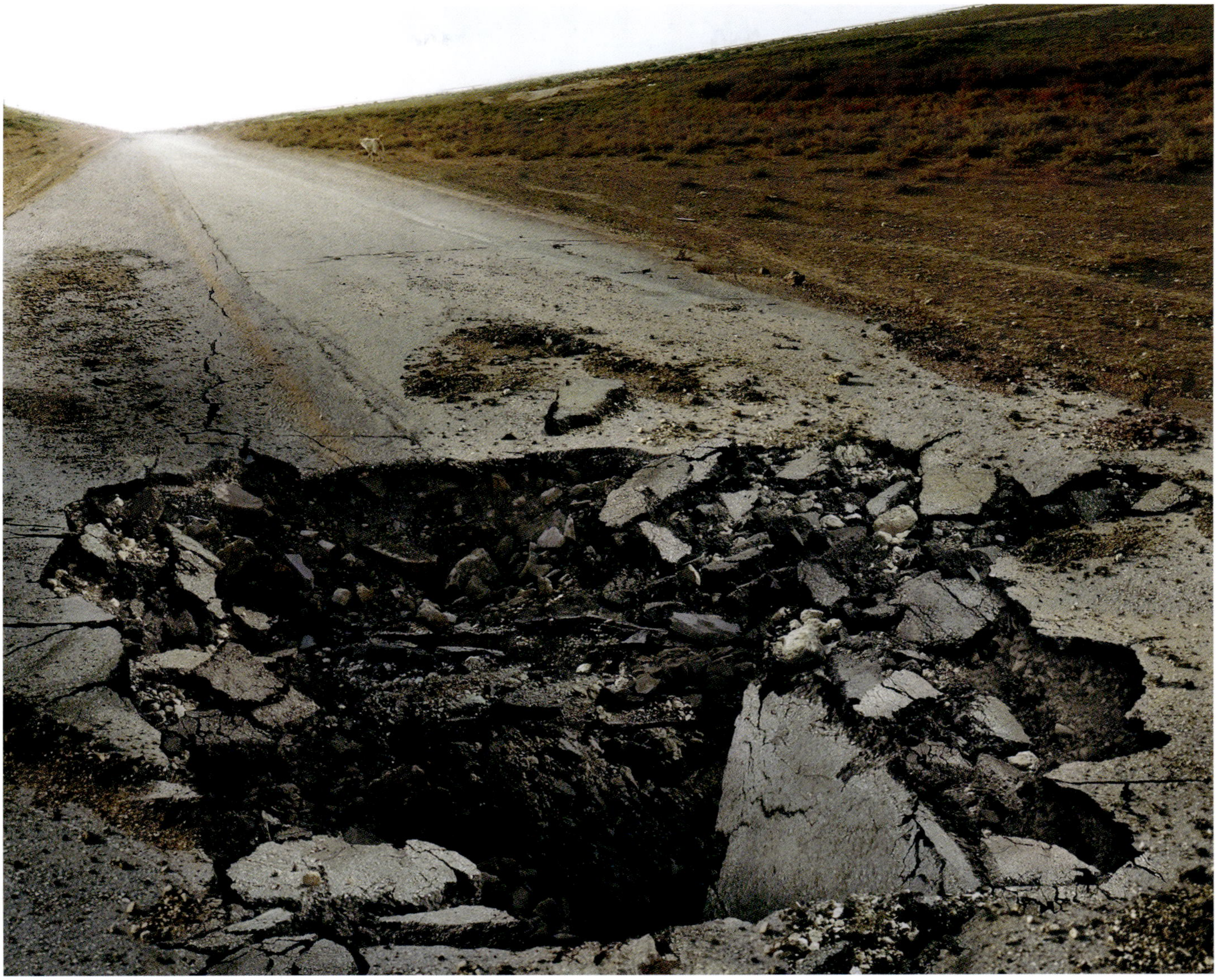

↖ 'Every One #14',
1994,
gelatin silver print,
London, Victoria & Albert Museum

↑ 'Eleven Blowups #1',
2006
colour photograph, silver print,
artist's collection

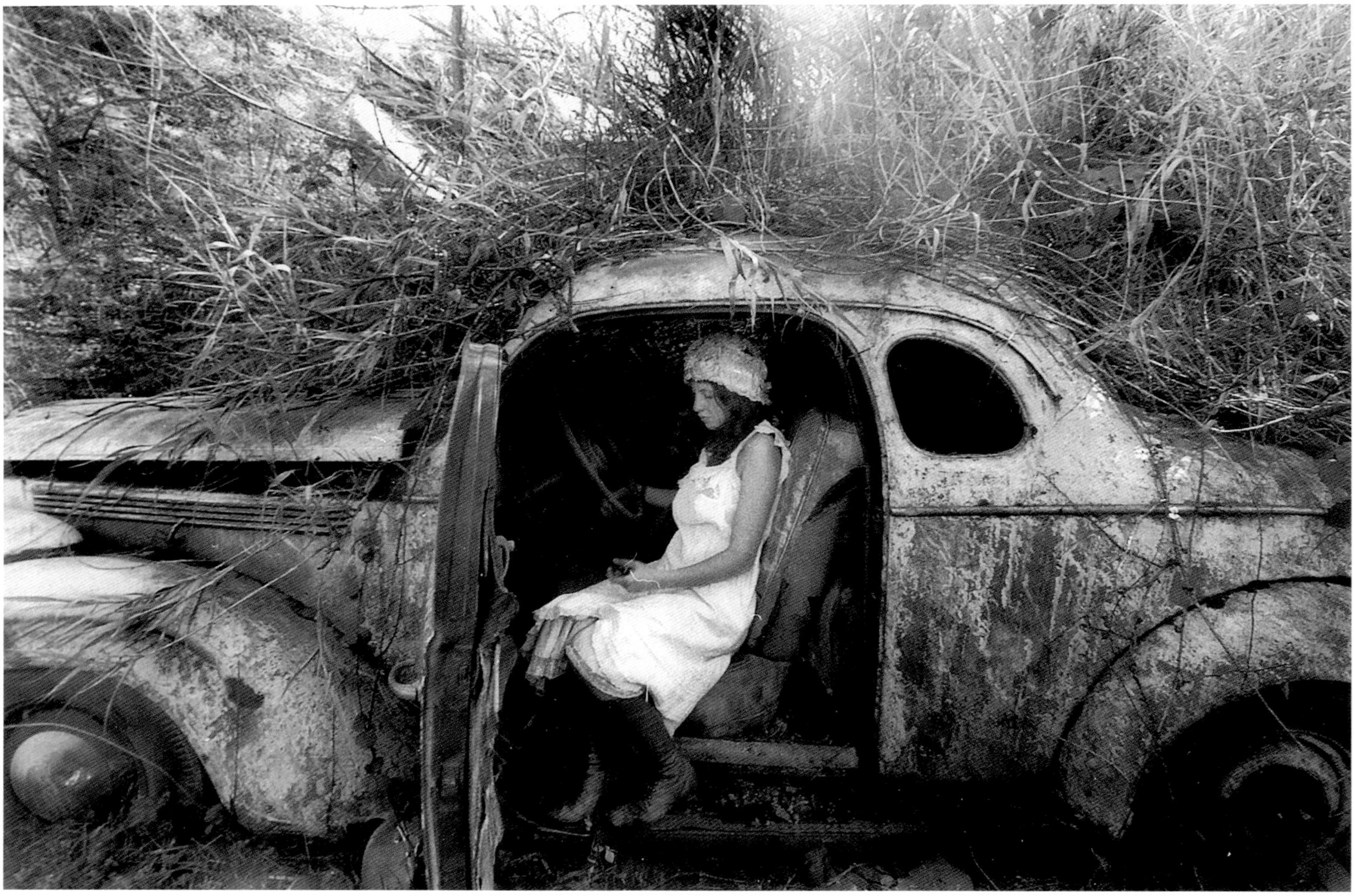

↑ 'Elizabeth, California, Spring', 1970, in *Les Femmes, les sœurs* [Women, Sisters], gelatin silver print, Paris, La Galerie Rouge

↗ 'Erica Lennard, *Paris, Winter, les* Sœurs', 1974, in *Les Femmes, les sœurs* [Women, Sisters], gelatin silver print, Paris, La Galerie Rouge

ERICA LENNARD

1950, USA

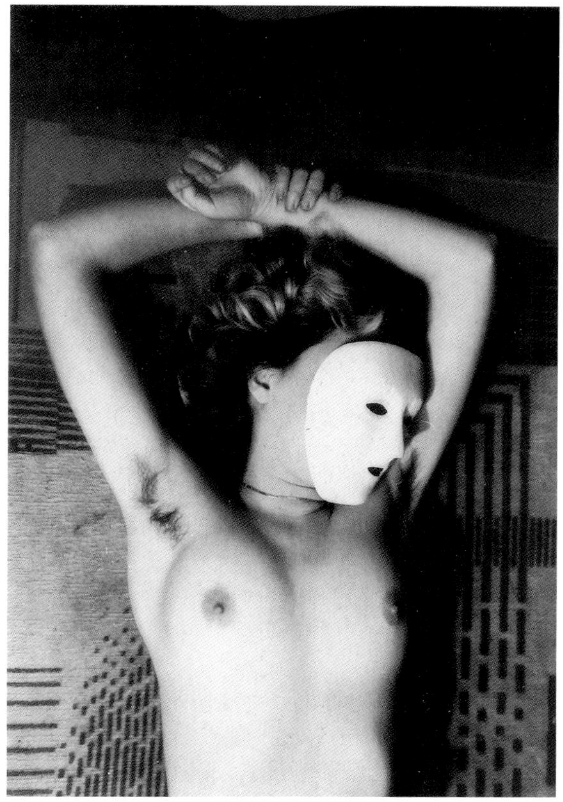

Erica Lennard grew up in Berkeley, California, amidst the ferment of student protests and the hippy movement. As an art student at the San Francisco Institute she met Ralph Gibson, who became her mentor, and she published her first book, *Sunday*, a children's story, through the latter's Lustrum Press. In 1973, she moved to Paris with her sister Elizabeth. In 1976, she exhibited at the Agathe Gaillard gallery and in conjunction with Les Éditions des Femmes published *Les Femmes, les sœurs* [Women, Sisters], which imagined a correspondence between a poem written by her sister and portraits of her and their female friends. In the book's afterword, the writer Marguerite Duras referred to 'a vertiginous harmony in its very disparateness'. This reflective, dreamlike ode places Erica Lennard's work under the sign of friendship and sisterhood. She wrote: 'I go with you and alone in the happy light of accomplished hours; without being the same as me, you are my reflection in these images. Elizabeth and I are sisters. We are all sisters.' The empathy linking her and her models gives her images an impression of spontaneity and tenderness and at the same time refreshes the genre of the female nude as a cross between deliberate crudity and theatrical staging.

She later turned her hand to garden photography. Her quirky gaze picked up the wildness bursting through the ordered symmetry of French-style parks or focused in close-up on botanical specimens. The author of 15 or so books on gardens and the houses of writers, she also worked in fashion and produced portraits of actresses such as Jeanne Moreau, Delphine Seyrig and Charlotte Rampling. The groundbreaking work of Erica Lennard offers a subtle and intimate vision of the tricky concept of sisterhood, nowadays reappropriated by a new generation of feminists.

DONNA GOTTSCHALK

1950, USA

The photographer and political activist Donna Gottschalk created a rare, and for a long time hidden, testimony of the relations between women and the lesbian communities in the USA from the 1970s onwards. She grew up in New York and started frequenting the places where gay people met and an alternative nightlife took place. A member of the Gay Liberation Front from the age of 17, she produced pamphlets and posters and photographed the protests and the activists. She studied at Cooper Union and joined a lesbian splinter group of the Gay Liberation Front, the Lavender Menace, named after the colour often associated with lesbianism. Their name also made reference to an expression of the writer Betty Friedman, the president of the National Organization of Women (NOW), who criticised the presence of lesbians in the feminist movement. In 1970, Donna photographed the Revolutionary Conference of Women organised in Limerick, Pennsylvania. Rather than show the events and the debates, she chose to make portraits of friends and lovers sharing a bed, inventing other ways of living together and creating political ties even in their sleep.

After moving to San Francisco in the mid 1970s, she documented the life of lesbian communities in Oregon. Her portraits of her own circle, taken over many years, offer intimate views of lesbian and trans people, particularly those who were working-class. The faces change over the course of time, like that of her younger sister, Myla, from her teenage years through her sex change to her death from AIDS at the age of 56. Donna Gottschalk uncompromisingly reveals the violence affecting stigmatised bodies but also the tenderness, mutual support and friendship uniting their normally invisible lives.

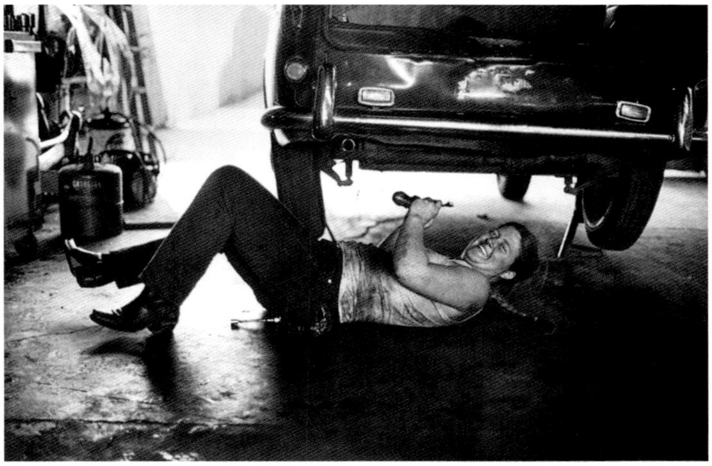

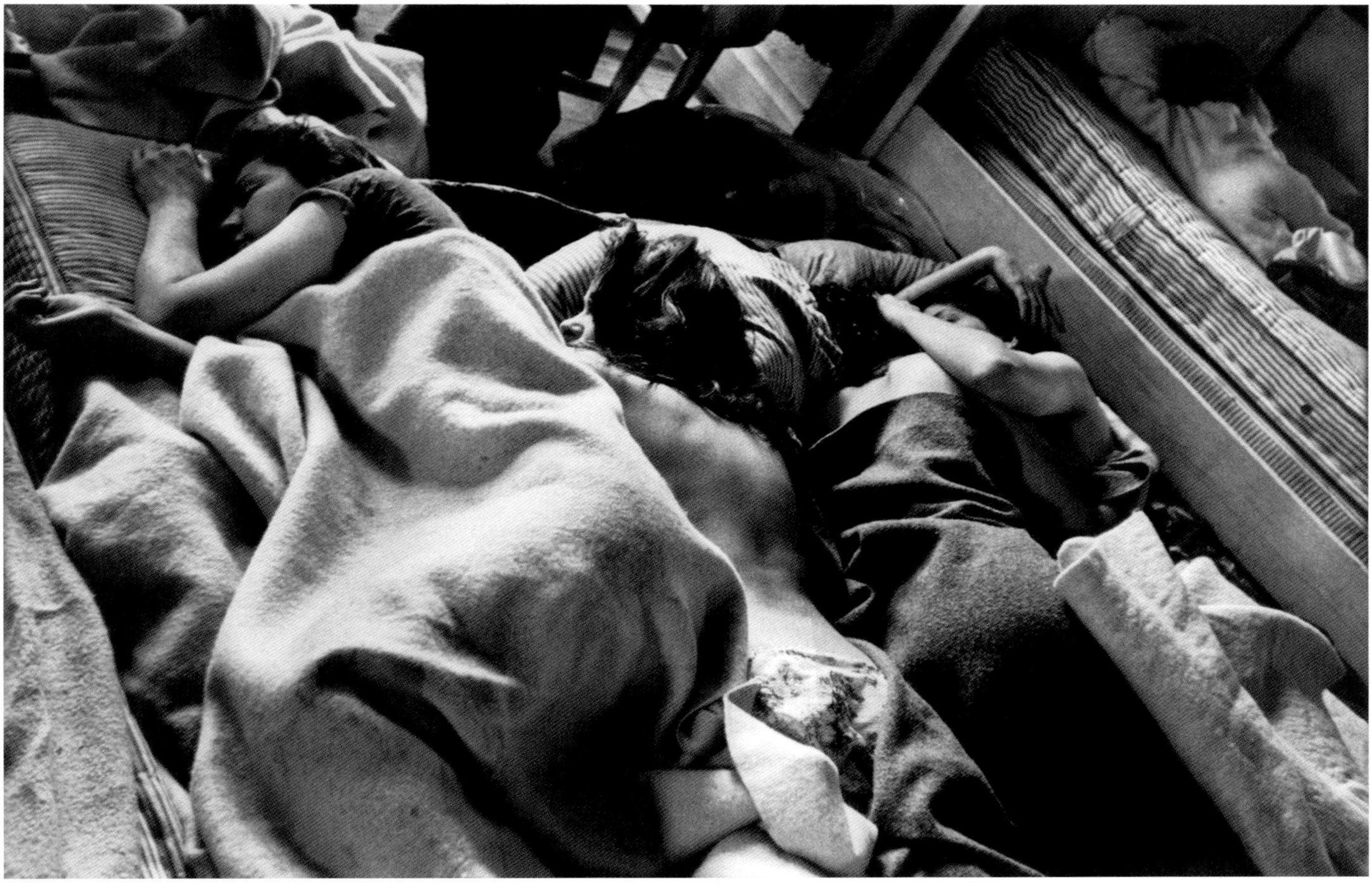

← Marlene Elling, Eugene, Oregon,
1974,
gelatin silver print,
Paris, Galerie Marcelle Alix

↑ 'Sleepers, Revolutionary Women
Conference, Limerick, Pennsylvania',
1970,
gelatin silver print,
Paris, Galerie Marcelle Alix

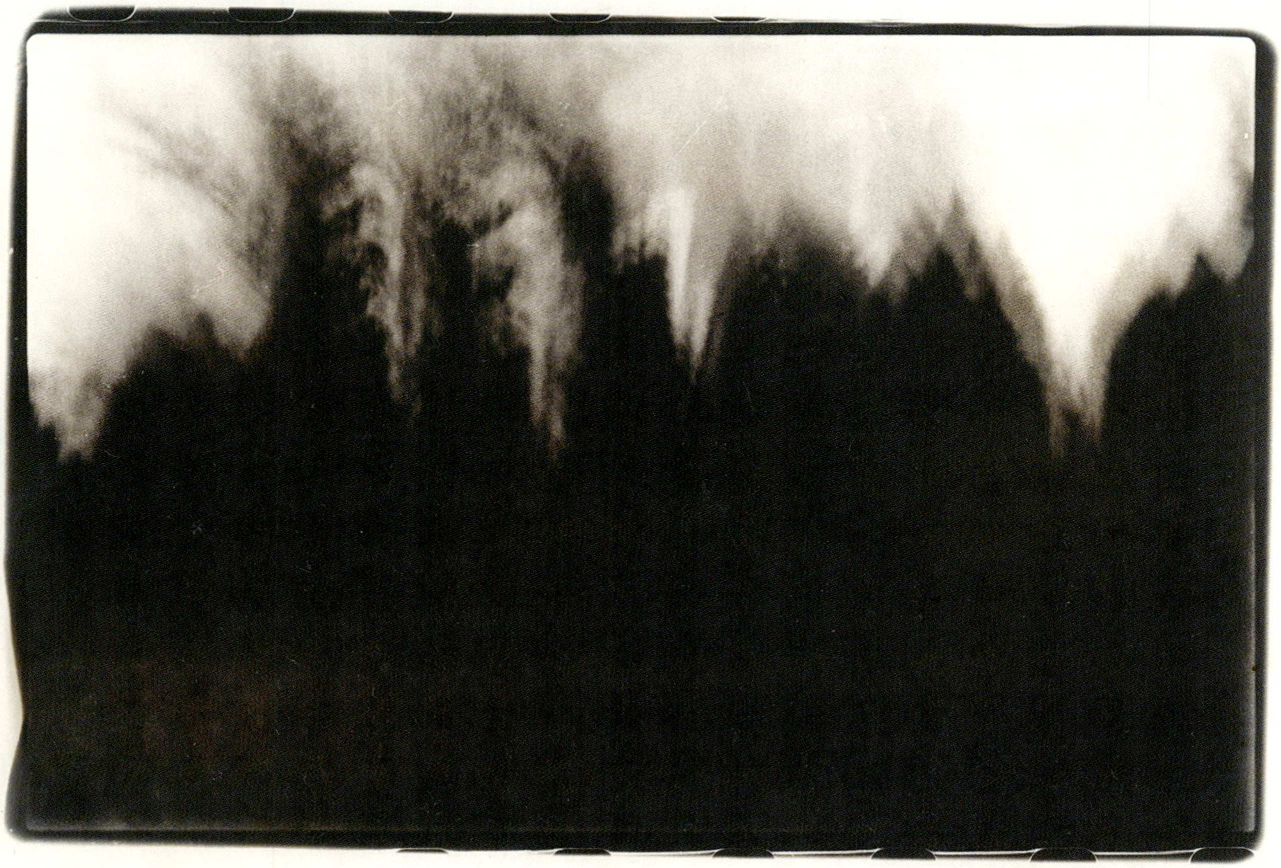

↑ 'Quinze minutes la nuit au rythme de la respiration' [Fifteen Minutes at Night to the Rhythm of Breath],
1980,
gelatin silver print,
Alix Cléo Roubaud collection

→ 'Correction de perspective dans ma chambre' [Correction of Perspective in My Bedroom],
1980–81,
gelatin silver print by superimposition,
Alix Cléo Roubaud collection

ALIX CLÉO ROUBAUD

1952, Mexico–1983, France

The dark silhouettes of the trees appear blurred, as if the wind were ruffling their foliage. But this scene is being agitated by neither wind nor rain: the landscape is breathing to the rhythm of the camera resting for 15 minutes on the chest of the recumbent photographer. The asthmatic Alix Cléo Roubaud transformed the darkened horizon into a mirror of her hidden breath. She used self-portraits to tell the story of the barriers in her everyday life, which was haunted by the death that took her prematurely in January 1983. Her *Journal*, published the following year by her husband, illustrates her aesthetic research, inspired by a study of the Austrian philosopher Ludwig Wittgenstein; her depression that led her to attempt suicide; and her photographic experiments. By manipulating the images as they developed, she interrogated the representation of her body, double exposing it or rendering it ghostly. Her emblematic series of 17 photographs *If Some Thing Black* announced her imminent death and inspired her husband, the poet and mathematician Jacques Roubaud, to publish a poetry collection, *Some Thing Black*, in a tombstone-shaped volume.

Rediscovered in the 2010s, her work was a mixture of conceptual, literary and philosophical research, self-portraits and darkroom work. She destroyed her negatives and kept only the prints, coming up with artisanal methods such as the 'luminous brush' to illuminate the paper directly in the laboratory. Her intimate, sometimes sensual, sometimes macabre work tested the limits of the photographic medium to try to distil its essential contours. The arrested temporality of the fixed image, this theoretical enigma that fascinates so many photographers, forms the matrix of a poetic and plastic meditation. The poems of Jacques Roubaud take up the fractured and arrested punctuation of the texts typed out by his wife and sketch the imprint as a negative, the interstices of an incomplete quest.

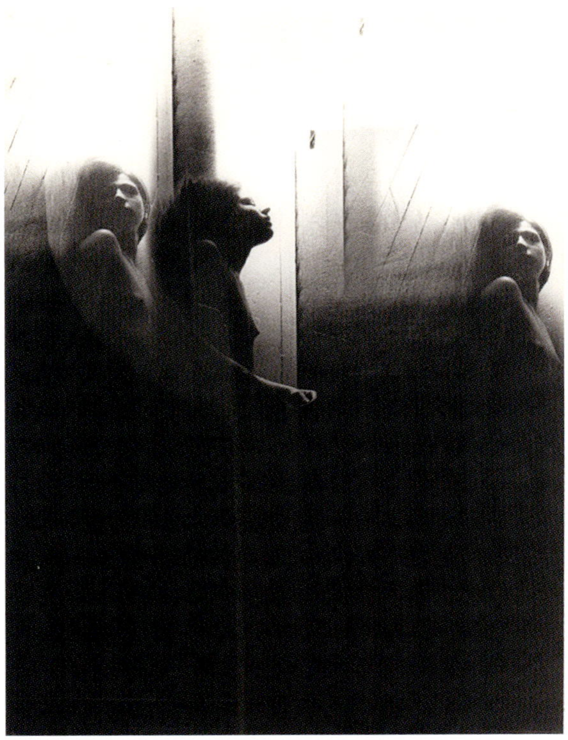

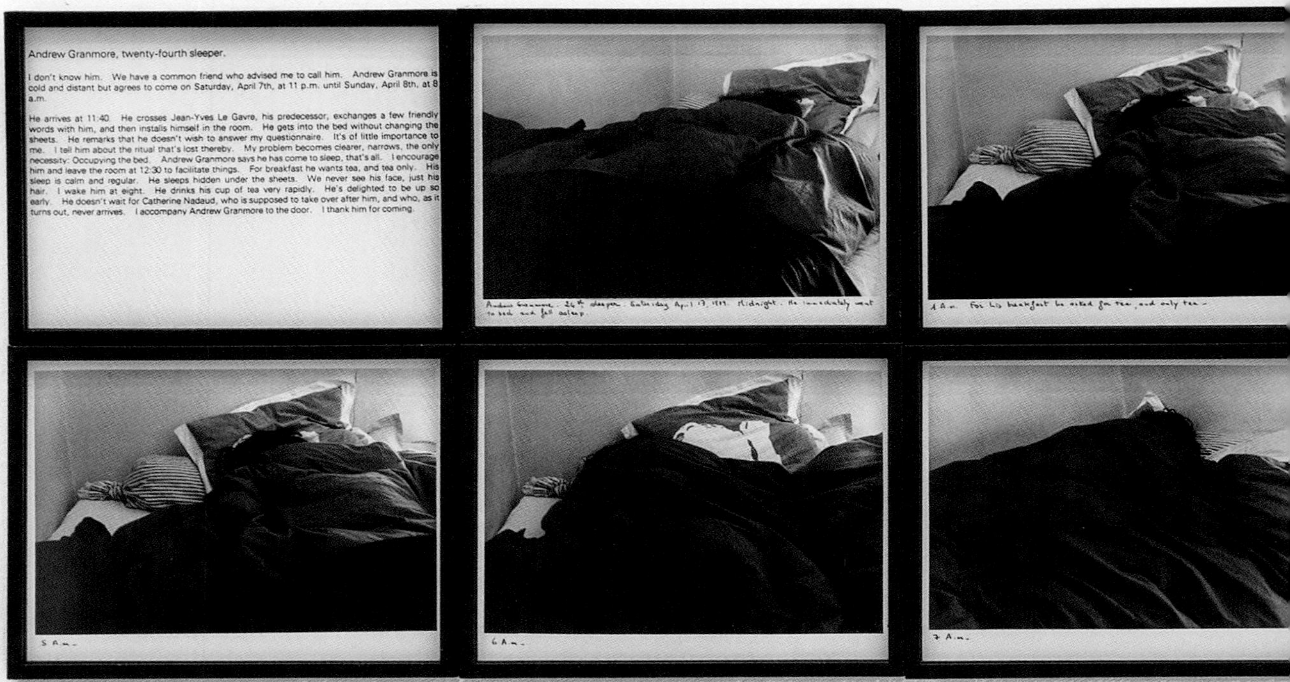

SOPHIE CALLE

1953, France

In 1979, Sophie Calle put her bed to radical use by inviting strangers to take turns sleeping in it, breaking down the barrier between public and private life. She documented her experiment in photographs and text. She then played with the conventions of photographic surveillance and the photo-novel by tailing a man to Venice, then asking her mother to hire a detective to follow her own movements. She took on a job as a chambermaid in a hotel and photographed the traces left by guests who had passed through. These vestiges formed the outlines of an absence, revealing the voyeuristic and partial character of photographic documentation. Her fascination with the limits of what can be captured, seen and listed inspired *Les Aveugles* [The Blind] and *La Couleur aveugle* [Blind Colour], collections of testimonies on sight loss.

Her own life provided material for her scenes and the creation of her intimate archive, as in the series *Rituel d'anniversaire* [Birthday Ritual], a documentation of the birthday presents given to her by friends and family between 1980 and 1993, or in *Régime chromatique* of 1997, in which she followed the same protocols as the heroine of a Paul Auster novel. In 2002, she installed her bed at the top level of the Eiffel Tower and asked visitors to tell her stories to prevent her from falling asleep.

In 2007, Sophie Calle represented France at the Venice Biennial. Her installation

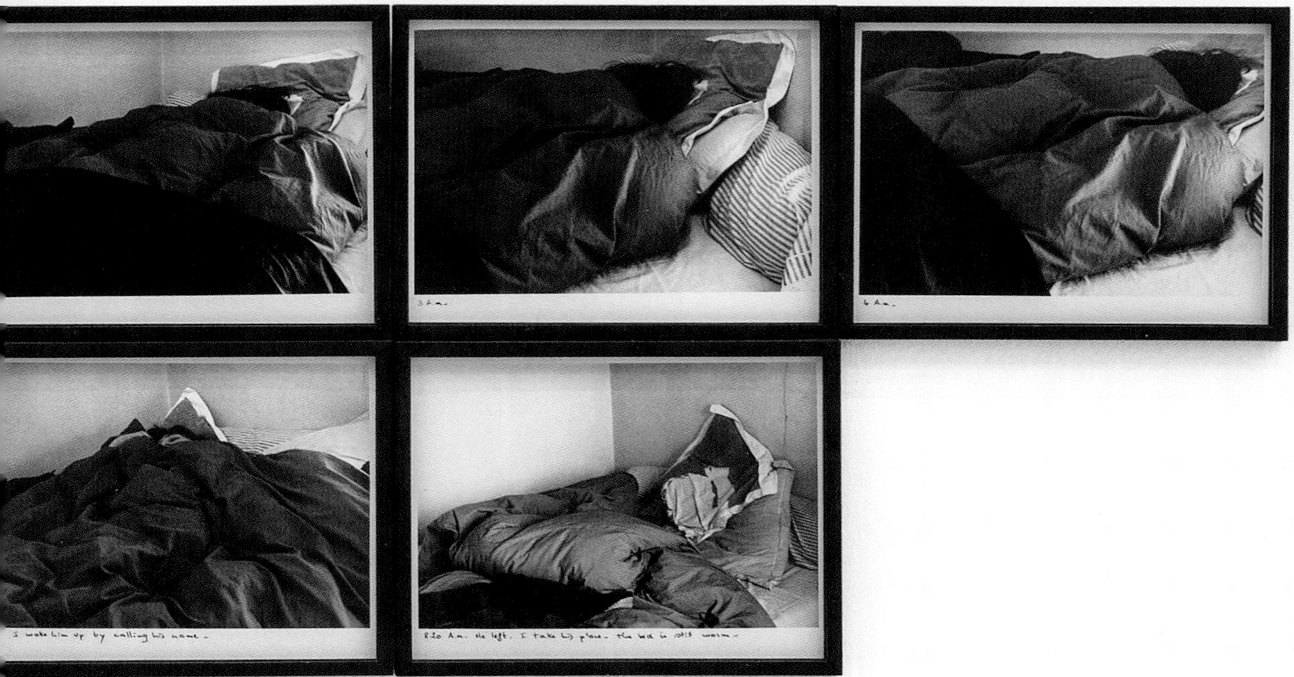

bore the title *Prenez soin de vous* [Take Care of Yourself], quoting the closing words of a break-up letter that had been addressed to her. She invited 107 women chosen for their profession – including actresses, an anthropologist, a Talmudic exegete, a clairvoyant and a psychoanalyst – to interpret this message – so banal, yet so difficult to understand and accept for the person who is dumped. Mixing fiction and autobiography, the books and installations of Sophie Calle assembled texts and images as so many signs and fragments charged with conjuring up absence and loss.

'Les Dormeurs – Andrew Granmore, vingt-quatrième dormeur' [The Sleepers – Andrew Granmore – 24th Sleeper],
1979,
gelatin silver print,
Paris, Galerie Perrotin

'I asked people to give me a few hours of their sleep. To come and sleep in my bed. To allow themselves to be photographed, to be seen. To reply to a few questions. I suggested a stay of eight hours to each of them. I contacted 45 of them by telephone: strangers whose names had been suggested to me by mutual acquaintances, some friends and people from the neighbourhood who slept during the day, such as bakers. My room would be fully occupied for eight days, with sleepers succeeding each other at regular intervals.

29 people accepted to come and sleep. Five of them didn't turn up: a babysitter booked at short notice and I myself took their place.
16 people refused. Either they weren't available or the idea didn't appeal to them.
The occupation of my bed began on Sunday 1 April 1979 at 5 p.m. and finished Monday 9 April at 10 a.m. 28 sleepers took it in turns. Some of them crossed over. They were all offered breakfast, lunch or dinner, depending on the time of day. Clean bedding was put at their disposal.

I asked a few questions of those who were willing to engage. It wasn't about knowing or enquiring but establishing a neutral and distant contact. I took photographs at all hours. I watched my guests sleep.'

NAN GOLDIN

1953, USA

In the early 1980s, Nan Goldin exhibited in a bar on Times Square in New York, where she worked as a waitress, a series of photographs of her friends in the LGBTQIA+ community. Her images with their acidic colours, lit by a blinding flash, were shown as a slideshow of more than 700 slides accompanied by songs. Breaking with the convention of glossy prints on museum picture rails, *The Ballad of Sexual Dependency* caused a sensation at the Whitney Museum of American Art in 1985 and at the Rencontres de la photographie d'Arles in 1987 and inspired whole new generations of photographers.

This intimate journal combining sound and images contained a recessed memory of her sister, whose suicide had blighted her adolescence. This prolific documentation of the links connecting her circle of friends transformed photography into a tool of resistance against loss and forgetting. Nan Goldin dealt uncompromisingly with themes such as love, sexuality, cross-dressing, drugs and the AIDS epidemic. In 1987, she published a book drawn from this series. The cover shows her lover Brian sitting on the edge of a bed, smoking, with his back turned, while she lies still recumbent in the bed straight after making love. Later, a self-portrait details with forensic precision her bruised and swollen face after being beaten by Brian, whom she subsequently left.

In 2004, Nan Goldin paid homage to her sister in her installation *Sister, Saints, & Sybils*, which documented her confinement in psychiatric facilities as well as Nan's own experience of such institutions receiving treatment for addiction and depression. She later campaigned against the Sackler family. Respected patrons of major museums, the Sacklers were the owners of the pharmaceutical firm that sold a highly addictive opioid that was implicated in the deaths of hundreds of thousands of Americans. This struggle and her life are the subject of a 2023 documentary by Laura Poitras, *All the Beauty and the Bloodshed*.

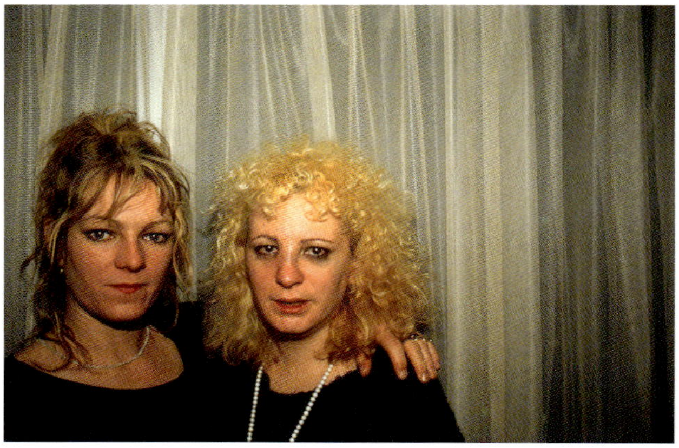

↑ 'Cookie with Me After I Was Punched, Baltimore, Maryland',
1986,
colour print,
artist's collection

→ 'The Hug, New York City',
1980,
colour print,
artist's collection

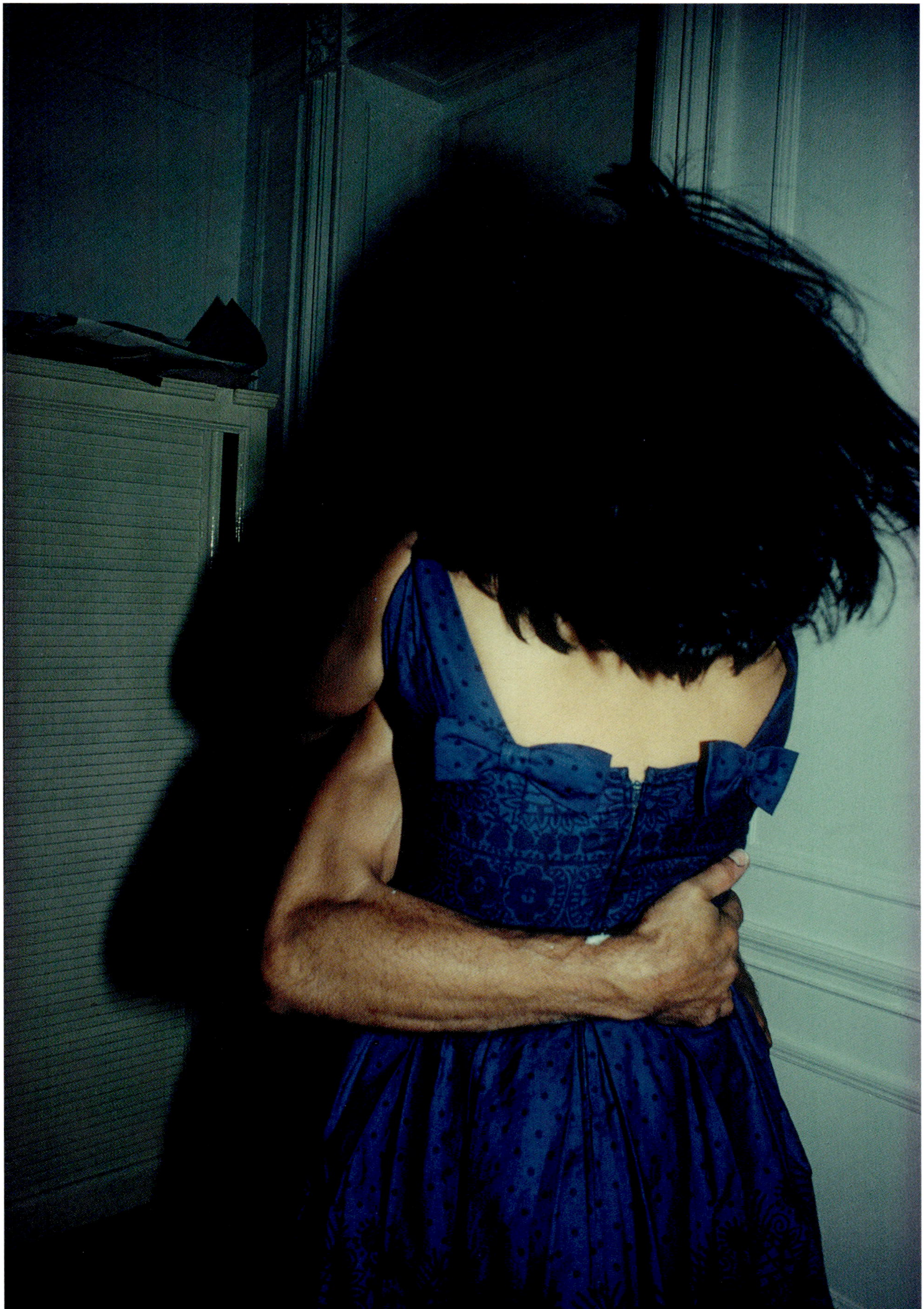

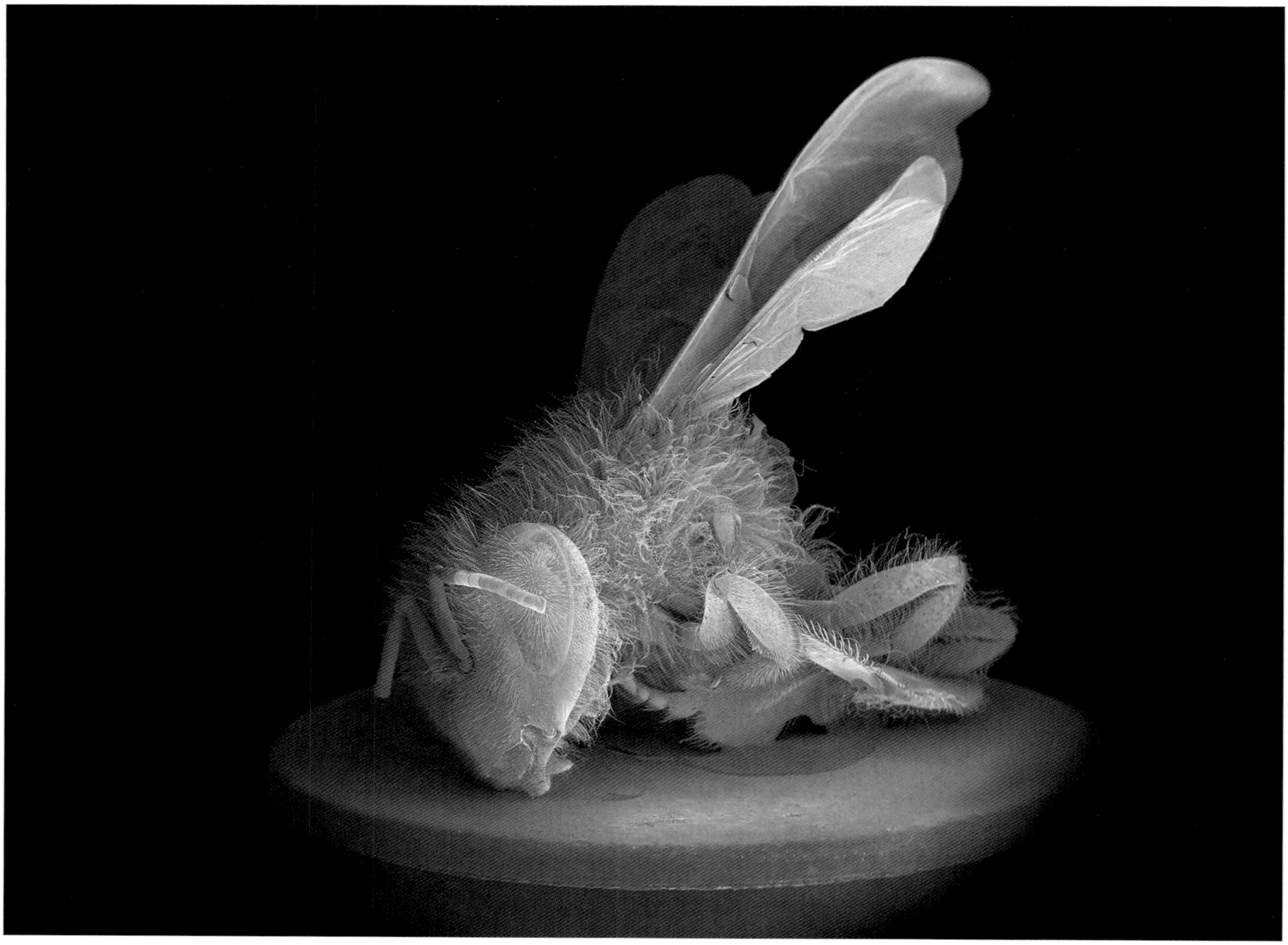

'Dead Bee Portrait #13',
2015,
pigment print,
artist's collection

ANNE NOBLE

1954, New Zealand

A dead bee lies on a pedestal, a statuesque museum exhibit of a species decimated by the use of pesticides. This funereal homage was part of an elegiac project conducted in the 2010s by the New Zealand photographer Anne Noble, which also included film stills and montages representing wings of bees. Fascinated by beekeeping and the way work is organised inside beehives, she used photography to interrogate our predatory relationship with the environment and other species.

Anne Noble became known in the 1980s for her black-and-white panoramas of the Wanganui River, near where she grew up, in which she developed her spiritual approach to landscapes. She turned her hand to nudes, to still lives, and produced work on a benedictine convent in the centre of London and on old people with learning disabilities.

In the late 1990s, she began a project with her daughter Ruby, seeking to subvert the smooth and stereotypical visions of childhood. Between 2001 and 2014, she produced work on the Antarctic, contrasting her photos taken over three journeys to the continent with the beautiful otherworldly snaps used by tourist agencies to promote polar exploration.

In 2021, she conducted a project at night time in the nature reserve of Tarapuruhi, not far from her hometown, where she explored how trees interrelate and communicate with each other via roots and fungi in the soil. In particular, she photographed Ratanui, a 500-year-old tree, representing a species endemic to New Zealand.

CINDY SHERMAN

1954, USA

A sense of déjà-vu: Cindy Sherman's photographs seem to be taken from black-and-white Hollywood films, replete with glamorous actresses and dramatic situations. They are, however, all staged. Her *Untitled Film Stills*, 1977–80, in fact do not come from actual films. In each case, the beautiful young woman is none other than the photographer herself, decked out in wigs to embody Hollywood stereotypes. These images reveal the hegemony on the screen of what Laura Mulvey in 1975 called the 'male gaze'. Women are seen as passive objects, offered for consumption, created by and for the pleasure of men.

These photos created from scratch and yet so familiar show how much we are saturated by visual mass culture. Cindy Sherman continued her exploration using advertising and media images, drawing on the worlds of pornography, fashion, fairy tales, monsters, dolls, masks and the history of art. Her transformations were achieved by use of extravagant toupees, prosthetics and make-up; they hover between the grotesque and the scary. The abused body becomes a support for fictional identities, exposing our obsession with ageing, our narcissism and our compulsive consumerism. She also incarnated archetypes from the middle classes or high society, reappropriating the expensive symbols of their power, and in 2017 subverted the tools used on Instagram for correcting and improving selfies. Her *Clowns* series (2002–03) crystallised the latent anxiety that haunts her work, as the deformed features scrawled on her face seem to obliterate any human expression, sad greasepaint disguising a collapse of entertainment.

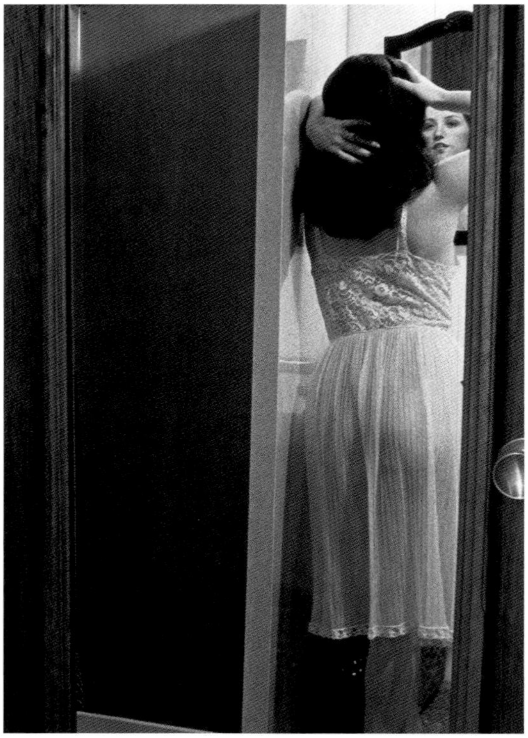

↑ 'Untitled Film Still #81',
1980,
gelatin silver print,
artist's collection

→ 'Untitled #414',
2003,
chromogenic colour print,
artist's collection

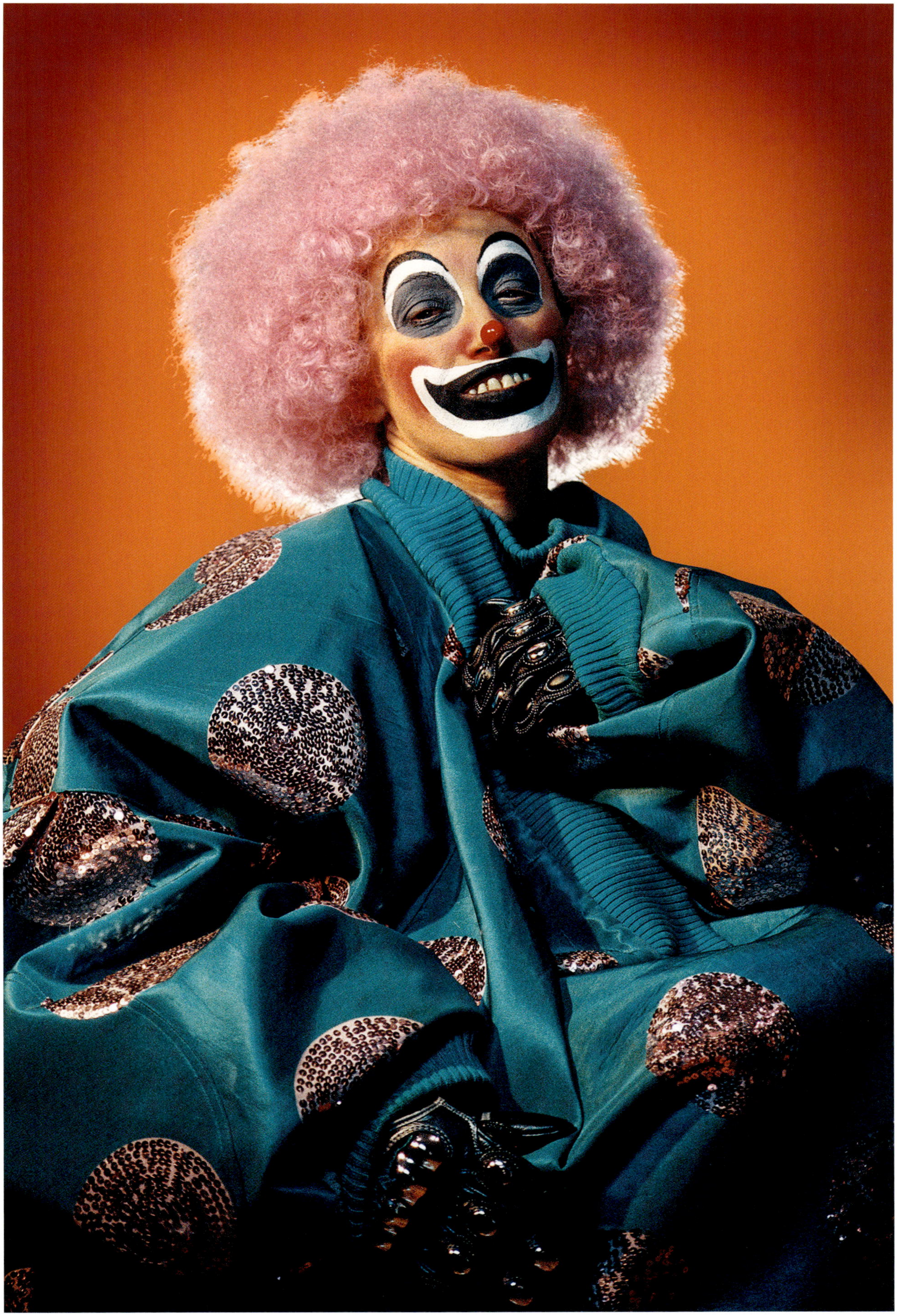

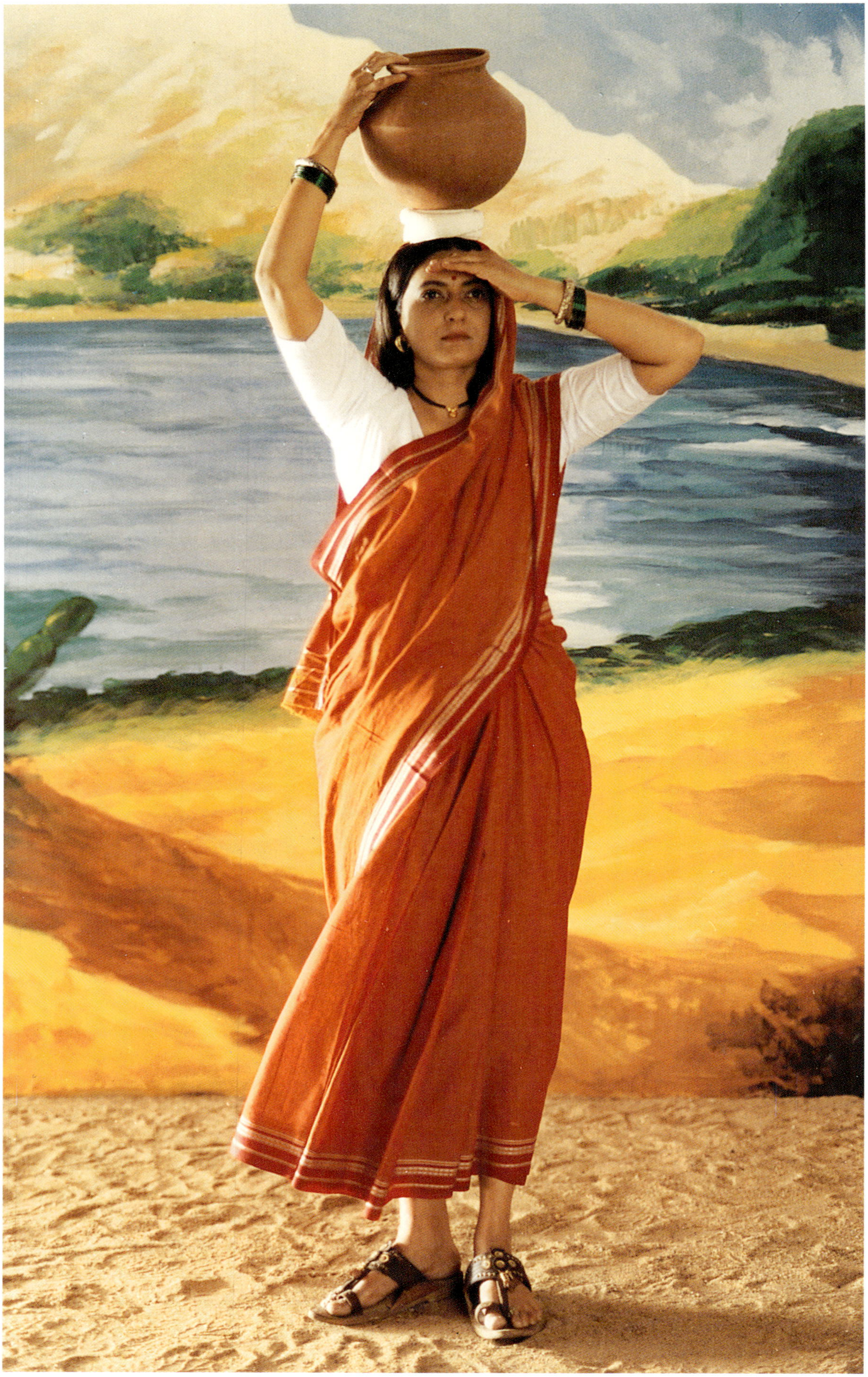

PUSHPAMALA N.

1956, India

Born in Bangalore, Pushmala N.'s first experiments in her art studies involved modelling with terracotta. She abandoned sculpture in favour of photography in the mid 1980s, employing masquerade, self-mockery and pastiche to great success. She presents herself in theatrical décors, parodying the photo-novel genre and the conventions of studio portraiture. Carrying a jug on her head, for example, in front of an obviously painted artificial backdrop, her gaze directed at some imaginary horizon, she ironically shields her eyes from the blinding glare of the spotlights – not the sun. Her self-portraits deconstruct the archetypal representations of 'exotic' or picturesque postcards. Her so-called 'ethnographic' series in 2004 mocked the methods of colonial explorers and administrators by hijacking their anthropometric measuring instruments. She also reveals her own shooting methods by displaying the work of costume designers, assistants, lighting technicians and camera operators who help her set up each shot (see p. 17). She variously adopts the personae of circus artists, film actresses or even goddesses in traditional costume, making reference to miniatures and religious iconography.

In 2009, she produced a series mocking the smooth and glossy finish of prints produced by the Parisian studio Harcourt, reprising the famous masked pose of the Countess de Castiglione, a composition by Ingres or *Liberty Guiding the People* by Delacroix. In 2012, she took her inspiration from orientalist paintings to tell the story of the abduction of Princess Sita by the demon Ravana, creating a dramatic atmosphere with the aid of smoke and expressive poses. Lying somewhere between performance, installation and photographic painting, the iconoclastic and provocative work of Pushpamala N. subverted the expectations of the most codified visual cultures.

In collaboration with Clare Arni,
'The Native Types / Returning from the Tank.'
Native Women of South India: Manners and Customs series,
2004,
colour print (2016),
artist's collection

OUKA LEELE

1957–2022, Spain

An octopus, a bird, a miniature plane, a ventilator, lemons, knives, shoes or tortoises disguised as hats: the portraits in the *Peluquería* series of 1979 make up an unusual and extravagant gallery. Photographed in black and white, her pictures were then hand-painted, mostly in watercolour. The garish, saturated, kitsch colours accentuate the acidic artifice of her drole and incongruous juxtapositions. These surrealist provocations demonstrate the subversive spirit of Movida, which was shaking off the shackles of the Franco era. In the democratic opening-up of the late 1970s, Ouka Leele was a leading figure in this movement of cultural liberation embodied in the cinema of Pedro Almodóvar, whom she was close to, and who showcased many of her works in his films.

After studying painting, drawing and sculpture, she trained at the Madrid Photocentro in 1976. Born Barbara Allende Gil de Biedma, she adopted the pseudonym Ouka Leele in the late 1970s, her 'war name, artist's name'. Moving between the fantastical, the absurd and burlesque, she tried her hand at nudes, still lives and portraits, but also video and poetry. A number of her compositions ironically combined female figures with household devices, subverting the conventions of advertising posters in an eccentric sublimation of the 'domestic goddess'. Ouka Leele reclaimed the blurring of genres and nonconformity: 'I am a photographer, but, as in Magritte's painting, this is not a photograph!'[1]

1. Interview with Élise Padovani and Annie Gava, 14 November 2013, published in *Zibeline* magazine on the occasion of the 12th edition of the Festival of Spanish Cinema in Marseille.

'Invraisemblances, Pulpo Rojo' [Unlikelihoods, Red Pulp], *Peluquería* [At the Hairdresser's] series, 1979

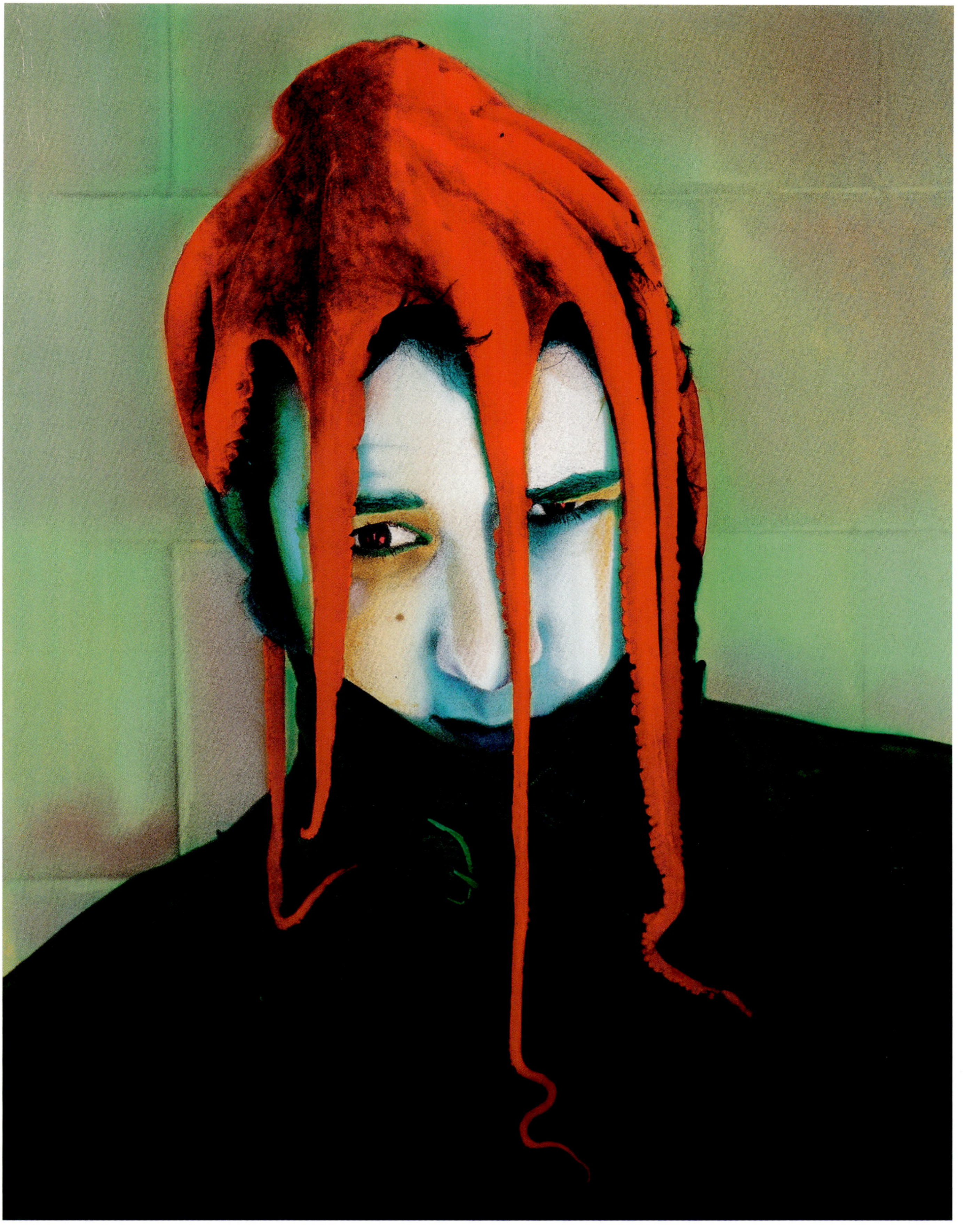

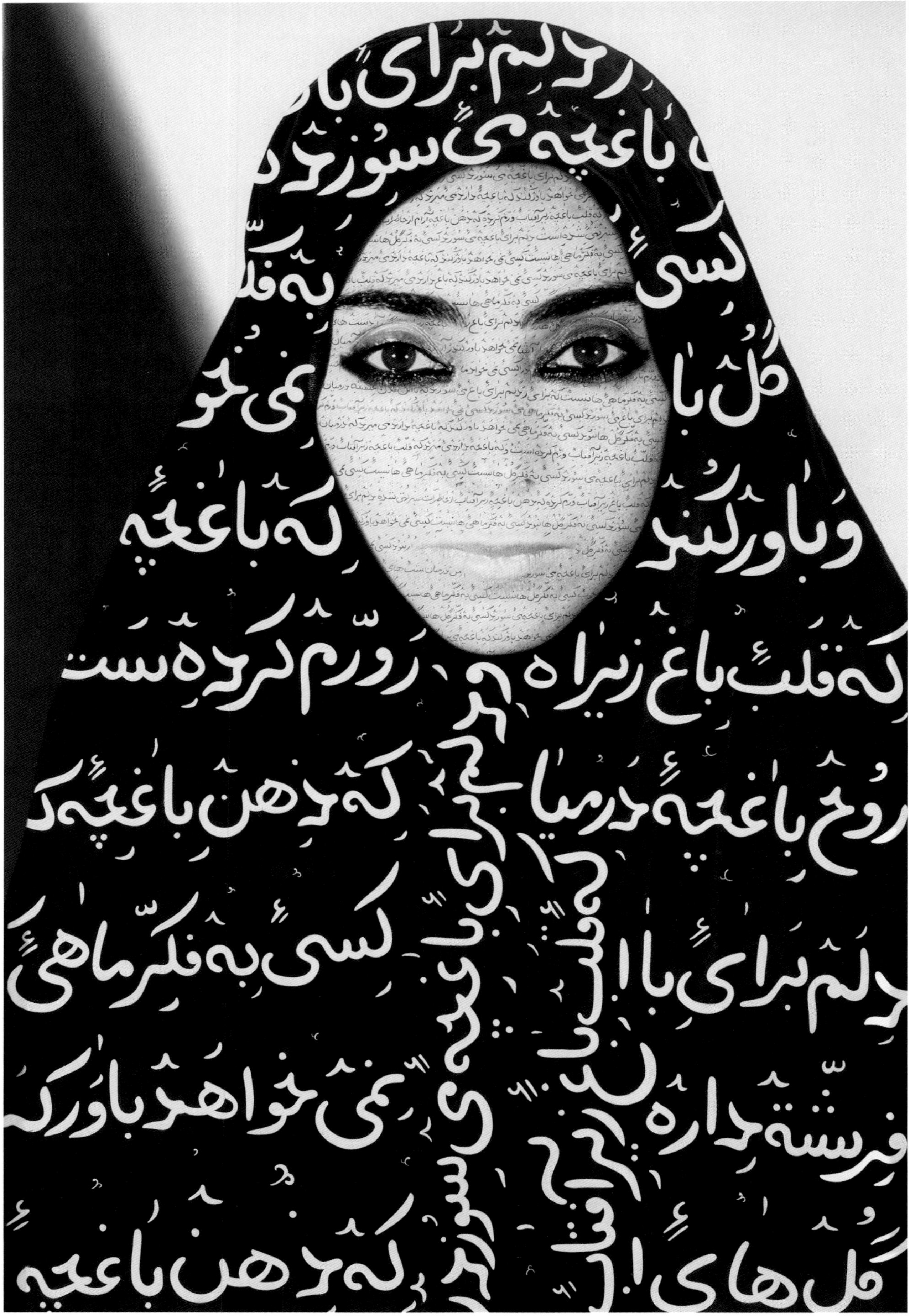

SHIRIN NESHAT

1957, Iran

Shirin Neshat went to the USA in 1974 to study art at Berkeley, before moving to the alternative art space of New York in 1983. A stay in Iran in the early 1990s inspired her to study the role of women during and after the Islamic revolution. Her photographs of veiled women had Farsi calligraphy quoting contemporary poetesses superimposed on the visible parts of their bodies, faces and hands. They demonstrated the effect of the religious culture of martyrdom, notably in the *Women of Allah* series, in which the models posed with weapons.

From the late 1990s, she turned to film and in 2009 adapted the novel *Women Without Men* by Shahrnush Parsipur, which was banned in Iran, for the screen. *The Book of Kings* (2012) took its inspiration from accounts by participants in the Arab Spring and the Green Movement in Iran in 2009. Using the title of a Persian epic, this series combined portraits, poetic calligraphy and mythological heroes, portraying present-day events through the mythical history of the region.

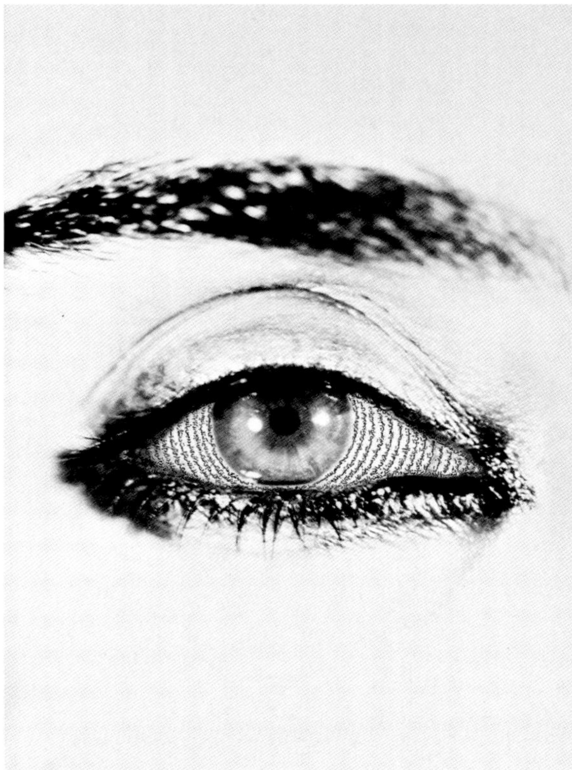

← 'Unveiling',
1993,
gelatin silver print and ink,
New York, Gladstone Gallery

↑ 'Offered Eyes',
1993,
gelatin silver print and ink,
New York, Gladstone Gallery

FRANCESCA WOODMAN

1958–1981, USA

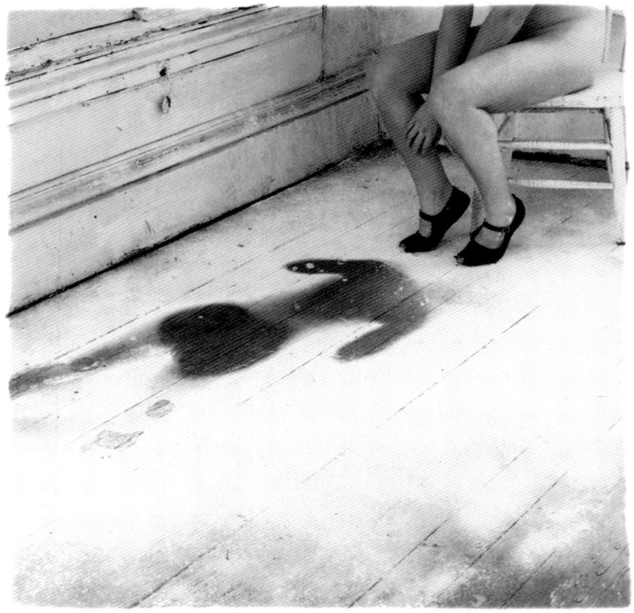

Francesca Woodman's parents were both artists – her mother was a ceramicist and her father a painter – and they passed on their fascination with Italy to her. They lived in Florence between 1965 and 1966 and spent their summers in Tuscany. She discovered photography at school and transformed her bedroom into a studio. She studied art at the Rhode Island School of Design in Providence and lived in a large apartment that doubled up as her studio. In this bare space she had little in the way of furniture but collected lots of objects which she used in her self-portraits, such as a mirror, some animal furs, a fishbowl… She lived in Rome in 1977–78 and created the series *On Being an Angel*, inspired by the baroque sculptures on Roman fountains.

She moved to New York in January 1979, where she worked as secretary, photographic assistant and model for a painter. She made photographic prints on blueprint paper normally used by architects to reconstruct the façade of an ancient temple with a collage of images of traditional bathroom tiling and of herself and her female friends as caryatids. In January 1981, she published *Some Disordered Interior Geometries*, combining her photographs with pages from an Italian geometry primer, setting up an unlikely correspondence between mathematical forms and the outline of her silhouette.

She took her own life on 19 January 1981. Her suicide was attributed to difficulties in her personal, professional and love life and was linked to the themes of disappearance and effacement in her work. She left a dazzling body of work, produced between the ages of 13 and 22, which is characterised by the ephemeral and the transitory, showing the ghostly and fleeting presence of her body in movement, fragmented and evanescent. She subverted the stereotypes of femininity but nonetheless retained a certain ambivalence, both a refusal and a desire to construct herself as an object of desire. Struggling with some tatty wallpaper or sitting in front of the imprint made by her back in a cloud of white flour, she demonstrates the simultaneous desire and impossibility of self-representation, of fixing one's body in an image.

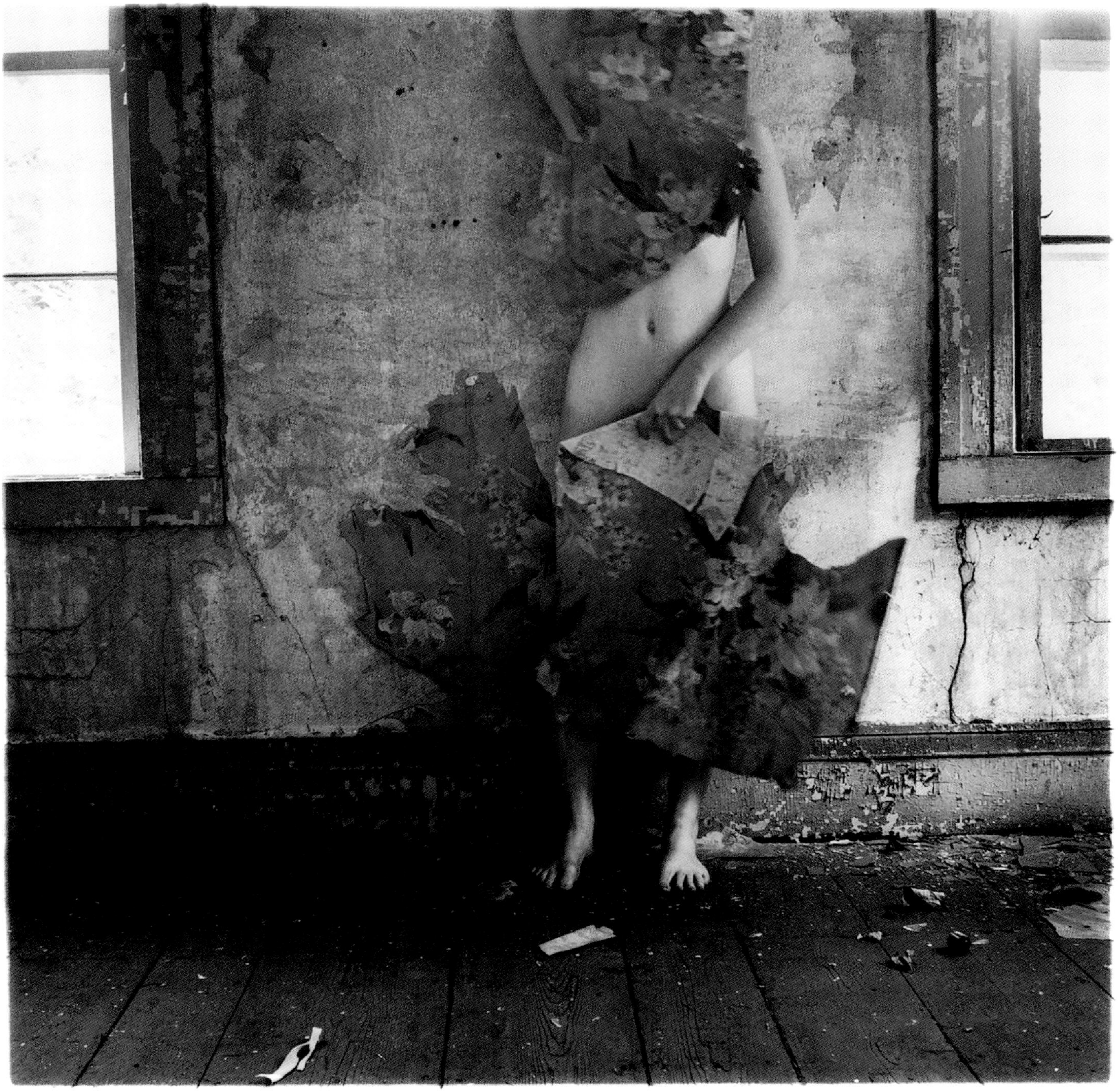

↖ 'Untitled',
1976,
gelatin silver print,
Woodman Family Foundation

↑ 'From Space²',
1976,
gelatin silver print,
Woodman Family Foundation

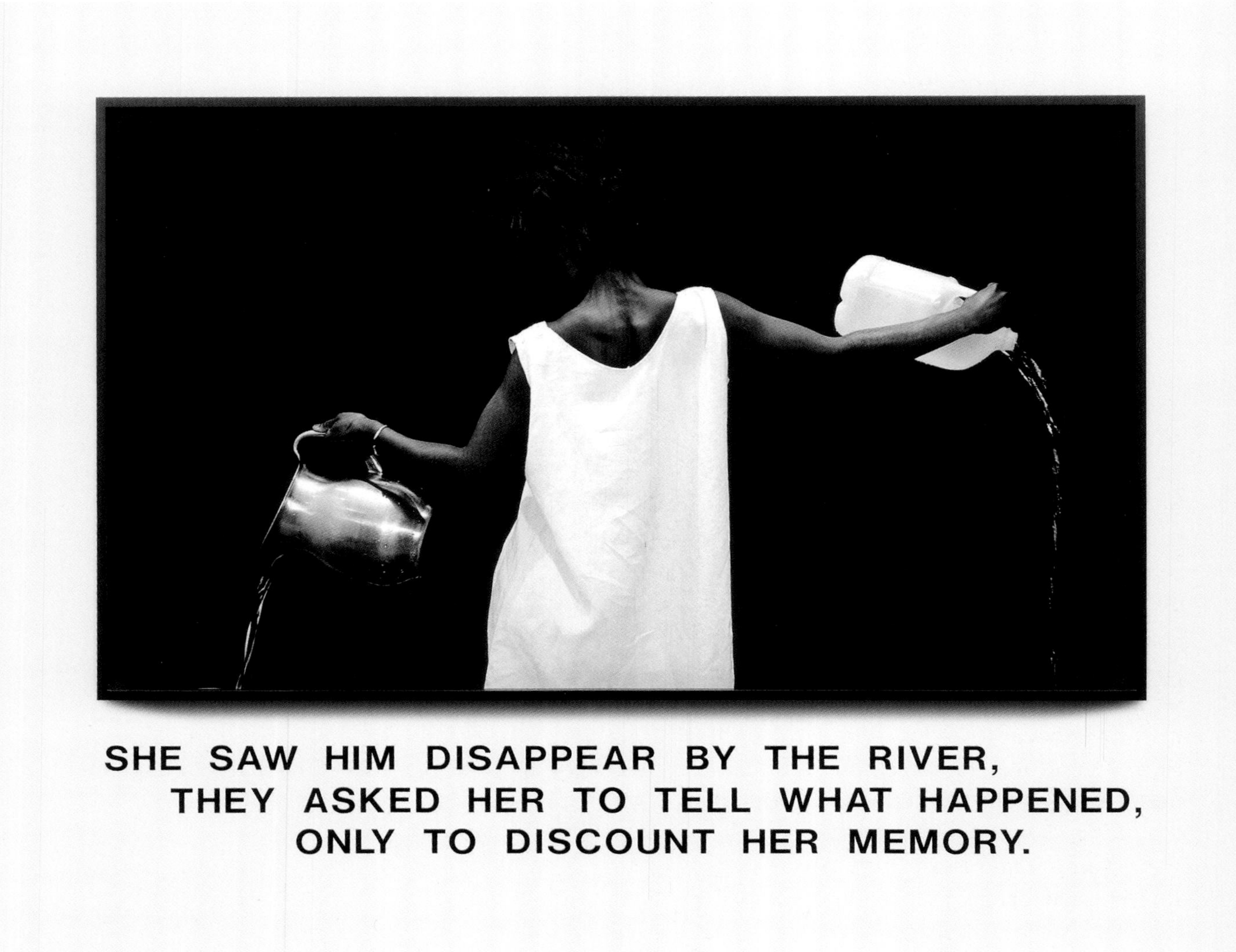

↑ 'Waterbearer',
1986,
gelatin silver print,
lettering in vinyl

→ 'Summer '57 / Summer '09 (Group 2)'
[detail],
Summer 57/09 series,
2009,
gelatin silver print

LORNA SIMPSON

1960, USA

Lorna Simpson is an African American artist who interrogates stereotypes of race and gender through installations that combine photography, film and sound. After studying art in New York and San Diego, she decided to combine her photographs with short pieces of text, sometimes simple words or phrases covering a part of the image and interrogating its content. She poses African American models with their faces partially hidden, offering a reflection on the place of black communities in contemporary culture and their representations. Thinking outside of documentary conventions, she creates troubling mismatches between her terse observations and her fragmented images. In 1986, she created a composition emphasising the elegant form of a water carrier dressed in a white dress, seen from behind, pouring the liquid in a sort of choreographed movement. The accompanying text tells an incomplete story of a woman whose identity slips away for want of being heard.

In the mid 1990s, she started to created photographs on felt, seduced by the thickness of the material. She created an inventory on the theme of wigs, which represent the ideal of a permed coiffure as opposed to natural Afro hairstyles. She made images based on multiple photo booth portraits collected online, then turned to video installations. She exhibited photographs retouched and covered with paint at the Venice Biennale in 2015; she also produced collages from images of African American women collected from magazine articles.

Her series *Summer 57/09* was inspired by photographs found on a small ads site. These dated from the 1950s and showed a young Black woman striking a pose. Simpson mixed these photographs with her own, in which she adopted the same poses and settings as the originals, making for an unsettling combination, halfway between documentary collection and fictional reconstruction.

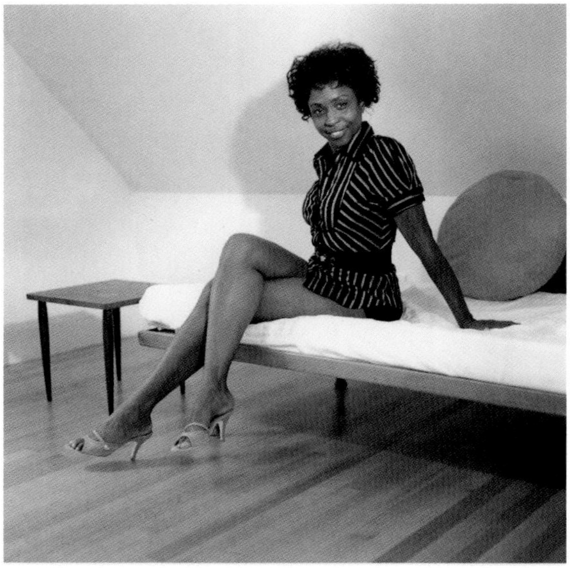

ANGÈLE ETOUNDI ESSAMBA

1962, Cameroon

Angèle Etoundi Essamba reappropriates representations of Black women, mixing a deconstruction of 'exotic' stereotypes with the invention of aesthetic forms amplifying power and independence or, to quote the title of her retrospective in Dakar in 2016, 'strength and pride'. From the late 1980s to the early 2000s, she used black and white to accentuate contrasts, the reflections and nuances on Black skin. She appropriates the tradition of the female nude and sets up dialogues between the profiles and her models with traditional African masks.

She then turned to colour – dazzling, saturated colour – to explore the headscarf and printed fabrics, paying homage to the art of drapery, the folds and layering of turbans or boubous. She also posed her models with stacked calabashes, painted or resewn with stitches evoking the process of suturing and healing.

In parallel with this, she pursued a number of documentary projects, such as *African Women in Action* on female workers in mining, textiles, agriculture and construction, or *Women of the Water* on the fragile ecosystem of the town of Ganvié in Benin, built on the shores of Lake Nokoué.

The series *A-fil-iations*, representing women weaving and unravelling balls of wool, makes reference to craft skills, to the mythical figure of Patience embodied by Penelope and to the traditions of braided hairstyles. In 2002–03, she used a Black model to reinterpret the famous Vermeer painting *Girl with a Pearl Earring*, a masterpiece of the Dutch Golden Age painted at a time of prosperity when the country was undergoing colonial expansion. While women are her subjects of choice, she has also turned her hand to abstraction by photographing plant matter, such as bark, or minerals, such as geological strata.

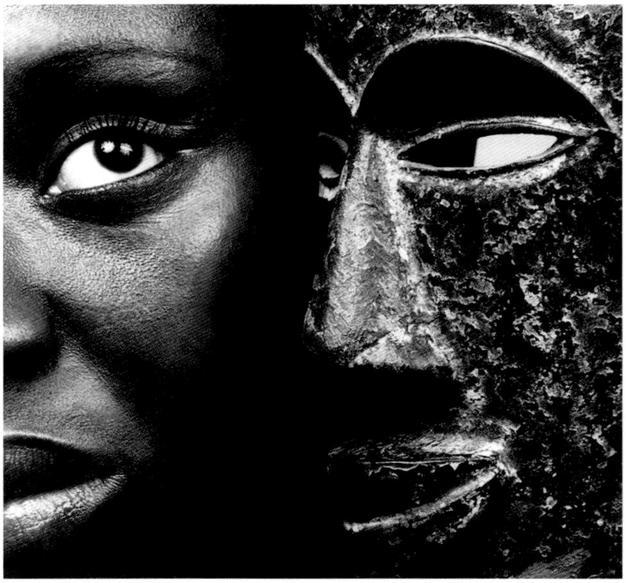

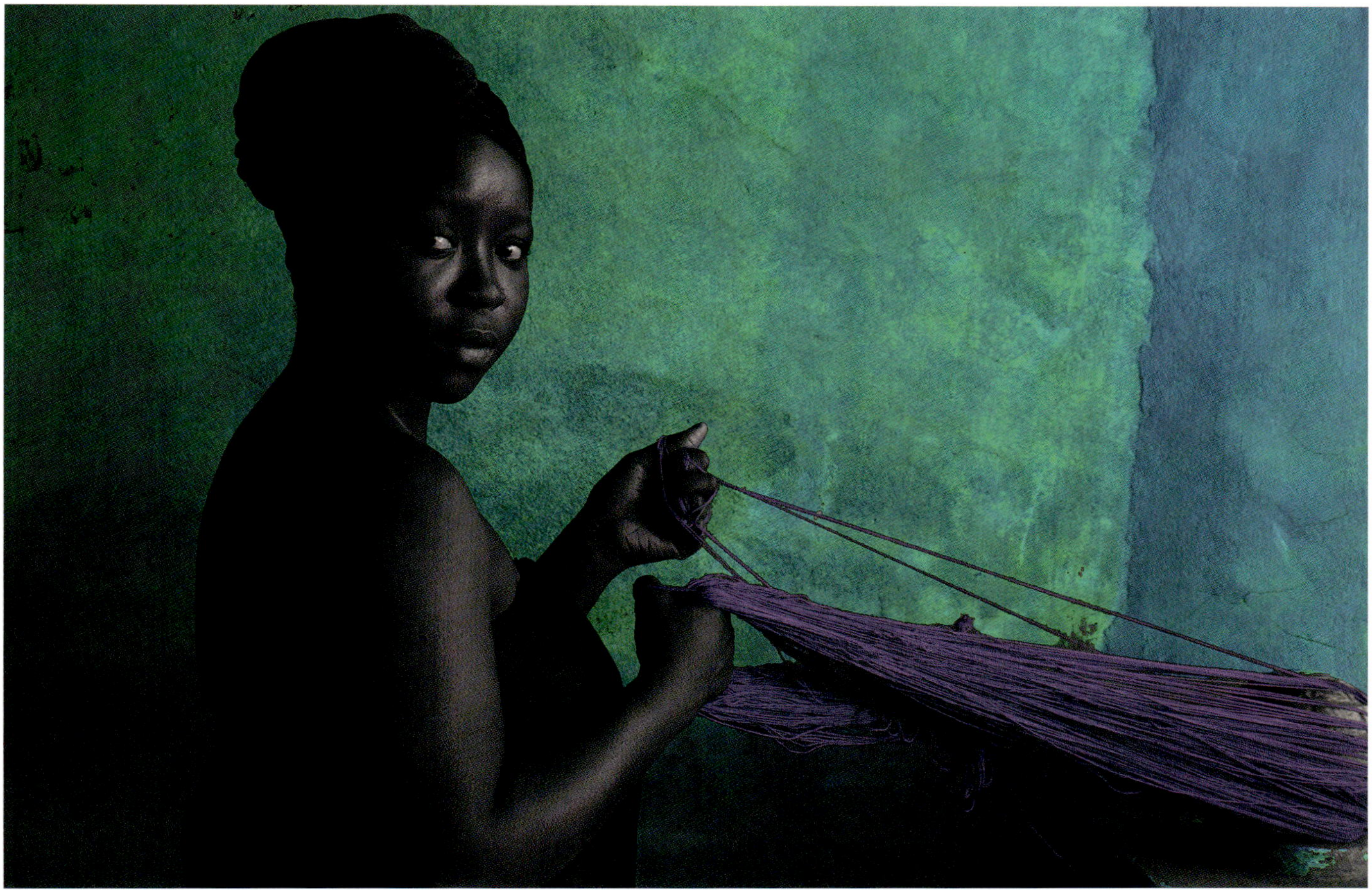

← 'Héritage 3',
1999,
gelatin silver print,
Paris Galerie Carole Kvasnevski

↑ 'A-fil-iation 25',
2002,
colour print

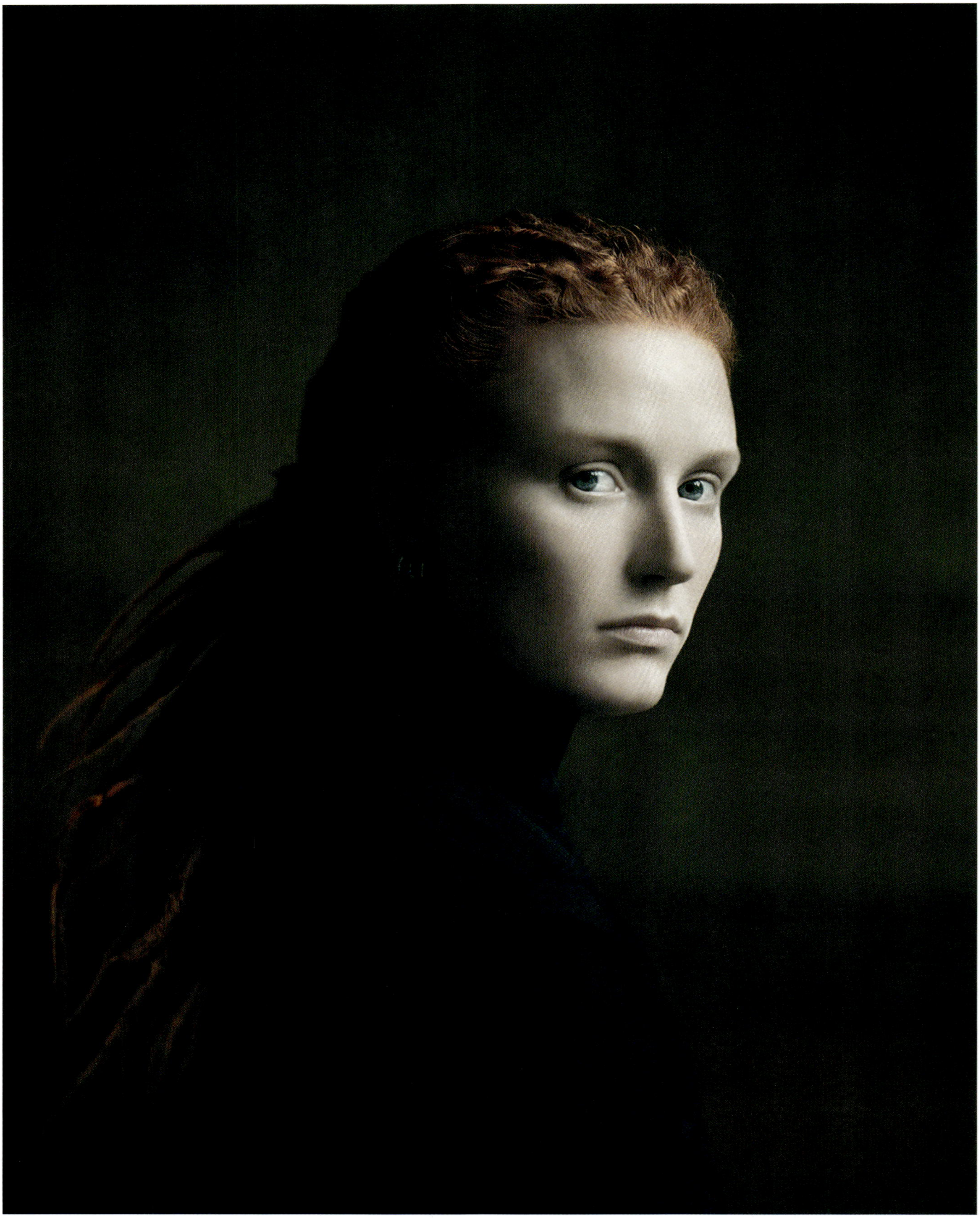

DÉSIRÉE DOLRON

1963, Netherlands

Throughout the 1990s, Désirée Dolron explored religious rituals in India, Pakistan, the Philippines, Malaysia, Thailand, Madagascar, Egypt and Morocco. Eschewing the conventions of the documentary, she created dreamlike visions to render her extreme experiences of trance and mutilation. At the end of the decade, she made a series of portraits of people immersed in water. Haloed by a fuzzy light, these submerged figures with their eyes closed seem to be suspended in an unreal blur. In 2001, she began the series *Xteriors*: portraits based on Flemish painting created with the help of digital tools. The diaphanous skin, the elaborate hairstyles and the sombre décors situate the characters in an indeterminate time: the distant past or, conversely, a science-fiction future. Suffused with melancholy, these austere and mysterious scenes are unsettling and bring into question the status of the photographic document.

Désirée Dolron was an innovator in the use of digital retouching and manipulation, against a background of uneasiness over the trustworthiness of images, nowadays exacerbated by the deployment of artificial intelligence. A pioneer of new technologies applied to photography, she interrogates the notion of truth by creating deliberately fake images.

She later used film to capture normally imperceptible dust particles. Magnified, they seem to adopt cosmic trajectories, inviting metaphysical meditation on our finite existence. In 2017, she recreated flocks of starlings flying in ever more sophisticated choreographed formations. The following year, she focused on the seasonal migrations of Monarch butterflies from North America to Mexico. Her pictures bristling with thousands of insects echo the journeys of human populations following the same routes.

'Xteriors IV',
2002,
artist's collection

GÉRALDINE LAY

1972, France

Géraldine Lay studied art history in Lyon and then photography in Arles. She became known for colour photographs of cityscapes, breathing new life into the genre of street photography. The elongated shadows and the sharp colours transform her images into graphic compositions like a film scene in which trivial events are acted out and anodyne and habitual activities take place. Capturing the gestures and movements of passers-by, she fastened on unusual details, like a piece of furniture abandoned on a street corner, cherry stones placed on a piece of paper or the alignment of tables at a café. Her method was to walk around, 'without knowing exactly where', stopping when the light 'threw a spotlight' on a scene.[1]

She has worked for the publishing house Actes du Sud since 1997, firstly in the production of illustrated books, then as editor of photography since 2019. She sees her books as objects and pays great attention to the choice of paper, the graphics and the quality of the reproductions, displaying her photographer's eye. She is also particular about the format of her own books and she has worked with several different houses, publishing *On commence la scène* [The Scene Begins] (2010) on the town of Beauvais; *Failles ordinaires* [Ordinary Faults] (2012), an ode to everyday anxieties; and *Impromptus* (2017), a poetic wander through several French cities. *North End*, which appeared in 2018, is the fruit of an exploration begun in 2009 in towns in Northern England and Scotland marked by deindustrialisation. *Far East*, in 2023, assembled the photographs she took over the course of four autumns spent in Japan. She also participated in the collective project *Mémoires* [Memories], which ran in tandem with the urban renovation plan in the Chêne-Pointu area of Clichy-sous-Bois.

1. As expressed to Jean-Baptiste Gauvin, *Blind*, 7 May 2019.

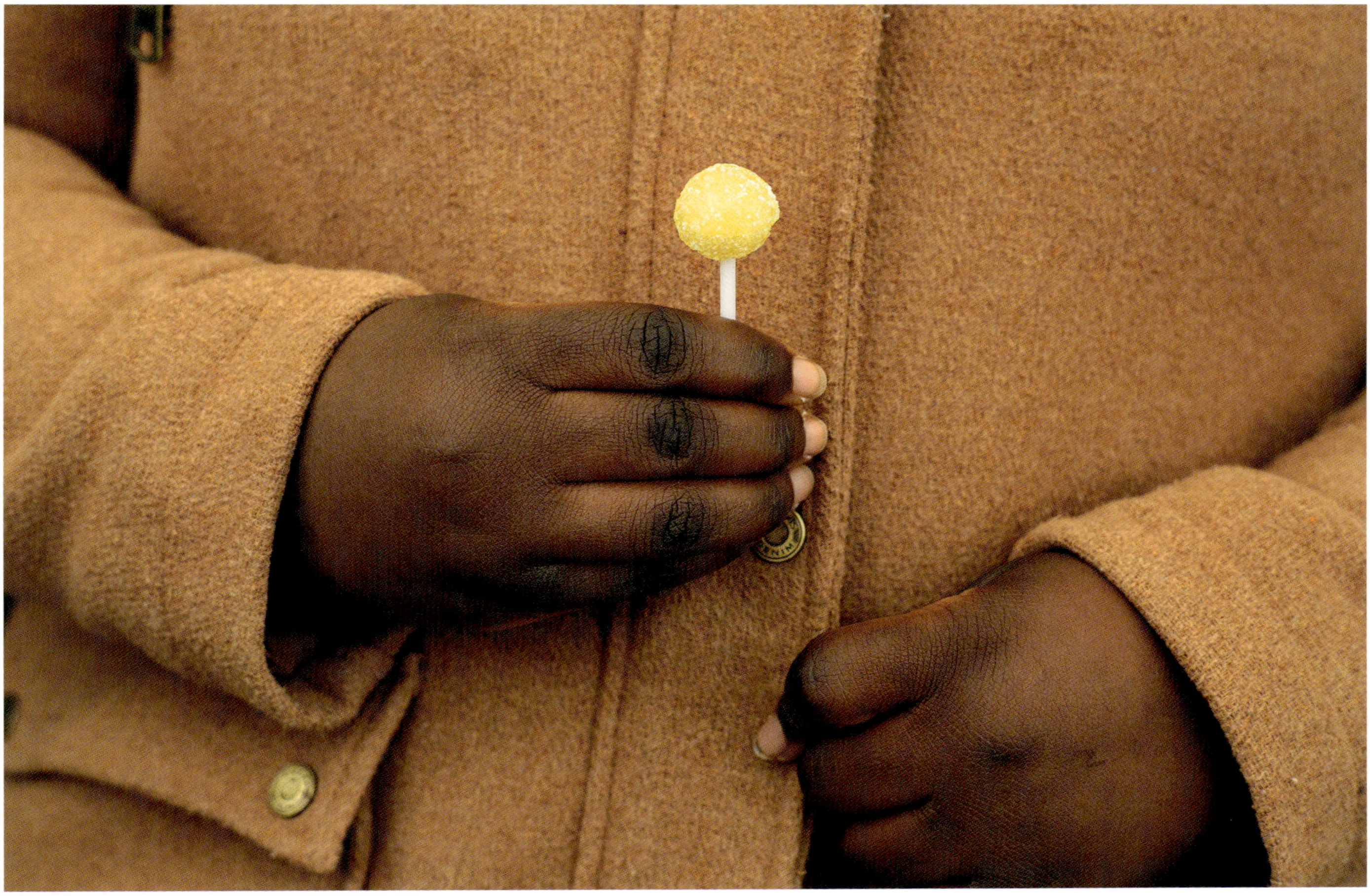

‘Chêne-Pointu, Clichy-sous-Bois’,
2021,
pigment print,
artist’s collection

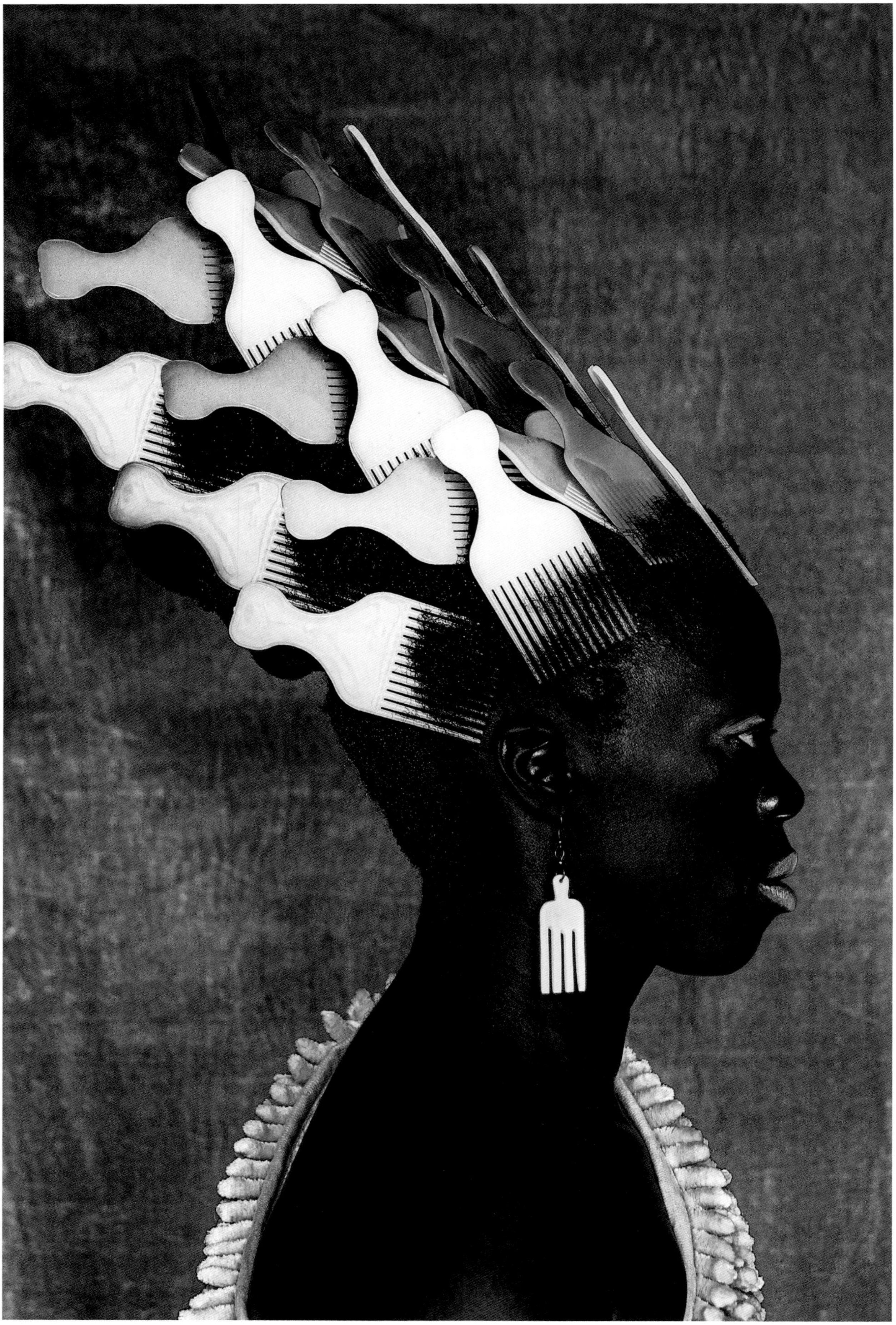

ZANELE MUHOLI

1972, South Africa

Zanele Muholi grew up in a Durban township and is an activist against the violence inflicted on lesbians and transgender people in Black South African communities, focusing on the punitive rapes that happen despite the fact that there has been a judicial framework in place since the 1990s banning discrimination on the basis of sexual orientation. As a non-binary person, Zanele Muholi wishes to be designated by the neutral pronoun *they/them* and describes themself as a 'visual activist'.

They co-founded the Forum for the Empowerment of Women in 2002 and then, in 2006, created Inkanyiso, the Zulu word for light, an online space for queer visual expression. They devote their photography to their activism and make portraits of LGBTQIA+ Black people. Working in cooperation with their models, they give a visibility and dignity to these people who are so often unseen and stigmatised, paying homage to their courage. Sometimes photographed over many years, the models participate in the progressive construction of their identity. In head-and-shoulder pose, looking straight at the camera, they assert their existence and their singularity. This collection of nearly 300 portraits constitutes a collective archive attesting to the diversity and solidarity of this community.

In 2012, Zanele Muholi began their series *Somnyama Ngonyama*, which in Zulu means 'Hail, black lioness'. They shot 365 self-portraits featuring monumental hairstyles including, for example, combs, clothes pins, sunglasses and string, playing with the prejudices underlying representations of racialised women. Subverting dress codes, they also used fabrics contrasting with the deliberately accentuated darkness of their skin to interrogate and reclaim their identity.

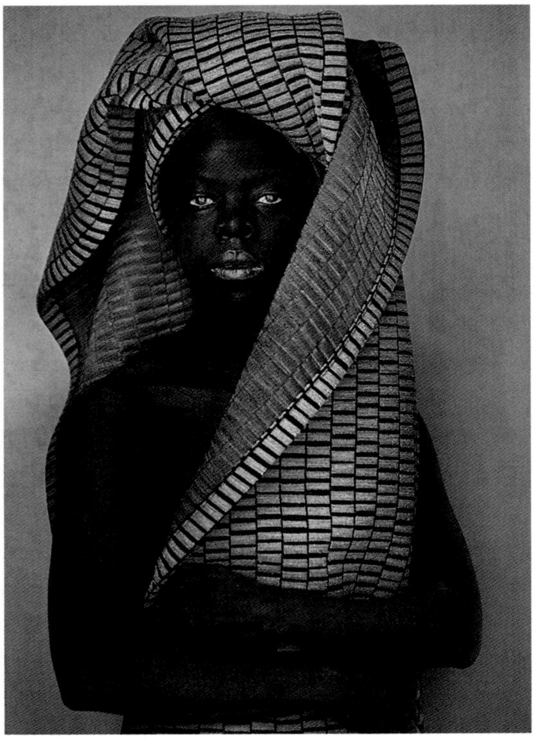

← 'Qiniso, The Sails, Durban',
Somnyama Ngonyama series,
2019,
gelatin silver print,
New York, Yancey Richardson Gallery

↑ 'Lena, London',
Somnyama Ngonyama series,
2018,
gelatin silver print,
New York, Yancey Richardson Gallery

SARA BENNETT

1955, USA

Sara Bennett worked for 18 years as a duty attorney in a law firm offering legal aid to all those who didn't have the means to defend themselves. Her first photographic project involved a detainee she was representing in her claim for remission of sentence. Sentenced to 70 years, Judith Clark was set to end her life behind bars. In her appeal for clemency to the governor, Sara Bennett created a portrait of her through the testimonies of her fellow prisoners, now released, who had interacted with her during their incarceration. The initiative grew and eventually led to her release in 2019.

When she realised how little the general public knew about life in prison and rehabilitation, Sara Bennett pursued other initiatives. She spoke out against the length of sentences handed down and the industrialisation of the penal system, which affected two million prisoners. *The Bedroom Project* featured former prisoners who had spent between 14 and more than 37 years in penitentiaries, usually posed sitting on their beds in their bedrooms. She asked her models to comment on the images and give their impressions in the form of handwritten notes in the margin. She also followed the progress of seven women after their release.

For example, Leah, 44, posed with a brush in the Brooklyn restaurant where she worked Sundays and evenings after her regular day job, in which she supervised and trained sales staff for a firm that provided first aid kits. In the face of a system that crushed individuals, Sara Bennett pays homage to the humanity of the prisoners and tries to restore their dignity in order to change perceptions of conditions in prison.

'Leah at Work at Mo's',
2019,
Artist's collection

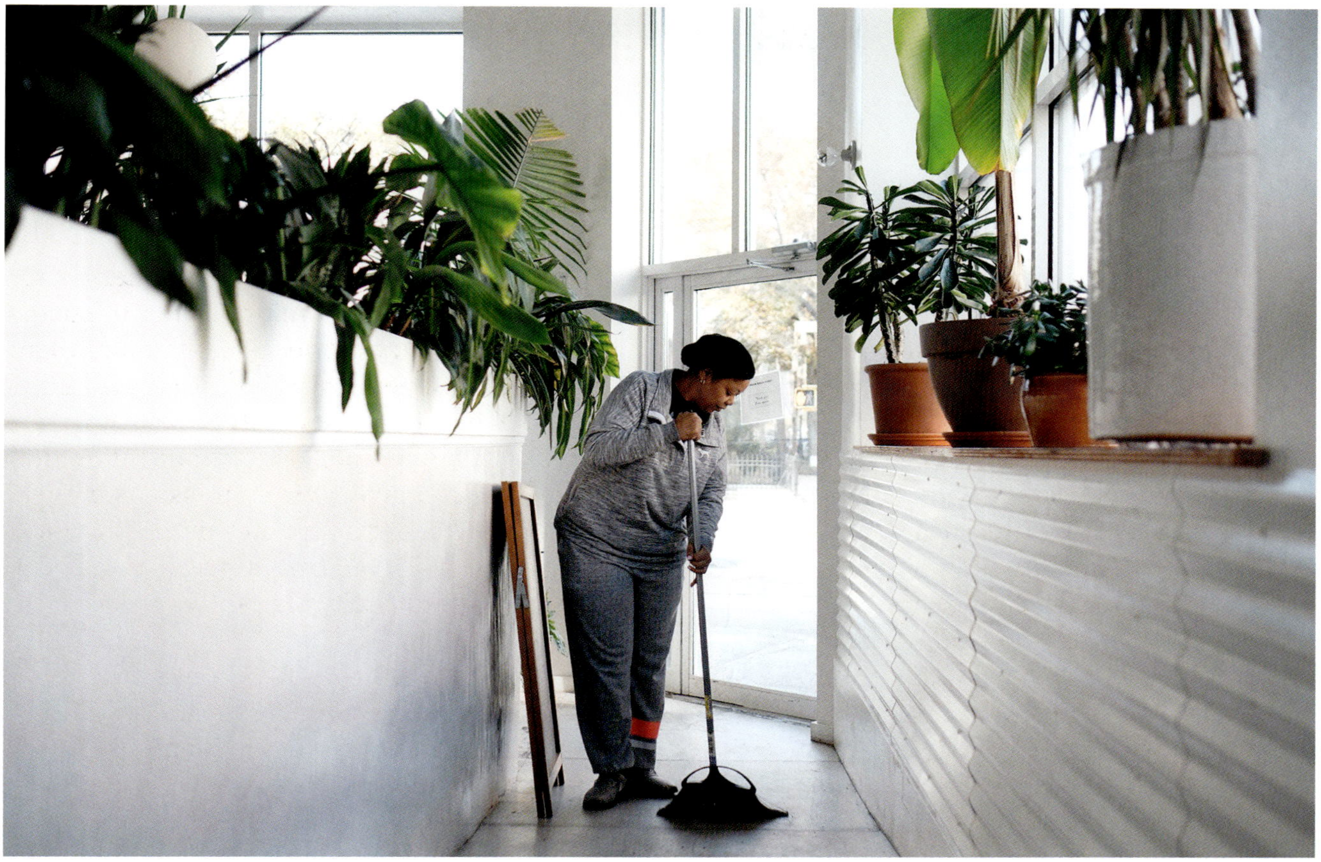

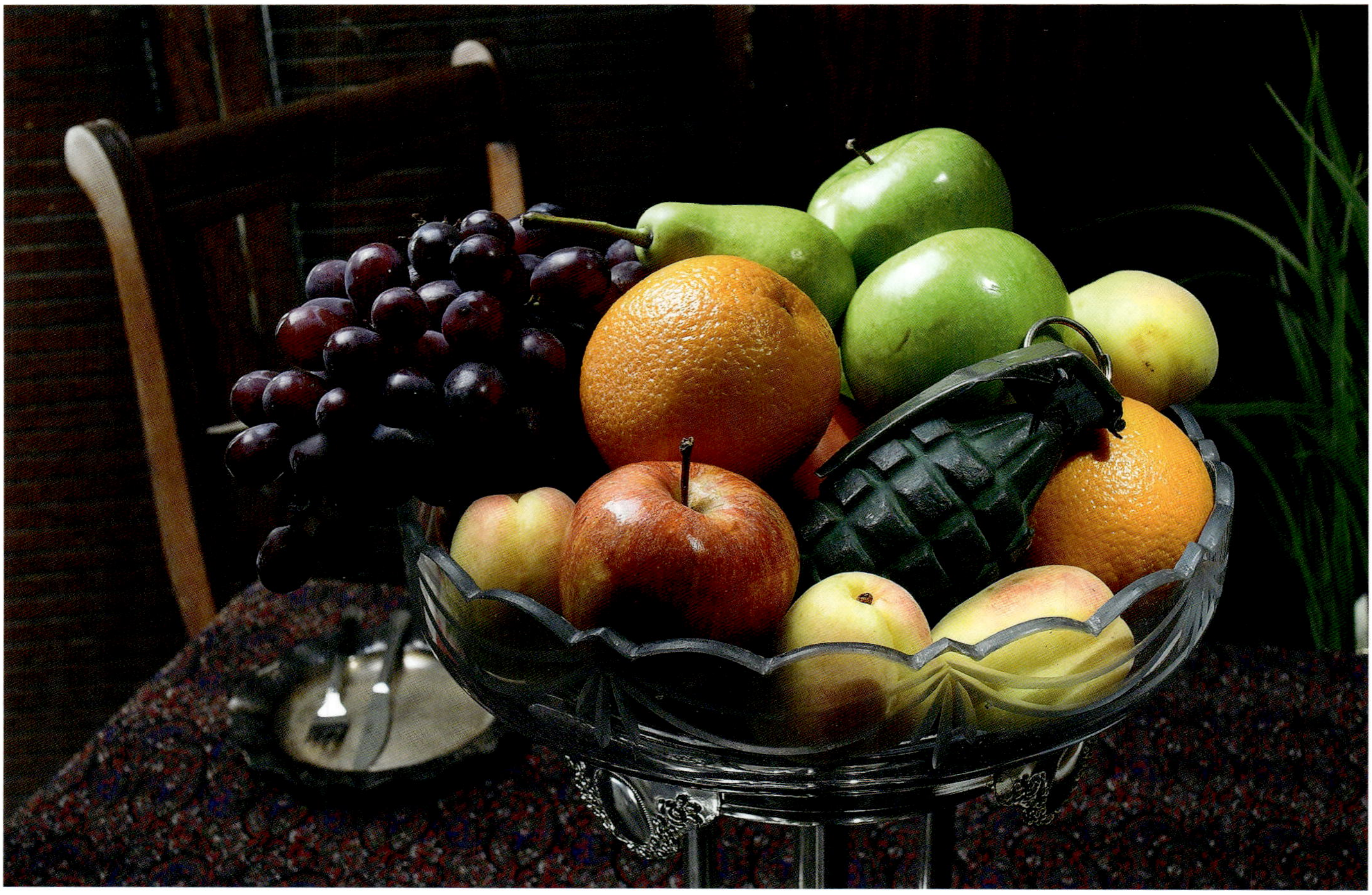

'Untitled',
Nil Nil series,
2008,
artist's collection

SHADI GHADIRIAN

1974, Iran

Shadi Ghadirian became known in 1998 through her series *Qajar*, from the name of the dynasty that reigned in Iran at the time that photography was first introduced. In her elegant black-and-white photos, veiled women pose in front of the luxuriously ornamental decors of classical studios. Reminiscent of ancient portraits, these set-ups point to the persistence of traditions alongside modernity, which is represented by the presence of objects such as transistor radios, bicycles, a vacuum cleaner or a can of fizzy drink. Many of her models carry the aluminium umbrella used to reflect the spotlights. In one of the images, there is a woman on a ladder in the background, painting the fictional landscape that forms the backdrop.

In 2000, she created portraits of women wearing veils with coloured motifs, their faces obstructed by a household utensil such as a rubber glove, a cheese grater, a pan or an iron. Placed between the model and the spectator, these objects create obstacles, in the same way in which domestic tasks close women off from the outside world. The series *Nil Nil* of 2008 used the image of a goalless draw to represent the stalemate of conflicts observed from behind the front. She brought the war into the most private spaces, revealing the consequences of combat even in the domestic setting: a cartridge alongside some cigarettes in a case, a grenade nestling between the sheets of a bed or buried in a fruit bowl. That same year, she tied ribbons around munitions and gas masks, turning them into deadly presents.

Miss Butterfly, in 2011, showed a woman busy weaving threads into the form of a spider's web separating her from the windows looking out onto the outside world. This same elegiac and enigmatic atmosphere pervades the series *Seven Stones* of 2023, which features an enormous rock washed up in a living room or a kitchen or stairwell, like an incongruous meteorite ignored by the unperturbed inhabitants.

TARRAH KRAJNAK

1979, Peru

The work of Tarrah Krajnak mixes photography and performance, using her own body in a subversion of the classic forms of modernism to interrogate her relationship with nature and with the conventions of landscape and femininity. In 2018 and 2019, she explored the story of her adoption by an American couple – who came across her in an orphanage in Lima – through self-portraits inserted into images from magazines that were published in the year of her birth. In 2020, she adopted the poses of models who appeared in the nudes of Edward Weston, revealing ironically how the framings cut out parts of the body to transform them into aesthetic objects. She then came up with an inventory of 'feminine poses', a continuation of an earlier list created in 2005 after she left art school: dressed in white in a plain studio hung in black, she alternately employed choreographed movement, theatrical exaggeration, apparent spontaneity and lewd suggestiveness, all the while holding the shutter release in her hand.

In 2021, she reproduced Victor Burgin's 1967 conceptual project in which he photographed the floor of a gallery then made prints to scale and re-covered the same floor with them, but in her case she photographed the soil of a forest floor scattered with twigs and leaves, mapping this living matter in the form of a photographic path. She also appropriated the surrealist process of automatic writing, combining images of her hands in contact with different rocks with the pages of her notebook inspired by her sensory experiences. Solarised stills obtained by placing excavated rocks on light-sensitive paper created constellations as a homage to the astronomical practices of the Andean peoples. The series *Ayni*, from the Quechua word meaning 'balance', referenced ceremonies using flowers, leaves and food using cyanotypes assembled into large-format compositions.

'#11 Self-Portrait as Weston/as Fay Fuqua (Bent Over)',
Master Rituals II: Weston's Nudes series,
1928/2020,
gelatin silver print,
Cologne, Thomas Zander Gallery

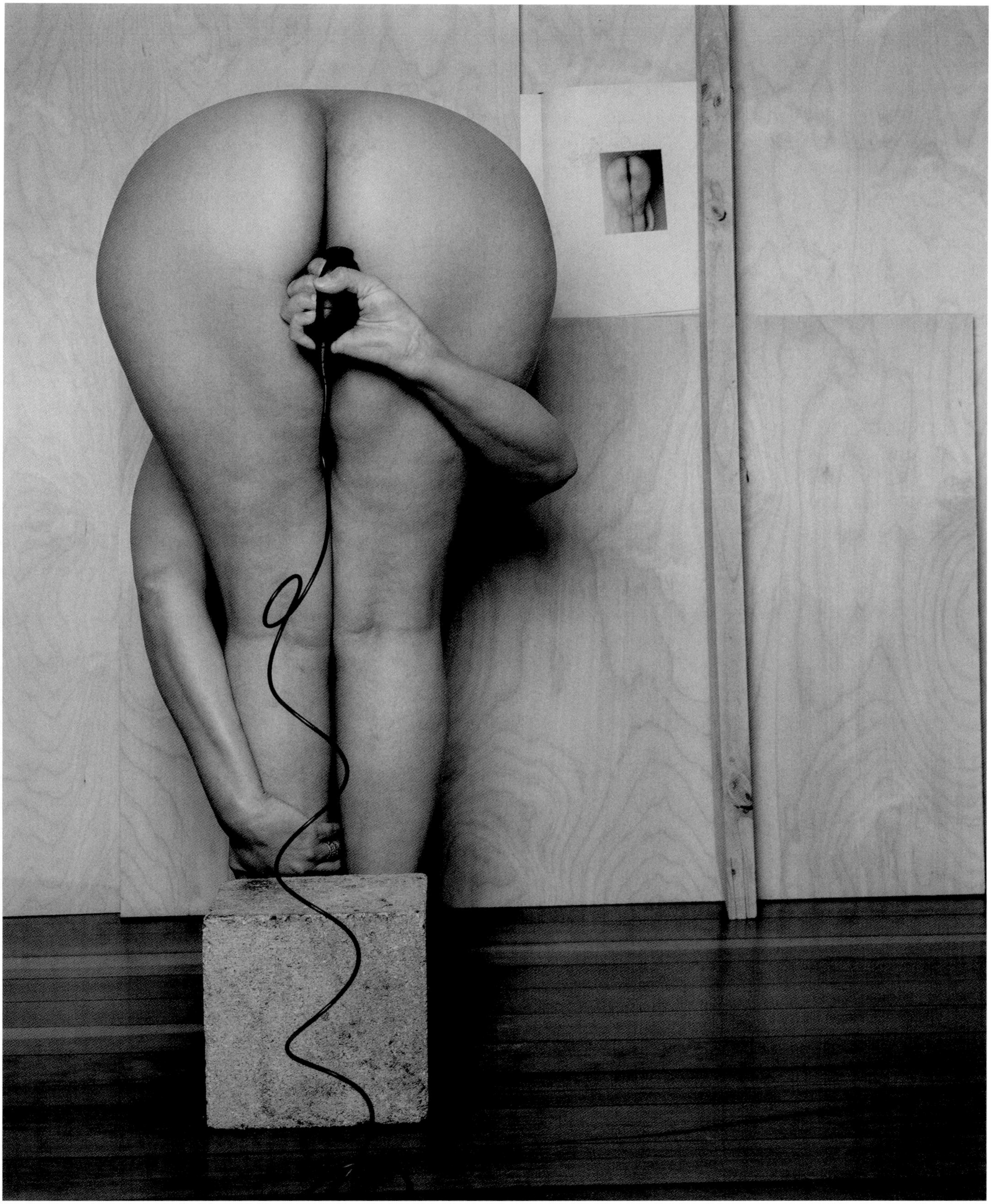

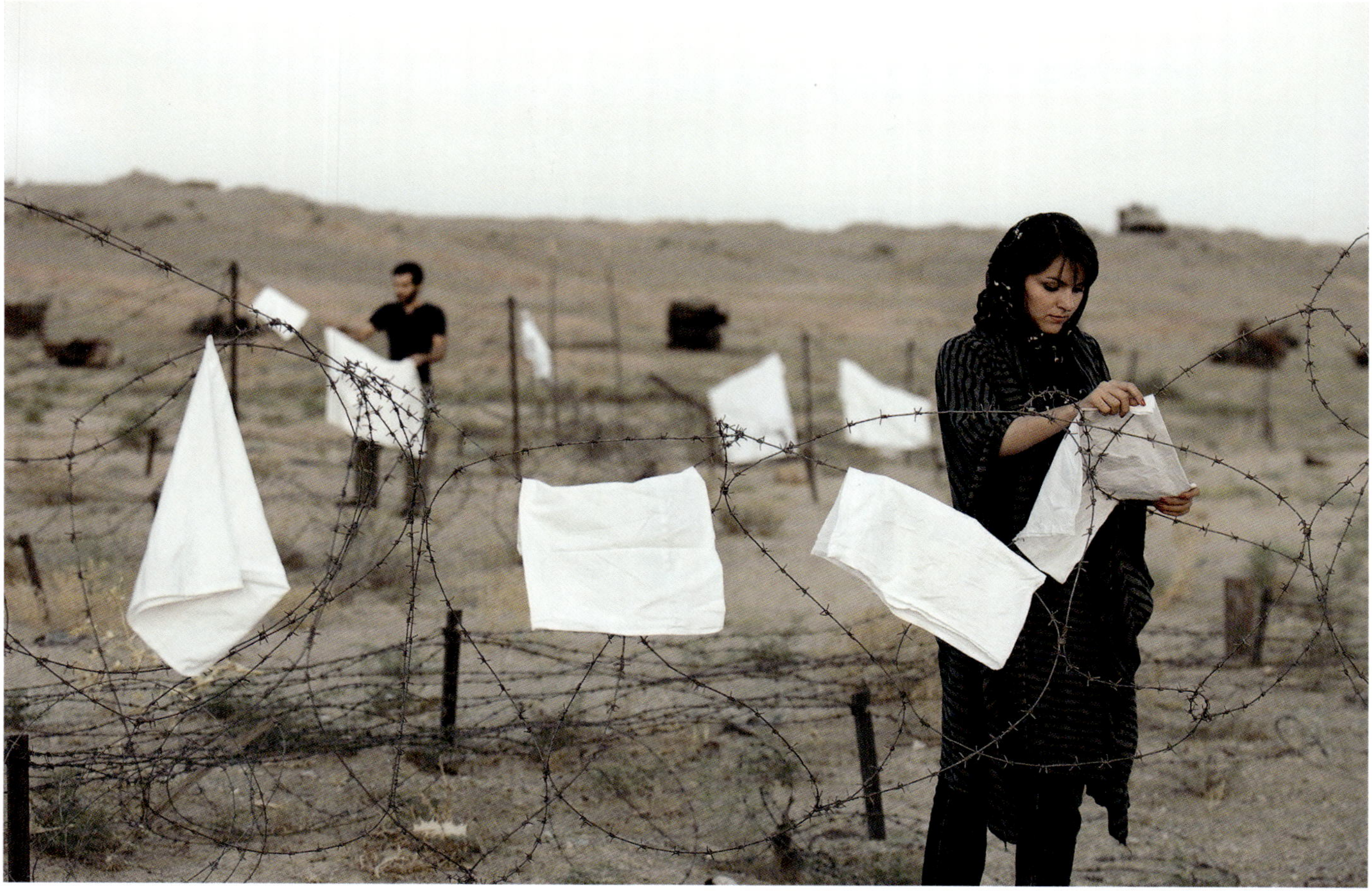

'Untitled #2',
Today's Life and War,
2008,
artist's collection

GOHAR DASHTI

1980, Iran

A young couple hang their immaculate washing on barbed wire. Their attempts at cleaning seem futile in this war-ravaged landscape. Gohar Dashti portrays their day-to-day life – they seem indifferent to their ruined environment – and evokes the latent memory of the Iran–Iraq war. Two years later, in 2010, she created fictions in which impassive characters, staring at the lens, stand with complete indifference next to bloodstains on the ground, on the walls or on their clothing, brutal outpourings of a silent suffering. The protagonists of her *Volcanoes* project in 2012 laugh openly while going about their business – renovating a house, hanging out washing or visiting an exhibition – paying no attention to the scaley tail of an animal that has invited itself into the frame. Their happy insouciance seems to co-exist with the threat of some imminent eruption. The characters in the series *Iran Untitled* of 2013 have been transported to the middle of the desert but continue to behave as if nothing were amiss. They queue up with their baggage in the middle of nowhere or squash together on a toboggan as if on an overcrowded escalator. The desert landscape also welcomes the refugees of *Stateless* (2014–15), stranded with a few bits of furniture or personal possessions with no walls to provide them with shelter. After 2017, these strange characters disappeared from the work of Gohar Dashti, and she turned her attention to nature and ecology. She produced cyanotypes of dissected plants and landscapes on Polaroid paper subjected to heat or degradation, foreshadowing the changes to come due to the effects of pollution and climate change. She photographed trees and vegetation invading rooms emptied of their inhabitants, demonstrating the resilience of nature after an imaginary catastrophe. Finally, she explored the relationship between the landscapes of her native land and those of her adopted country, the USA, by combining images taken either side of the Atlantic in geometric patterns inspired by Islamic art, eschewing the tradition of perspective and vanishing point. Bewildering and poetic, Gohar Dashti's work is based on tragicomic juxtapositions, interrogating the mystery of the human condition in an absurd world.

Marta Photonovel, 'Illegal Stories on Abortion',
2016,
artist's collection

'On 2 January 2015, I travelled to Slovakia to have an abortion. I was too scared to take abortion pills on my own, DIY-style. What if something went wrong? So, I decided to go for a surgical abortion in a clinic abroad. I had trouble borrowing the money for the procedure and felt isolated and frustrated because I couldn't tell anyone what was going on. The hardest bit was facing my boyfriend, who was opposed to abortion. In spite of everything, I felt stronger and more grown up afterwards.' Abortion is legal in almost every country in the European Union except Poland, Ireland and Malta. In Poland, abortion is illegal except in cases of rape, serious deformity of the foetus or threat to the life of the mother.

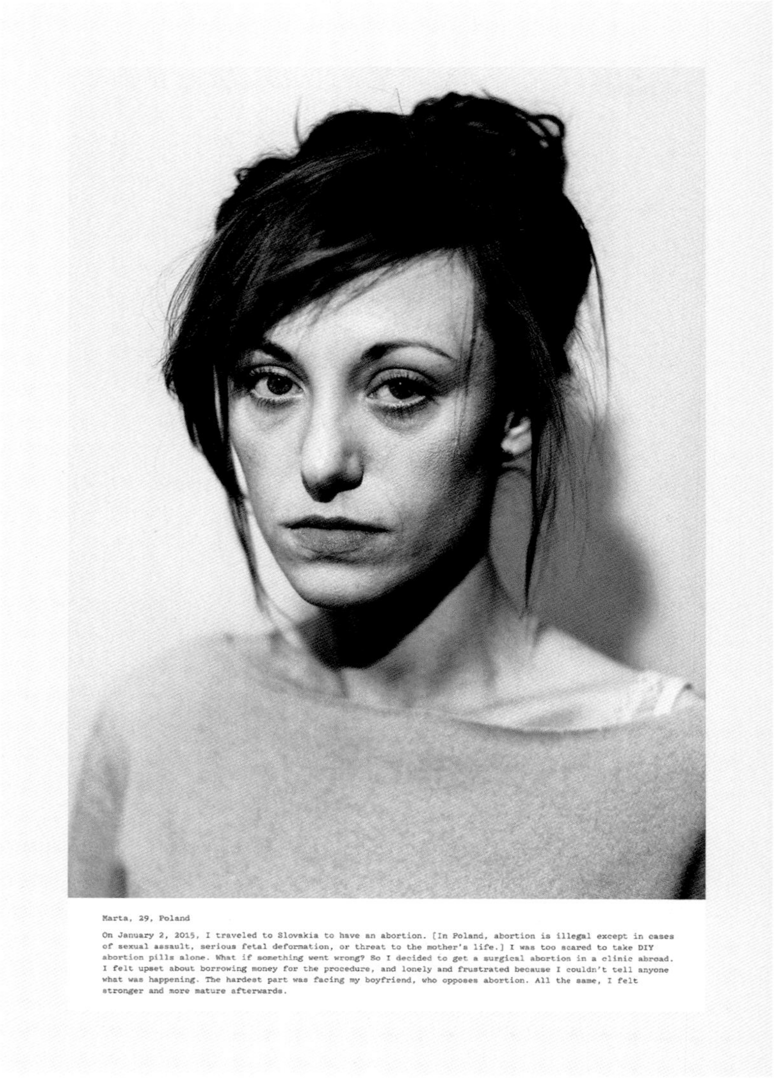

LAIA ABRIL

1986, Spain

Laia Abril studied journalism before moving to New York, where she documented the lesbian community, in particular the everyday lives of a couple of women. She then launched a huge study of the abuses, injunctions and discriminations affecting women in wide-ranging themes split into chapters.

One early topic comprised projects on eating disorders. She explored the culture of dieting and the circulation on the internet of images promoting anorexia. Her book *The Epilogue* (2014) recounted the life of Cammy Robinson, who died at the age of 26 of heart failure connected to her bulimia.

Another topic collected research on the history of misogyny. She addressed the prohibitions, the rituals and the sufferings surrounding menstruation, as well as the phenomenon of collective hysteria interpreted as a form of unconscious protest. She also produced

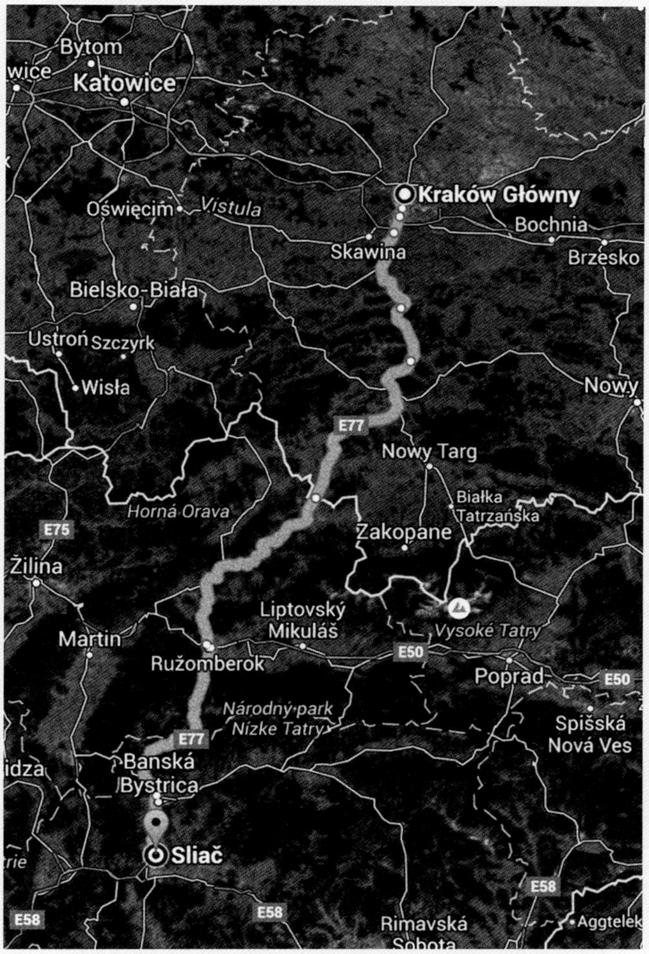

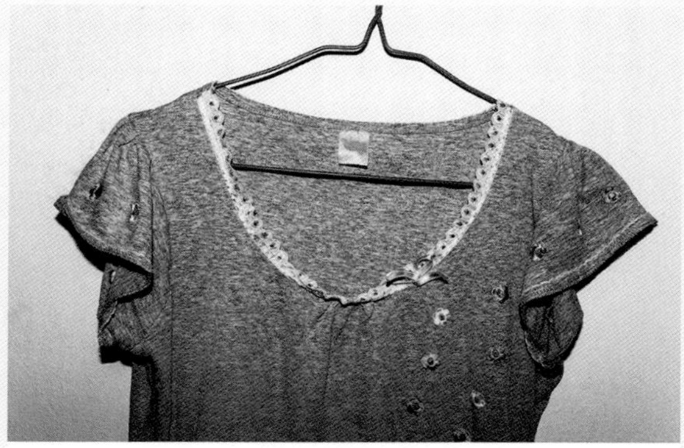

I got pregnant during Christmas, then I had to wait a few weeks before I could make the trip. I was so anxious to avoid the process and save the money, that I first tried to end the pregnancy myself. The night before departing, I took a bath in very hot water and swallowed many aspirin to induce miscarriage. I wanted to feel stronger than the law. But I did not succeed because I was afraid of hurting myself. When I packed for the 15 hours trip, I took only underwear, this nightdress that I hate and €445 to pay for the procedure (all the money I had at that time).

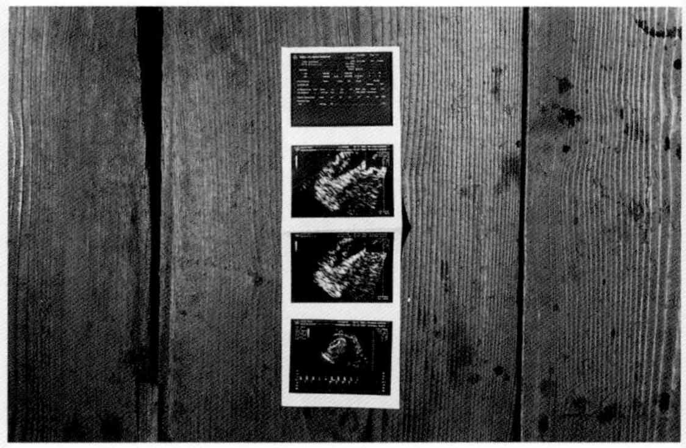

I was seven weeks pregnant when I finally made the trip. I waited at a gas station in Krakow, and then jumped into a van with two other pregnant girls. We drove about three hours into Sliac, where there's an abortion clinic that specializes in welcoming Polish women.
All in all, the experience took almost 15 hours without incident. I called my (now ex-) boyfriend from the road, and he begged me to not do it. When I mentioned the stuffiness and throng, he answered me: "That seems right, murderers should be treated like cattle."

work on the consequences of a lack of access to abortion, which results in the deaths of 47,000 women forced to resort to illegal means annually throughout the world. The direct gazes of the women who agreed to share their experiences were combined with snaps of objects and places connected to their abortion to reconstruct their stories. She was also interested in rape, turning her focus not on the victims but on the perpetrators and on the five feminicides committed on the island of Réunion in 2019. Her book *Lobismuller*, published in 2016, revisited the story of Manuel Blanco Romasanta, who was accused in 1853 of the murder of nearly 20 women and children but was convinced that he had acted while transformed into a sort of werewolf.

In her books and installations Laia Abril assembled testimonies, portraits, documents and objects organised in an up-front and systematic way. Using the conventions of medico-legal inquests, police procedure and even the photo-novel, she represents subjects that normally engender unease, stigmatisation or fear, inscribing them in a shared history, the antithesis of the usual suppression of the female experience.

BIEKE DEPOORTER

1986, Belgium

The inventor of a form of photographic couch surfing, Bieke Depoorter asks random strangers she encounters on her peregrinations to put her up for the night. She thus enters into the privacy of their homes and puts herself in their debt and in a position of vulnerability, since she has been invited by them. Her first books were a type of log of her journeys in Russia on board the Trans-Siberian Express in 2009, then hitchhiking in the USA in 2012.

In 2011, she went to Egypt at the start of the revolution: rather than document the public demonstrations in Tahrir Square, she continued her sleepovers, trying to show how the political debates also played out in the home. Dissatisfied by the layout of her book, she returned to Egypt in 2017 to gather testimonies and handwritten comments from her models and various other people to add to her images. Each page then included a dialogue and personal interpretations, quips, the occasional critique. Some observers identified with the situations or the people and evoked their own family history. The photographs portrayed daily routines, ordinary moments, redolent with expectation, fatigue or tenderness, which resonated with many readers.

Mumkin – Est-ce possible? [Mumkin – May I?]: The title of the book quotes the first words of the Arabic phrase that allowed her to ask permission to take photographs. The response to this question unfolds through the course of the conversations that make up the book, offering unknown people the chance to debate and share in a collective reflection.

'Mumkin – Est-ce possible?' [Mumkin – May I?], published by Éditions Xavier Barral (Paris), 2017, p. 21, Magnum Photos Archive

Phrases in French are written on the back of the photograph.

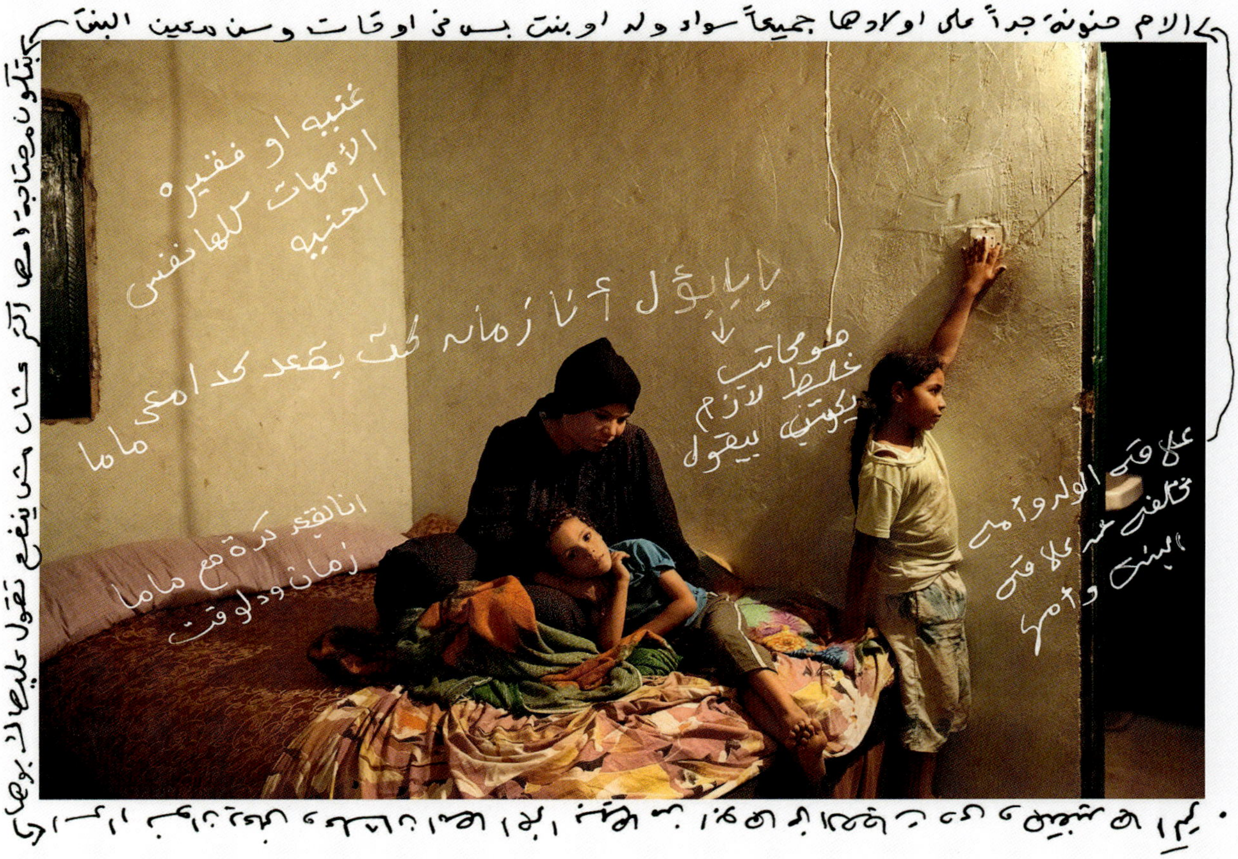

Les mères éprouvent de la tendresse pour tous leurs enfants, garçons ou filles, mais parfois, à un certain âge, une fille a plus besoin de sa mère parce qu'il y a des choses dont elle ne peut pas parler à son père – je veux dire, des secrets de femmes – et sa mère en sait plus à propos de ces choses que son père et elle pourra mieux l'aider.

Riches ou pauvres, toutes les mères éprouvent la même tendresse.

Papa *dite* : j'avais l'habitude de m'asseoir comme ça avec ma mère, il y a des années de cela.

Il l'a mal écrit, il faut mettre « dit ».

Je m'assieds comme ça avec ma mère, depuis toujours.

La relation entre une mère et son fils est différente d'une relation entre une mère et sa fille.

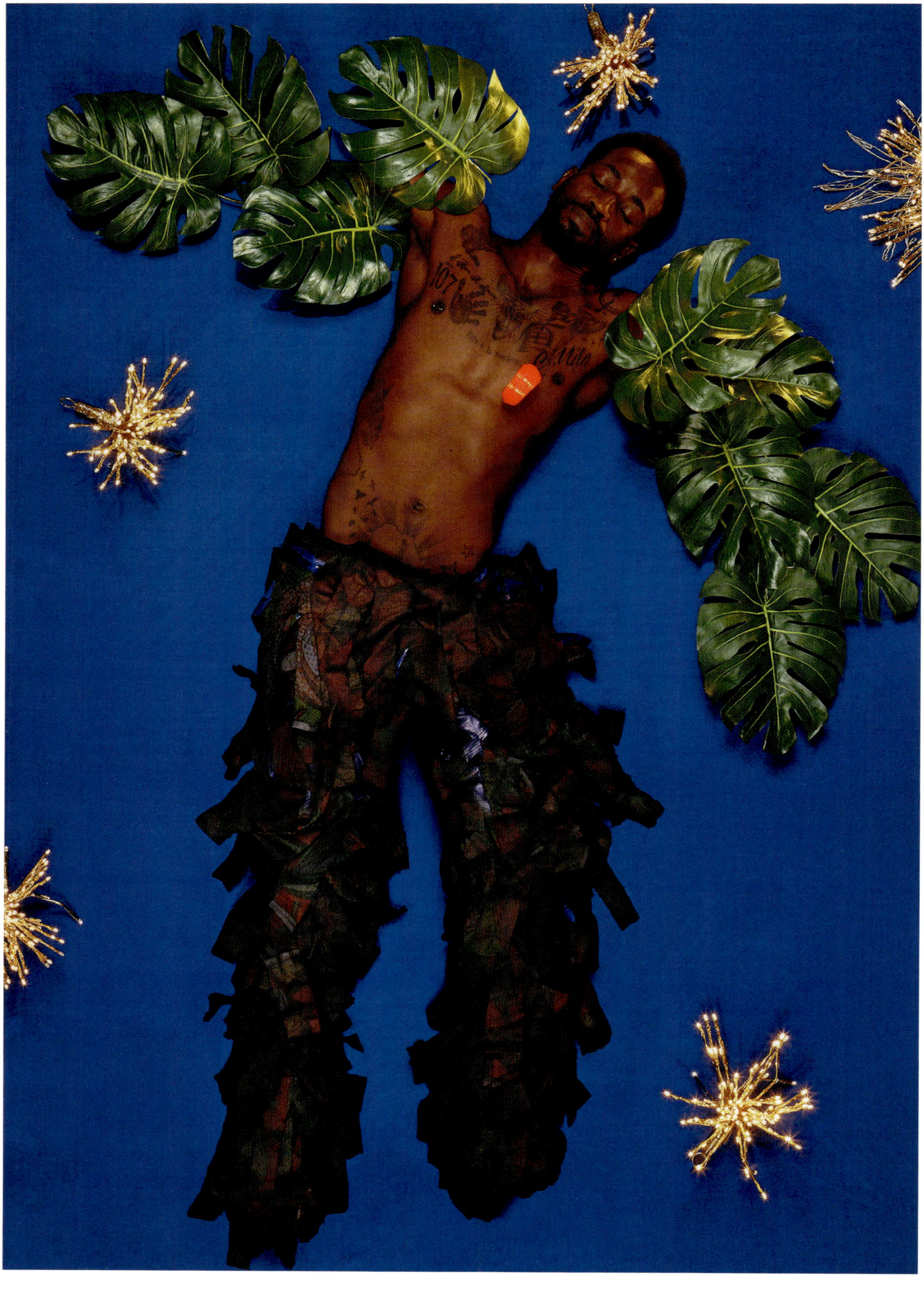

MAYA INÈS TOUAM

1988, France

The granddaughter of Algerian immigrants, Naya Inès Touam interrogates her cultural heritage between France and the Maghreb. Drawing her references from the history of art, she presents a daring creolisation of artistic traditions. *Icare, le revenant* [Icarus the Ghost], for example, cites a celebrated gouache découpage by Henri Matisse representing the fallen Greek hero, punished for flying too close to the sun. The Black man with the leafy wings, open against a blue background, relates to current political events, evoking exile and the crushed hopes of the migrants who drowned in the Mediterranean.

She describes the dazzling deep colours that characterise her work as a form of 'photographic fauvism'. This is particularly evident in her still lives in the series *Ready-Made*, an assembly of Moroccan objects revealing contemporary vanities, or the project *Sanctuarium*, in which she collects religious objects from various regions of the African continent such as statuettes, rugs or candlesticks, whether from monotheist religions or nomadic rituals. The prints are inserted as panels in altarpieces that open like windows on a heteroclite spirituality.

Maya Inès Touam is also interested in Arabic femininities, with her portraits of Algerian women displaying a diversity of cultural practices, and the different ways in which they wear or don't wear the veil; these portraits are accompanied by testimonies. Her work is not confined to photography exclusively. Her sculpture *Burqafacette* represents the silhouette of a woman covered in a mosaic of mirrors, twirling like a glittering disco ball. In *La France est tissu de migrations* [France Is Woven by Migrations], she constructs a map of France made of sewn-together fabrics from the former colonies. The work of Maya Inès Touam employs the canons of western art to open up a rich hybrid visual space illustrating contemporary cultural fusions.

'Icare, le revenant' [Icarus the Ghost],
2020,
pigment print,
Paris, Galerie Les Filles du Calvaire

Photo Credits

© Cindy Sherman – Courtesy of the artist and Hauser & Wirth: **front cover, p. 18, 126 and 127**

© akg-images / Album – © all rights reserved: **p. 6**

© Agnès Varda estate – the Agnès Varda collection deposited at l'Institut pour la photographie: **p. 8, p. 81**

Courtesy of Glenbow Archives: **p. 11**

Courtesy of Throckmorton Fine Art, New York: **p. 13, back cover**

© Inge Morath/Magnum Photos: **p. 14**

© Pushpamala N. in collaboration with Clare Arni: **p. 17, p. 128**

© VERBUND COLLECTION, Vienna – © Renate Eisenegger: **p. 21**

Library of Congress, Prints & Photographs Division, Farm Security Administration/Office of War Information Black-and-White Negatives: **p. 23**

Spencer Collection, The New York Public Library. The New York Public Library Digital Collections.1849-11 – 1850-06: **p. 25, endpapers**

Digital image courtesy of Getty's Open Content Program: **p. 26, back cover**

The Metropolitan Museum of Art, New York. Gift of George Davis, 1948. Accession Number: 48.188: **p. 29**

© Photo12/Alamy/History and Art Collection: **p. 30, p. 31, back cover**

Library of Congress Prints and Photographs Division Washington D.C. 20540 USA: **p. 32**

© Digital image, The Museum of Modern Art, New York/Scala, Florence: **p. 33**

© akg-images: **p. 34, p. 35**

© IWM (Q 8074): **p. 37**

© BnF – © Laure Albin Guillot: **p. 38, p. 39**

© 2024 Imogen Cunningham Trust / www. ImogenCunningham.com: **p. 40, p. 41**

© Centre Pompidou, MNAM-CCI, Dist. GrandPalaisRmn / Jacques Faujour – © all rights reserved: **p. 42**

© The Dorothea Lange Collection, the Oakland Museum of California, City of Oakland. Gift of Paul S. Taylor: **p. 45**

Courtesy of Colección y Archivo de Fundación Televisa / Fundación Televisa Collection and Archive: **p. 46**

© Berenice Abbott/ Getty Images: **p. 49**

© The Anita Conti collection – Archives de Lorient – 24 Fi 10537: **p. 50**

© Lisette Model, with the kind permission of Baudoin Lebon and Avi Keitelman: **p. 52, p. 53**

© Margaret Bourke-White / The LIFE Picture Collection / Shutterstock: **p. 54**

© The Estate of Grete Stern, Courtesy of Galeria Jorge Mara – La Ruche: **p. 57**

Photo © Christie's Images / Bridgeman Images – © Adagp, Paris, 2025: **p. 58**

Photo © Centre Pompidou, MNAM-CCI, Dist. RMN-Grand Palais / Georges Meguerditchian – © Adagp, Paris, 2025: **p. 59**

© Julia Pirotte/ Mémorial de la Shoah – © all rights reserved: **p. 60**

Photo © Paris – Musée de l'Armée, Dist. RMN Grand Palais / Marie Bour – © all rights reserved: **p. 61**

© Lee Miller Archives, England 2025. All rights reserved. leemiller.co.uk: **p. 62, p. 63**

Edith Tudor-Hart © Families Suschitzky / Donat courtesy FOTOHOF archiv: **p. 64, p. 65**

© Gerda Taro © International Center of Photography/Magnum Photos: **p. 66**

© Eve Arnold/Magnum Photos: **p. 68, p. 69**

© Film Documents LLC, courtesy of Zander Galerie, Cologne: **p. 70, p. 71, back cover**

© Janine Niepce / Roger-Viollet: **p. 72, p. 73**

© The Estate of Diane Arbus: **p. 75**

© Martini & Ronchetti, courtesy of Archivio Lisetta Carmi: **p. 76, p. 77**

© Estate of Vivian Maier, Courtesy Maloof Collection and Howard Greenberg Gallery, New York: **p. 78, p. 79**

© Claudia Andujar – Courtesy Galeria Vermelho: **p. 82**

© Claude Batho/courtesy La Galerie Rouge: **p. 84, p. 85**

© Archivio Letizia Battaglia: **p. 86, p. 87**

Courtesy of the artist and Tanya Leighton, Berlin and Los Angeles: **p. 89**

© Martine Franck/Magnum Photos: **p. 90**

© Sarah Moon: **p. 93**

© Sandra Eleta / courtesy of La Galerie Rouge: **p. 94, p. 95, back cover**

© Estate of Abigail Heyman: **p. 97**

Photo: courtesy of ROSEGALLERY © Graciela Iturbide: **p. 98**

© Paz Errázuriz: **p. 100, p. 101**

© Dotation Catherine Leroy: **p. 102, p. 103**

© Christine Spengler: **p. 104, p. 105**

© Paola Agosti: **p. 106, p. 107**

© Ishiuchi Miyako, courtesy of The Third Gallery Aya: **p. 109**

© Susan Meiselas/Magnum Photos: **p. 110, p. 111**

Courtesy of Sophie Ristelhueber – © Adagp, Paris, 2025: **p. 112, p. 113**

© Erica Lennard – © Adagp, Paris, 2025: **p. 114, p. 115**

Donna Gottschalk and © Courtesy of gallery Marcelle Alix, Paris: **p. 116, p. 117**

© The Alix Cléo Roubaud collection: **p. 118, p. 119**

© Sophie Calle / ADAGP, Paris 2025. Courtesy of Perrotin – © Adagp, Paris, 2025: **p. 120–121**

© Nan Goldin, courtesy of the artist and Gagosian: **p. 122, p. 123**

© Anne Noble: **p. 124**

© Ouka Leele / Agence VU: **p. 131**

© Shirin Neshat – Courtesy of the artist and Gladstone Gallery: **p. 132, p. 133**

© Woodman Family Foundation / ADAGP, Paris – © 2025 Woodman Family Foundation / ADAGP, Paris: **p. 134, p. 135**

© Lorna Simpson. Courtesy of the artist and Hauser & Wirth: **p. 136, p. 137**

Courtesy of Galerie Carole Kvasnevski and the artist: **p. 138, p. 139**

© Désirée Dolron: **p. 140, back cover**

© Géraldine Lay, courtesy of Galerie le Réverbère: **p. 143**

© Zanele Muholi, Courtesy of the artist and Yancey Richardson, New York: **p. 144, p. 145**

© 2019 Sara Bennett: **p. 147**

© Shadi Ghadirian: **p. 148**

© Tarrah Krajnak, courtesy of Zander Galerie, Cologne: **p. 151**

Courtesy of the artist, © Gohar Dashti: **p. 152**

© Laia Abril / Les Filles du Calvaire: **p. 154, p. 155**

© Bieke Depoorter/Magnum Photos: **p. 157**

Courtesy of the artist & the gallery Les Filles du Calvaire, Paris – © Adagp, Paris, 2025: **p. 158**

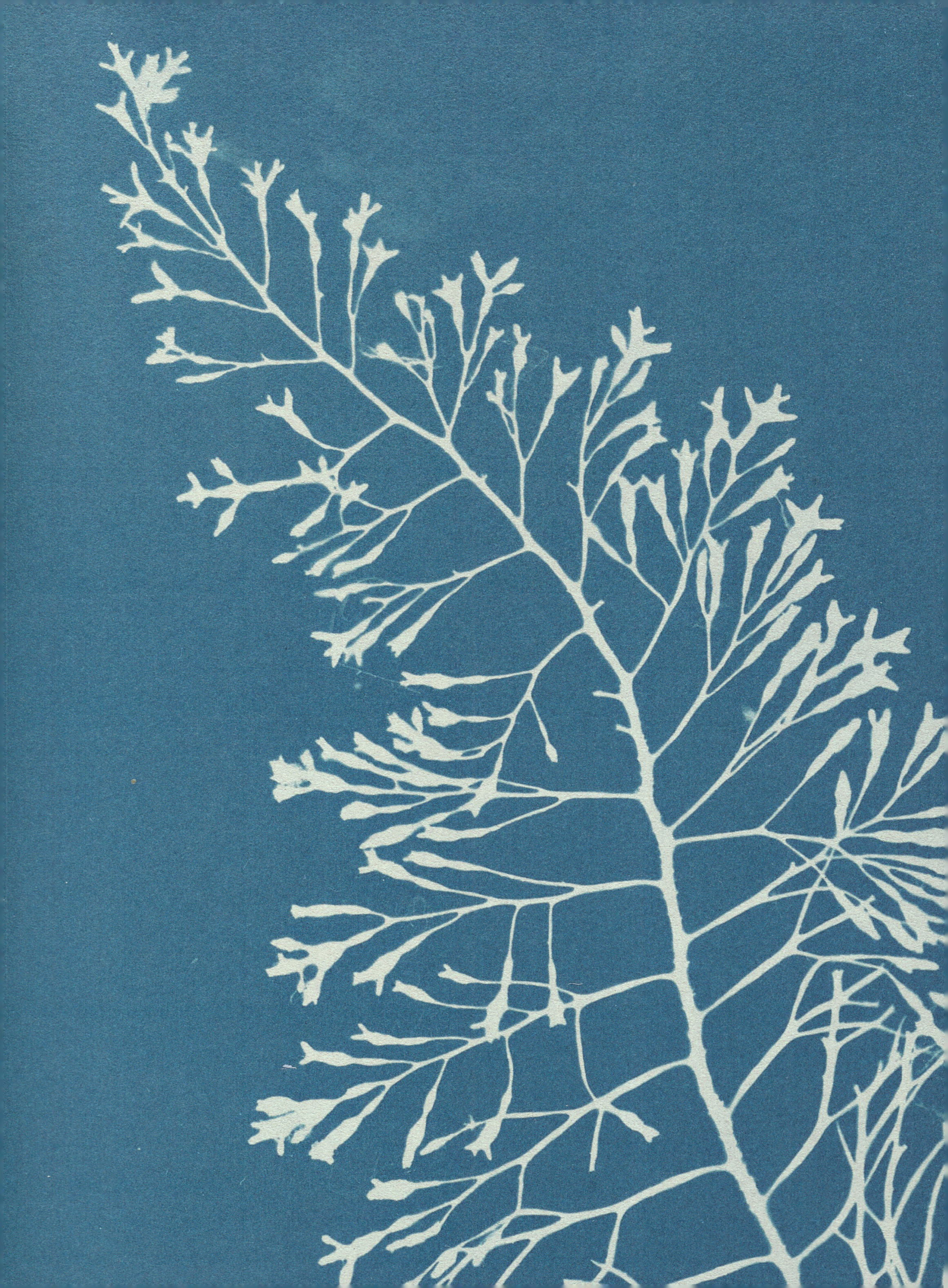